*Republican Ascendancy in
Southern U.S. House Elections*

TRANSFORMING AMERICAN POLITICS

Lawrence C. Dodd, Series Editor

Dramatic changes in political institutions and behavior over the past three decades have underscored the dynamic nature of American politics, confronting political scientists with a new and pressing intellectual agenda. The pioneering work of early postwar scholars, while laying a firm empirical foundation for contemporary scholarship, failed to consider how American politics might change or to recognize the forces that would make fundamental change inevitable. In reassessing the static interpretations fostered by these classic studies, political scientists are now examining the underlying dynamics that generate transformational change.

Transforming American Politics brings together texts and monographs that address four closely related aspects of change. A first concern is documenting and explaining recent changes in American politics—in institutions, processes, behavior, and policymaking. A second is reinterpreting classic studies and theories to provide a more accurate perspective on postwar politics. The series looks at historical change to identify recurring patterns of political transformation within and across the distinctive eras of American politics. Last and perhaps most important, the series presents new theories and interpretations that explain the dynamic processes at work and thus clarify the direction of contemporary politics. All of the books focus on the central theme of transformation—transformation both in the conduct of American politics and in the way we study and understand its many aspects.

BOOKS IN THIS SERIES

Republican Ascendancy in Southern U.S. House Elections

Seth C. McKee
*University of South Florida
at St. Petersburg*

A Member of the Perseus Books Group

Copyright © 2010 by Westview Press
Published by Westview Press,
A Member of the Perseus Books Group

All rights reserved. Printed in the United States of America. No part of this
book may be reproduced in any manner whatsoever without written
permission except in the case of brief quotations embodied in critical
articles and reviews. For information, address Westview Press, 2465
Central Avenue, Boulder, CO 80301.

Find us on the World Wide Web at www.westviewpress.com.

Every effort has been made to secure required permissions to use all
images, maps, and other art included in this volume.

Westview Press books are available at special discounts for bulk purchases
in the United States by corporations, institutions, and other organizations.
For more information, please contact the Special Markets Department at
the Perseus Books Group, 2300 Chestnut Street, Suite 200, Philadelphia,
PA 19103, or call (800) 810-4145, extension 5000, or e-mail
special.markets@perseusbooks.com.

A CIP catalog record for this book is available from the Library of Congress.
ISBN 978-0-8133-4407-2

10 9 8 7 6 5 4 3 2 1

To Esther, Jesse "Bear," and Jasper;
you are my dearest southern constituency.

Contents

Tables and Illustrations

Tables

Maps

Introduction

Republican Ascendancy in Southern U.S. House Elections is a story of tremendous political transformation in the eleven former Confederate states. Not that long ago, many white southerners would profess they would rather vote for a yellow dog if it ran on the Democratic ticket than cast a Republican ballot. Times have changed. These so-called "Yellow Dog" Democrats are now exotic, if only for the fact that they are so endangered. And, although it took some thirty years after the initial switch (among southern whites) to Republican voting in presidential contests, by the 1990s what had been a long pattern of incremental growth and then stagnation was finally punctuated by a Republican surge in southern U.S. House races. When change finally arrived, it was swift—the GOP held a third of southern House seats after the 1990 elections, but just four years later it was the majority party. Since taking over after the 1994 midterm, the Republican delegation has solidified at the direct expense of white Democratic Representatives. The erstwhile one-party Democratic Solid South is now a historical relic. In the contemporary South, the Republican Party has a viable presence in elections from top to bottom, from president down to sheriff. This truly ain't your daddy's Dixie.

The drastic shift in partisan control of the southern House delegation warrants attention for several reasons. First, the study of political change is a worthy endeavor in its own right because it is the business of political scientists to understand the factors shaping partisan transformations. In this regard, southern House elections from 1990 to the present encompass a striking episode of political change. For decades, students have looked to the New Deal realignment as the quintessential example of partisan transformation in electoral politics. We now have a much more recent account of realignment—one that most political observers have been fortunate to witness firsthand. Indeed, most students are aware that the Republican Party has a commanding presence south of the Mason-Dixon Line, but they are not sure why.

Second, the ascendancy of southern Republicans has substantial consequences for national politics. For six consecutive elections (1994–2004), the large southern GOP contingent was critical for securing U.S. House majorities. Beginning in 1996, with the base of the Republican Party anchored in the American South, southern gains compensated for the decline in Republican seats outside the region. And since Republicans relinquished their majority status by losing thirty seats in the 2006 elections, it is evident that the South remains a Republican redoubt. In fact, compared to the North, the relatively modest congressional losses in the South in the 2006 and 2008 contests highlight the permanency of the southern partisan realignment. By contrast, outside the South it is now apparent that the rightward shift of the Republican Party, which was mainly due to its southern leadership, made northern Republicans especially vulnerable to electoral defeat. With the benefit of hindsight, it is now apparent that Republican ascendancy in southern House races has directly and indirectly contributed to partisan polarization in the Congress and the reemergence of the national Democratic Party.

Finally, changes in partisan control mean changes in representation, particularly with respect to policy outputs. With the re-sorting of voters and candidates into the political parties that better reflect their ideological dispositions, the quality and type of representation provided by southern Republicans is a major determinant of how long the GOP can maintain its dominant status in the region. Notable demographic changes, particularly with the growing presence of Hispanics and the continual in-migration of residents from outside the South, may foretell a Democratic revival, especially if Republicans do not adopt positions more accommodating to these newer residents. This book addresses all three aforementioned reasons for studying partisan change in southern House contests: (1) explaining the factors shaping political change, (2) understanding the national consequences of southern Republican ascendancy, and (3) the future of southern congressional politics.

The book proceeds in six chapters. Regarding the question of political change, Chapter 1 ("Explaining Republican Ascendancy") presents a tripartite explanation of Republican advancement in southern House elections that, in its broad contours, is parsimonious and unique. The macro-pattern of Republican ascendancy is an instance of punctuated equilibrium. Punctuated equilibrium is a dynamic process; it begins with a stable state that is disrupted by a period of rapid change that ends in a new equilibrium drastically different from its predecessor. In the case of southern House elections, party competition was in equilibrium in the late 1980s, with the Democrats in the majority. The period of punctuated change occurred when the GOP netted twenty-five seats after the 1992 and 1994 elections. After 1994, Republican gains leveled off, and a new equilibrium has held ever since with the GOP firmly in the majority.

Three temporally sequential and interdependent factors account for this instance of punctuated equilibrium in southern House elections: (1) the steady increase in Republican identification among white southerners, (2) the impact of redistricting, and (3) the emergence of viable Republican candidates. Although these three factors have been investigated in the literature independently of one another, I depart from extant scholarship by advancing a synthetic analysis of these causes. I argue that the GOP's attainment and maintenance of its majority status is a function of the interaction between the structural and behavioral conditions listed above.

Specifically, the increasing Republican identification of southern white voters provided a necessary foundation for Republican gains, but it was the destabilizing effect of redistricting that explains the sudden increase in Republican victories that occurred in the 1992 and 1994 House elections. Redistricting weakened the incumbency advantage of many Democrats and created more Republican districts, thus triggering an elite response: the emergence of Republican candidates who were adept at campaigning on a message more in step with the views of southern whites.

After presenting the explanation for political change in Chapter 1, Chapters 2, 3, and 4 provide empirical evidence for how each of the three above-mentioned factors account for partisan change in southern House contests. Chapter 2 ("The Dynamics of Party Identification") focuses on the role of long-term partisan change in southern House elections by documenting and interpreting the steady increase in the number of white southerners who identify with the Republican Party. The growth in southern Republicanism is a function of the interaction of elites and the mass public with respect to the positions the parties take on politically salient issues. Both conversion and generational replacement account for the increasing number of Republican identifiers.

Chapter 3 ("Electoral Effects of Redistricting") highlights the critical role that redistricting played in the ascendancy of the Republican Party. Redistricting disrupted the electoral status quo by directly weakening the incumbency advantage of Democrats through the altering of congressional boundaries that contained large numbers of redrawn voters. Apart from the newly created majority-minority districts that ensured the election of minority candidates, redrawn voters in neighboring districts swung Republican in their vote choice. They did so for at least three reasons: (1) redrawn Republican voters no longer split their tickets (Republican for president and Democratic for House) because they lacked a bond with their new Democratic representative, (2) short-term political factors like public opinion favored the GOP, and (3) redistricting conditioned the emergence of Republican candidates who had the resources to wage competitive campaigns and thus win the votes of many erstwhile Democratic supporters.

Chapter 4 ("Republican Candidate Emergence") investigates the role of elites by examining patterns of Republican candidate emergence and campaign spending. Redistricting clearly impacted candidate emergence, with better funded and thus more viable Republicans running in those districts that were most competitive. There was an increase in the number of Republican candidates with prior elective experience running in 1992, the first election proceeding redistricting. Yet in subsequent elections, particularly 1994, previous elective experience was not as relevant because of the nature of the political climate and the reality that the GOP did not possess a pool of experienced candidates able to run at a time when the party was rapidly ascending. When Republican growth leveled off after the 1996 elections, a more conventional pattern returned, as more experienced Republicans emerged to contest House seats.

Whereas Chapters 2–4 center on the periods of stability and punctuated change ending with the 2004 elections, Chapter 5 ("National Implications of Southern Republican Ascendancy") considers a longer time span as well as the electoral significance of the 2006 and 2008 contests. The chapter shifts away from a regional focus to illustrate how partisan change in the postwar South affects national congressional politics. An important and prominent consequence of Republican success in the South is the widening interparty polarization of Congress.

Drawing on several data sources, I contend that because the southern realignment was so strong and enduring, and since this episode of partisan change was not duplicated outside the region, southern control of the House's legislative agenda ultimately led to the party's defeat in the 2006 elections. The reason for this is because after the GOP attained majority control in 1994, its leadership was comprised of southerners (Speaker Gingrich, Majority Leader Armey, and Majority Whip DeLay) who were not representative of the median congressman or even the median Republican member for that matter. With the legislative agenda controlled and shaped by the GOP's more ideologically extreme members, the rightward shift in policymaking exposed the party's more centrist representatives to electoral defeat. These were Republicans who disproportionately represented districts outside the South, where voters were considerably more moderate.

It is in the South where redistricting fostered the safest GOP-held districts. This allowed southern Republicans to pursue a conservative reformist agenda (as outlined in the Contract with America) without electoral reprisal. Outside the South, the absence of a long-term shift in favor of the GOP meant that these districts were not as politically insulated. Hence, when short-term conditions in 2006 shifted decidedly in favor of the Democratic Party, northern Republican incumbents suffered the bulk of political defeats. Like 2006, the 2008 elections benefited the Democratic Party at the national level because extant political conditions continued to favor the party. But the 2006 and 2008 elections also demonstrate that the Democratic advantage remains less pronounced in the South, where racial polarization in vote choice is greatest, and the white majority population is decidedly more Republican.

Finally, Chapter 6 ("The Future of Southern Congressional Politics") concludes with an assessment of the future state of partisan competition in southern U.S. House contests. Demographic change, redistricting, and party performance are identified as key factors impinging on the status of two-party competition in southern congressional elections. Most important however, is strong evidence that subregional differences are threatening Republican hegemony. A possible revival of the Democratic Party is contemplated, and specifically what kinds of events and conditions are necessary for this to happen.

Acknowledgments

This project has its roots firmly planted in my dissertation at the University of Texas at Austin. As such, the core of the thesis remains intact, but thanks to Larry Dodd, the scope of the book has broadened to include an examination of how the southern transformation affects national electoral politics. To anyone who has not had the pleasure of getting to know Larry, just as Louisiana is considered sui generis, so is Larry. I have not met another scholar who rivals Larry in terms of his quest for understanding politics in all its many forms and to convey his passion so forthrightly to his students. When I was briefly enrolled at the University of Florida, having a class with Larry left me with a firm belief in how to properly evaluate the quality of political science scholarship. Larry is a catholic scholar—a scholar who appreciates all kinds of approaches to political inquiry—so long as the work is rigorous and insightful. Thanks to Larry, I too am a catholic scholar.

Given the dynamic process that is contemporary southern politics, I saw the *Transforming American Politics* series as the ideal outlet for this work. Fortunately, Steve Catalano, the editor at the time, was convinced that this was an important undertaking with wide-ranging appeal for undergraduate and graduate students, as well as for American politics scholars more generally. Toby Wahl took over as editor last year and, thanks to his tremendous accessibility and vigilance in overseeing my progress, the manuscript was delivered on a date that seems improbably early.

There are several scholars and colleagues in the discipline who deserve specific mention. First, Daron Shaw, my advisor at the University of Texas at Austin, encouraged me to pursue writing a book. I owe a debt of gratitude to Daron for socializing me into the profession, explicitly and implicitly instructing me in the finer points of what it means to be an academic and a teacher. It was Daron who introduced me to Jim Gimpel, an extremely generous and indefatigable political scientist. Jim has become a friend and mentor, and I thank him specifically for finding a congressional map that I was able to present in chapter three. I would be remiss and in trouble if I did not thank Danny Hayes and Trey Hood, my frequent coauthors. Perhaps these guys could not possibly be any more different, but they, like me, love to do research, and our collaborations on southern politics have clearly left their imprint on this study. I also am thankful for the brilliant insight of Earl and Merle Black; their *Rise of Southern Republicans* (2002) proved the foremost resource for advancing the argument and analyses in this book. Finally, I want to acknowledge the efforts of Larry Moreland, Bob Steed, and DuBose Kapeluck—the Citadel triumvirate in charge of the biennial Symposium on Southern Politics. Over the years, this conference has become an invaluable setting for sharing scholarship on the politics of the American South.

With any long-term, large-scale project, there are roadblocks and hurdles that are insurmountable and yet others that can only be overcome with the proper assistance. Specifically, in the case of Texas House elections, so much of the analyses were possible because of the data that Charles Eckstein of the Texas Legislative Council made available to me. If only every other state kept the kind of data the Lone Star State has regarding redistricting and had someone like Charles, who always gave me access to what I needed. I fancy myself an amateur geographer, and thus the assistance of a real geographer, Pete Reehling at the University of South Florida, graciously produced all of the South-wide congressional maps. For better or for worse, Pete knows I will turn to him again (and again) for technical expertise when it is time to display geographic renditions of political phenomena.

Lastly, I thank my family for their patience and encouragement. In hindsight, I realize that the only one truly surprised by the completion of this book is me. Needless to say, when a manuscript is due at the turn of the new year, and in the meantime you have your first baby, a small home full of relatives, and classes to teach—someone is giving you a pass on otherwise nonnegotiable responsibilities. Thank you, Esther.

Seth C. McKee
St. Petersburg, Florida
February 2009

1

Explaining Republican Ascendancy

The onset of GOP southern growth can be readily identified and tracked. The causes are subject to greater debate. (1996, 451)

—Charles S. Bullock III

The rise of southern Republicans in U.S. House elections is one of the most remarkable developments in the history of American politics. For decades, scholars have contemplated the possibility for GOP ascendancy in congressional contests in the states of the old Confederacy.[1] In the 1990s, what was long anticipated finally became an abrupt reality. Indeed, the sheer rapidity of Republican growth took political observers by surprise. Consider this comment in a *Social Science Quarterly* article published in the spring of 1992: "Undoubtedly, the Democratic dominance of the region's congressional voting is not going to change overnight" (Thielemann 1992, 143). Maybe not overnight, but after the next two elections, the GOP comprised a majority in the South and the U.S. House of Representatives. And the leader of the 1994 Republican takeover was speaker-elect Newt Gingrich, who in 1990 was the lone Republican House Representative in Georgia's ten-member delegation.

To put it mildly, contemporary southern congressional elections look nothing like they did a half-century ago, or as they did as late as the 1980s. The presence of Republicans in the southern House delegation was virtually nonexistent fifty years ago, and their numbers stagnated at approximately a third of the membership in the late 1980s. But in the 1990s, a swift reversal of political fortune occurred, with southern Republicans attaining majority status in 1994 and then continuing to expand on their number of seats for the next decade (through 2004). What accounts for the rise of the Republican Party in southern House elections? More specifically, how can one explain the unique pattern of advancement, in which the GOP is the preferred party among most white southerners in presidential elections since 1968,[2] and yet they don't take control of the House until twenty-six years later in an unexpected surge of victorious candidates? In this chapter, I offer an explanation for the ascendancy of the Republican Party in southern House elections in the 1990s. Essentially, the explanation can be condensed into three temporally sequential and interdependent factors: (1) increasing Republican identification among white southerners, (2) the partisan impact of redistricting implemented prior to the 1992 elections, and (3) the emergence of viable Republican candidates who struck the right chords with an electorate primed for representational change.

Before laying out the specifics of the explanation for Republican ascendancy, it is appropriate to first discuss what other scholars have noted as being factors that account for the stagnation and eventual rise of southern House Republicans. As the introductory quote in this chapter attests, the palpable evidence of partisan change in the South is much easier to document than it is to explain. In fact, even the leading account of Republican ascendancy in southern congressional contests, Black and Black's *The Rise of Southern Republicans* (2002), has been vigorously disputed (see Shafer and Johnston 2006). Simply put, there is no consensus with respect to the sequential influence of factors shaping political change, the essential factors in this process, and the relative importance of the factors thought to produce Republican gains. And in this vein, one should not expect that this account will unify expert opinion regarding the causes of southern Republican advancement. However, by focusing specifically on the pattern of GOP growth in southern House elections and its national implications, this study provides new insight into the causes and consequences of partisan change in America's most recent electoral realignment.

Because past research clearly informs and contributes to the thesis posed in this book, the first half of this chapter proceeds with a review of that literature on party competition in House elections both before and after the Republican takeover of Congress. The latter half of the chapter then discusses the specific pattern of GOP advancement in the 1990s and presents a theoretical explanation for Republican ascendancy in southern House elections.

Previous Research: Before Republican Ascendancy

Right up until the Republican victory in 1994, the apparent permanent minority status of the GOP spawned several hypotheses for the failure of the party to win back the U.S. House of Representatives. Most of these studies either implicitly or explicitly seek to address the persistence of a split-level alignment in American politics. In other words, what explains the perpetual minority status of House Republicans whereas the GOP usually wins the presidency? The preeminent congressional elections scholar Gary Jacobson (1990) offered two explanations to account for Democratic dominance: (1) the Democratic party contested more districts and ran better candidates, as measured by previous office-holding experience, and (2) the nature of congressional service, with its heavy emphasis on redistributive politics, was thought to be more philosophically suitable to Democratic candidates who generally embrace the notion that government should provide a bounty of services to their constituents.

In making his argument for a party-based electoral order, Byron Shafer (1991) argued that a divided government was a function of the different partisan preferences that voters held toward a particular institution. According to Shafer, the GOP controls the presidency because it deals with cultural values and foreign policy. The Senate, however, is not dominated by either party because it deals with issues that advantage both parties, for example, Republicans with respect to foreign policy and cultural values, and Democrats with respect to social welfare and service provision. And lastly the House, in keeping with the view of Jacobson, provides a distinct advantage for Democrats because it deals primarily with social welfare and service provision.

Alan Ehrenhalt's (1991) explanation for Democratic superiority in congressional elections jibes with the arguments of Jacobson and Shafer. Ehrenhalt makes the observation that the Democratic Party is the party of government in the sense that Democrats believe that government plays a necessary role in improving the lives of citizens. So, unlike many Republicans (perhaps most according to Ehrenhalt), Democrats are not conflicted in their role as representatives because they believe in the pork barrel when it is done to improve the welfare of constituents. Ehrenhalt writes, "Congressmen . . . are judged by how well they deliver—how good they are at providing federal money for the district and personal service for the constituency. Democrats are the ones who know how to do that, and voters reward them accordingly" (1991, 224). Ehrenhalt claims that the Democratic Party attracts better candidates because "it is the obvious magnet for people who think running for office is worth the considerable sacrifice it entails" (224).

In addition to superior candidates and a philosophy of government more congruent with the mission of representation, we must of course add the role of incumbency. Among other things, incumbency affords a candidate at least two major advantages. First, incumbents deter strong challengers because strong challengers act strategically in the sense that they prefer to run for a seat when their chances are most favorable (Jacobson and Kernell 1983)—and that is when a seat is open. Second, based on their previous electoral performance and campaigning, incumbents have cultivated a core of supporters (Fenno 1978). By virtue of holding office and performing constituency service, incumbents enjoy high name recognition and the ability to raise much larger sums of money (Abramowitz 1991)—particularly from political action committees (PACs) who seek influence by placing the bulk of their campaign contributions on incumbents since they have a better chance of winning. The incumbency advantage has loomed largest in the South because of its history of having a one-party system. Likewise, the hegemony of the Democratic Party had the effect of perpetuating itself because ambitious politicians seeking a career in electoral politics would naturally identify with and run as candidates of the dominant party.[3]

According to Jacobson (1990; 1991), the GOP was relegated to its minority status because Republicans "have fielded inferior candidates on the wrong side of issues that are important to voters in House elections" (1991, 640–641). Jacobson is accurate up to a point because, in an age of candidate-centered elections, the Democratic Party ran superior candidates, especially with respect to previous elective experience. Jacobson argues that the reason the Republican Party was the minority party for so long was not structural, but rather political. Structural arguments pointed to gerrymandering, campaign finance, and incumbency as the advantages afforded to Democrats. Jacobson, however, dismisses each of these explanations. In the 1980s, gerrymandering was found to have little overall partisan bias (although there were exceptions, such as in California with a Democratic bias, and in Indiana with a Republican bias that did not pan out). Neither party gained or lost more than a handful of seats because of redistricting. And in the case of campaign finance, on average, Republican candidates were better funded.

As for incumbency, Jacobson shows that Republican candidates performed no better in open-seat contests (even those open seats that were held by Republicans), where of course, incumbency is not a factor. This evidence, however, is not satisfactory for dismissing incumbency as an advantage for Democrats. As Davidson and Oleszek (2000, 70) put it: "In politics, nothing succeeds like success." And in the South, since the end of Reconstruction up until the 1990s, to say that Republican candidates did not have much success is the ultimate understatement. Losing on a massive scale takes its toll on a party, and this is reflected in the historically large number of seats southern Republicans did not even bother to contest (Black and Black 2002). Strategic candidates avoided running as Republicans because candidates are (by definition) rational political actors whose goal is to win, not put up a good fight. So on the one hand, there is indeed a connection between fielding quality candidates and a track record of electoral success, and this is in line with Jacobson's argument that the main problem with the Republican Party was its failure to run quality candidates. But on the other hand, the reason why there were relatively fewer quality Republican candidates was because so many Democrats held seats in the southern House delegation (Black and Black 2002). Incumbency was a key factor in prolonging Democratic hegemony because these members used their incumbency status to ward off quality challengers and to cultivate political support across party lines (e.g., Fiorina 1977).

With the benefit of hindsight, after the GOP captured a majority of House seats in the 1994 elections, it appears that at least in the South, the Democratic Party was not better positioned on the issues. Instead, it may have been the case that southern Democrats were able to maintain their seats because they proved adept at deflecting issues that would prove electorally harmful, particularly those sorts of "values" issues (school prayer, abortion, crime, gun control, gay rights, affirmative action) that have marked the demise of Democratic presidential candidates (Rae 1994). Thus, southern Democratic representatives and candidates were not necessarily on the right side of the issues, but in so many instances they were blessed with an inferior Republican opposition that was ill-equipped to exploit the political weaknesses of the Democratic Party. In this respect, candidate emergence is a crucial variable. The GOP needed to run strong candidates who could exploit the unpopular political positions of southern Democrats.

Linda Fowler (1993) has noted the key role of candidate emergence in the context of southern House elections. She states that,

> If political elites fail to provide meaningful alternatives to the status quo or to structure cleavages in an intelligible and coherent fashion, then the public can hardly be faulted for aborting the periodic adjustment in the party system that political scientists have predicted with such certainty. (35)

Furthermore, according to Fowler, the missing ingredient for a Republican takeover in the South was the absence of strong candidates willing to expose the vulnerabilities of the Democratic Party:

> Indeed, the long-predicted Republican realignment has not taken place in the 1980s, despite substantial GOP gains among voters, because a

high incidence of uncontested seats and uncompetitive Republican challengers has prevented the party from capitalizing on its strength at the top of the ticket, particularly in the South. (1993, 35–36)

Both Jacobson (1990; 1991) and Fowler (1993) are correct in citing the deficit of viable Republican candidates as being fundamental to the reason why the GOP was unable to attain a House majority in the 1980s. But what these scholars and others have overlooked is that a structural change was necessary for the emergence of viable candidates capable of ushering in a Republican majority. Redistricting implemented for the 1992 elections was just the sort of structural change needed for the advent of these formidable candidates.

Previous Research: After Republican Ascendancy

For three consecutive elections (1986–1990), there was no change in the partisan balance of the southern House delegation. The political system was in a state of short-term equilibrium induced primarily by the incumbency advantage accruing to both Democrats and Republicans. For the GOP to increase their number of House seats (one-third of the delegation in 1986, 1988, and 1990), a shock to the political system would be necessary—the kind of shock that could upset the electoral status quo by weakening the incumbency advantage of Democrats. Redistricting proved the perfect remedy.

Reapportionment led to improved political opportunities for Republican House candidates. The Department of Justice (DOJ) enforced a majority-minority maximization agenda on nine southern states (Alabama, Florida, Georgia, Louisiana, Mississippi, North Carolina, South Carolina, Texas, and Virginia) for the decennial redistricting that was undertaken before the 1992 elections (Bullock 1998, 2000; Butler 2002; Clayton 2000; Cunningham 2001). African American voters were "packed" into thirteen newly created black majority districts, meaning that a lower minority district percentage would still have allowed these voters to elect a Democratic representative—though not necessarily an African American (Cameron et al. 1996; Epstein and

O'Halloran 1999a, 1999b, 2000). Several of the districts adjacent to these majority-minority districts were of course made proportionally whiter, and many became Republican pickups in 1992 and subsequent elections (Bullock 1995a, 1995b; Hill 1995; Lublin and Voss 2000; Mc-Kee 2002).

Earl and Merle Black (2002) point out that race-based redistricting was just the kind of destabilizing mechanism the GOP needed to make gains in House races:

> Before redistricting, 53 of 116 southern House districts—fewer than half of the region's seats—had been carried by Bush in 1988 with 60 percent or more of the vote. After redistricting, 65 of the South's 125 congressional seats—a clear majority—had given Bush a landslide vote in 1988. (330)

So not only did more districts reflect a Republican advantage (based on the district-level 1988 Republican presidential vote) after the 1991/1992 round of redistricting, but this advantage also materialized into Republican gains in southern House elections. As a result of redistricting, the new racial foundations "improved the southern Republicans' presidential foundations" (Black and Black 2002, 337), and this in turn contributed to Republican success in southern House races. Between the 1988 and 2000 presidential elections, there was a 71 percent decline in the number of white southerners who voted Republican for president and Democratic for the House and a 65 percent increase in the proportion of white southerners who voted a straight Republican ticket.[4] The 1992 House contests marked the beginning of a swift end to the Democratic Party's majority status in the South.

The reconfiguration of congressional boundaries fostered greater Republican voting in House races by increasing the likelihood that white southerners would vote in line with their presidential preferences. Why? The literature on race-based redistricting has grown tremendously in no small part to explain why Republican candidates have disproportionately benefited.[5] For instance, Kevin Hill (1995) measured the impact of racial redistricting in the eight southern states (Alabama, Florida, Georgia, Louisiana, North Carolina, South Carolina, Texas, and Virginia) that each added at least one new black ma-jority district before the 1992 elections. Based on a district-level analy-sis (using Gelman and King's [1994] JudgeIt program) of the 1992 Democratic House vote in these states,[6] Hill's model correctly predicts the four seats in these states that switched to the Republican Party "due to racial redistricting: Alabama 6 and Georgia 1, 3, and 4" (1995, 397). A shortcoming of Hill's work, however, is that he does not address whether or not white voting behavior was essentially constant before and after redistricting. Thus, it appears he is suggesting that the reduc-tion in the black population of districts is great enough for a Republi-can candidate to win based solely on the more favorable racial composition of the district.

John Petrocik and Scott Desposato (1998) take issue with Hill's analysis. They find that a reduction in black population alone was not sufficient for Republican candidates to win in so many southern dis-tricts in 1992, and especially 1994. Rather, white voters who had previ-ously supported Democratic candidates had to defect in large enough numbers for Republican candidates to win. Further, the most likely white voters to switch (vote Republican) were "new" voters, those vot-ers districted into seats represented by white Democratic incumbents. Coupled with a GOP tide in 1994 and the severance of the incum-bency bond, these new voters cast GOP ballots at a rate high enough for Republican candidates to win seats that were affected by racial dis-tricting. The explanation put forth by Petrocik and Desposato is more complete and plausible than Hill's, but they perhaps place too much emphasis on the importance of the Republican tide and downplay the significance of candidate emergence (a topic given little discussion).

Redistricting certainly led to an increase in Republican voting, but there would not have been greater Republican support if redistricting did not produce the impetus for the emergence of viable Republican candidates. On this point, Jacobson (1996, 2000, 2001, 2004) has con-tributed greatly by offering a supply-side or candidate-centered expla-nation for Republican ascendancy in congressional elections. Jacobson demonstrates convincingly that those Democratic incumbent-held districts that were more Republican at the presidential level (he takes the district's average GOP two-party vote for the 1988 and 1992 elections) were targeted by the strongest Republican candidates. Compared with Democratic-leaning districts (based on the presidential vote), the Republican challengers in Republican-leaning districts were more experienced and better funded, and it paid off as a greater number of these seats were won by Republicans in 1994 (Jacobson 1996).[7]

Alan Abramowitz (1995) provides corroborative evidence with NES survey data, showing that better funded Republican challengers targeted those districts with more Republican identifiers, and the increase in spending resulted in more political support. Black and Black (2002, 338) also point out that these presidentially Republican districts represented by Democrats were in the GOP's crosshairs:

> Encouraged by their initial success in 1992, Gingrich and Armey intensified their efforts to find, fund, and foster GOP congressional candidates ready to run in districts where Reagan and Bush had previously attracted landslide majorities.

Turning away from analyses of incumbent House contests, Ronald Keith Gaddie and Charles Bullock (2000) focus solely on open seats and find, interestingly, that Republican amateurs (no prior elective office-holding experience) in contested southern primaries did better than experienced GOP opponents in 1994. This phenomenon certainly speaks to the anti-incumbent, anti-careerist, anti-politics mood of the electorate, documented so thoroughly by Jacobson (1996) and Ladd (1995). Nonetheless, from 1982 to 1994, with respect to open-seat *general* elections, Gaddie and Bullock also find that the most successful Republican candidates were well funded and had previous political experience—winning more than 80 percent of the time against Democratic opponents lacking these two vital resources.

Gaddie and Bullock (2000) present rich data on candidate quality and spending. They argue cogently, picking up on the finding of Jacobson (1990), that prior to the 1990s, the Republican Party fielded inferior candidates even in those districts that were Republican in presidential voting, and this partially accounts for their inability to win open seats in the 1980s. As Jacobson (1990) argued, because they failed to win so many seats when they became open contests, Republicans could not blame their minority status on a structural explanation like incumbency. Instead, Republicans did not win these contests because the Democrats fielded superior candidates. In effect, Republican candidates were less "strategic" because, compared with Democrats, not as many Republican candidates were well funded and experienced, even in those districts where the odds of winning were certainly more favorable based on the partisanship of the district.

Before the 1990s, the percentage of quality Republican challengers in the South (about 9 percent for each election) remained the same since the early 1960s (Jacobson 1990, 63). Of course Jacobson (2001) points out that the largest pool of future House members is supplied by state legislatures and, unfortunately for the Republican Party, there was a meager supply of Republican contenders because southern state legislatures were historically dominated by Democrats. More specifically, Gaddie and Bullock (2000, 71) point to the even lower likelihood of finding a Republican state legislator who represented territory that overlapped with the local congressional district. This was a fundamental problem with top-down Republican advancement. By the late 1990s, however, the Democratic advantage "in candidate development and promotion has become less pronounced . . . almost to the point of disappearing" (Gaddie and Bullock 2000, 71). In other words, because of the recent success of the Republican Party, especially in congressional elections, their numbers have substantially improved in state legislatures, and this has put in place a farm system for candidate recruitment.

Thus far, we have discussed the role of redistricting and candidate emergence with respect to the advancement of the GOP in southern House elections in the 1990s. Redistricting triggered an elite response by fostering the emergence of viable Republican candidates and in turn increased the rate of Republican voting, particularly among redrawn or so-called new voters. That said, a Republican House majority would not have been possible without the presence of one more condition: an increase in the number of Republican identifiers. Growing Republican mass partisanship in the southern electorate (see Black and Black 2002; Wattenberg 1991) provided a necessary foundation for GOP ascendancy in House elections in the 1990s. The work of Green et al. (2002) shows that the increase in Republican identification was both a function of conversion and generational replacement—with younger cohorts more likely to identify with the GOP.

Similarly, Alan Abramowitz and Kyle Saunders (1998) contend that southern Republican ascendancy was the culmination of an ideologically driven secular realignment in party identification (party ID). Recognizing that the literature points to presidential vote choice and retrospective evaluations as factors that can impact party identification, Abramowitz and Saunders argue that neither factor can account for "long-term shifts in the party loyalties of the electorate" (636). What they say can explain a long-term change in party ID is the effect of policy preferences. Because the parties have taken clear and opposing positions on salient issues, over the years voters have responded by lining up their party identifications with their ideological positions on the issues advocated by the parties.

The evidence is strongly supportive of their theory, especially based on a path analysis that shows that ideology drives partisanship and not vice versa. Based on panel data (1978 and 1992–1994 NES), it is evident that among conservative respondents in 1994 who had Democratic parents, they were much more likely to be Republicans than were their counterparts in 1978.[8] Furthermore, Abramowitz and Saunders find that among respondents of different levels of political awareness (low, moderate, and high) regarding party-issue differences, the correlation between party ID and ideology is substantially greater in 1994 than it was in 1978.

The work of Abramowitz and Saunders also meshes with the evidence presented by Jacobson (2001, 2004), who finds that the parties in government have become more polarized (see also Aldrich and Rohde 1997–1998; Rohde 1991; Stonecash et al. 2003; Theriault 2006) and their electorates, albeit to a lesser extent, have followed suit (but see Fiorina et al. 2005).[9] Jacobson notes that the "southern strategy" "emerged because Republican candidates sensed an opportunity to win converts among conservative white southerners" (2001, 252). He goes on to explain:

> In adopting positions, then, politicians are guided by the opportunities and constraints presented by configurations of public opinion on

political issues. Party polarization in Congress depended on the expectation that voters would reward, or at least not punish, voting with one's party's majority. (Jacobson 2001, 252)

Black and Black (2002, Chapter 7) show that the election of Ronald Reagan ignited the partisan realignment of white conservatives (especially those of the religious right) into the GOP and also prompted the dealignment of white moderates away from the Democratic Party (see their Figure 7.2, p. 223). Based on exit poll data, 70 percent of conservative white southerners identified with the GOP in 2000, and white moderates were a little more likely to side with the GOP (just under 40 percent) than with the Democratic Party. Black and Black (2002) point to the importance of ideology as a key determinant in understanding the current party system in the South. If one only looks at party ID, then Democratic strength is overstated and thus Republican strength is underestimated.

Republican identifiers are currently a plurality of the southern electorate and a majority among whites. A recent study by Hayes and McKee (2008) showed the continuing growth in southern Republican identifiers through the 2004 elections. A notable feature of their analysis is that the political ideology of southerners has remained virtually constant for over thirty years, leading to the expectation that ideology is fueling the partisan re-sorting of southern voters. Future Republican House prospects—and hence the long-term status of the southern GOP—will depend on the portion of Republicans comprising the party in the electorate.

Sizing Up the Literature

What can we conclude from the literature on party competition in House elections both before and after the Republican Party became the majority in Congress and in the South? First, it is not plausible that the southern GOP was relegated to minority status before the 1994 elections because voters preferred candidates who delivered the pork barrel and thus chose Democrats over Republicans. Perhaps Republicans changed their tune with respect to performing constituency service after they won a majority of seats, but most likely this was not the basis for deciding elections. The GOP may present itself as the more fiscally conservative party, but this is often hard to reconcile with the empirical evidence of congressional spending undertaken by both Republican and Democratic House members.

Instead, a more convincing explanation is that Republicans were able to shift the terms of the electoral debate from one about constituency service, where the Democrats had the advantage, to one about ideologically based issues where the GOP had the edge. The message of conservative reform (Fenno 1997; Gimpel 1996; Rae 1998) as outlined in the GOP's Contract with America served to nationalize (Fiorina 2005; Jacobson 2001) House elections and shined the spotlight on how out of step the Democrats were with the values held by white southerners.

To be sure, the positions outlined in the Contract with America purposely avoided some hot-button social issues like abortion and school prayer,[10] but the overall theme was that the Democratic congressional majority was out of touch with rank-and-file Americans because of the party's profligate behavior (e.g., the House Bank Scandal, President Clinton's actions, gays in the military, the 1993 budget, and health care). In fact, constituency service came to be seen as a liability because Republicans were able to frame it as an instance of Democratic largesse. The Republican Party, under the leadership of Representative Newt Gingrich, promised to bring back responsible governance, and if they failed, then they expected and demanded the voters to throw them out of office. Thus, in contrast to the 1980s, in the early to mid-1990s the Gingrich-led Republican Party touted a message of political reform favored by a white southern electorate that came to recognize stark differences between the major party candidates running in House elections.

As Morris Fiorina (2005) (also see Aldrich 1995) contends, in the contemporary House there are more members who possess strong policy commitments, and consequently issues have become more important and more nationalized in House elections. In response, the cue of partisanship becomes decidedly more salient than the cue of incumbency. Candidates who are able to show that incumbents are out of touch with the views of their constituents face defeat (Erikson and Wright 2005). By the 1990s, constituency service became relatively less important because there was an expectation of constituency service irrespective of a candidate's partisanship (Fiorina 2005). Therefore, ideologically based issues came to the fore, and on these issues Republicans were more appealing to white southerners.

Not surprisingly, the literature on House elections after the GOP secured its majority in 1994 is more accurate in terms of pointing to the causes that brought about Republican ascendancy. As mentioned, there are several important works that explain the influence of redistricting and candidate emergence on Republican gains in House elections. Furthermore, the research of Abramowitz and Saunders (1998) and Green et al. (2002) demonstrates the importance of a partisan realignment among white southerners in favor of the GOP as being a fundamental component of Republican success. Additionally, the work of Black and Black (2002) is by far the most comprehensive in documenting the rise of the southern Republican Party in congressional elections since the end of World War II.

Yet despite a tremendous amount of high-level scholarship on party competition in contemporary southern House elections, no one has offered an integrated explanation to account for party system change. Instead, the causes for Republican ascendancy are typically identified in piecemeal fashion, or the reasons given for the growth of southern Republicanism are thought to be too varied and complicated to be distilled to a set of necessary and sufficient factors. Or, even worse, the explanation for partisan change is simplified to such an extent that the fundamental details of the causal process are virtually absent (see Shafer and Johnston 2006). In this respect, I depart from extant scholarship by presenting an explanation for Republican ascendancy in southern House elections that is explicitly reducible to three sequentially and temporally interdependent factors: (1) growing Republican identification among white southerners, (2) the electoral effects of redistricting implemented prior to the 1992 elections, and (3) the emergence of viable Republican candidates who campaigned on a message that was in step with the views of white southerners.

My explanation can account for the S-curve pattern of Republican advancement in southern House elections from 1988 to 2004. The increasing Republican identification of southern white voters provided a necessary foundation for Republican gains, but it was the destabilizing effect of redistricting that explains the sudden increase in Republican victories that occurred in 1992 and 1994. Redistricting weakened the incumbency advantage of many Democrats by infusing their districts with a large share of redrawn constituents, and this triggered the emergence of Republican candidates who were adept at campaigning on a message that would be embraced by southern whites. Thus, both long-term (realigning party identification) as well as short-term (redistricting and the emergence of viable Republican candidates) factors converged in the 1990s to create the perfect electoral storm for southern Republicans. Before this, party competition was in equilibrium in the late 1980s, with Democrats in the majority. Then, with the onset of redistricting in 1992 followed by the GOP netting twenty-five seats after the 1992 and 1994 elections, the period of punctuated change occurred. After 1996, however, Republican gains leveled off and a new equilibrium has held ever since with the Republican Party maintaining a comfortable majority.

A Theoretical Explanation for the Rise of Southern Republicans

Before 1994, the last time the GOP was the majority in the U.S. House was after the 1952 elections. The Democratic Party's forty-year reign in the U.S. House, from 1955 to 1995, is the longest span of party control in American history and is two-and-one-half times longer than any other span of party control (there have been three durations when a party was a majority for sixteen consecutive years—Republicans from 1859–1875, Republicans from 1895–1911, and Democrats from 1931–1947 [Connelly and Pitney 1994, 2]). This may seem an impressive streak, but prior to 1994 the last time the GOP was a majority of the southern House delegation was after the 1872 elections (Black 1998).

Figure 1.1 shows the total number of Democrats and Republicans in the southern House delegation from 1946 to 2004. The vertical axis on the left-hand side denotes the raw party total whereas the vertical axis on the right-hand side indicates the Republican percentage of the southern House delegation. At the start of the time series, Republicans were practically nonexistent, with only two Tennessee Republicans in the 105-member southern House delegation from 1946 to 1950. Beginning in the 1950s, however, the GOP started to register gains, which increased markedly in the 1960s and then leveled off in the 1980s. Thus, from 1946 to the mid-1980s Republican growth generally tracks a linear pattern.

By contrast, Republican advancement from the mid-1980s through 2004 is characterized by punctuated change, which exhibits an S-curve or jump-shift pattern. There was a remarkable period of partisan stability from 1986 to 1990, with seventy-seven Democrats and thirty-nine Republicans serving in the southern House after each of these elections. Then, this electoral equilibrium was disrupted in 1992, when Republicans picked up nine seats and followed up with sixteen more in 1994, thereby giving southern Republicans a House majority. Republicans won seven more House seats in 1996, and at this point their rate of advancement leveled off until the 2004 elections.

What accounts for this S-curve pattern of Republican advancement in southern House contests from 1988 to 2004? Or rather: Why, after 120 years in the minority, did Republicans *suddenly* win back the southern House in the mid-1990s, and what explains their steady gains ever since?

The seeds of southern Republican ascendancy were sewn a half-century ago by the actions of political elites, which led to a change in the composition of the groups comprising each party's voting coalition. This change in the social bases of the parties is a consequence of voters lining up their preferences with the policy positions advanced and supported by candidates and officeholders (Carmines and Stimson 1989; Petrocik 1981, 1987; Stimson 2004; Sundquist 1983).

Because voting behavior is more responsive to short-term effects than is the more durable concept of party identification, it is a leading indicator of change (Campbell et al. 1960). In the South, we find that

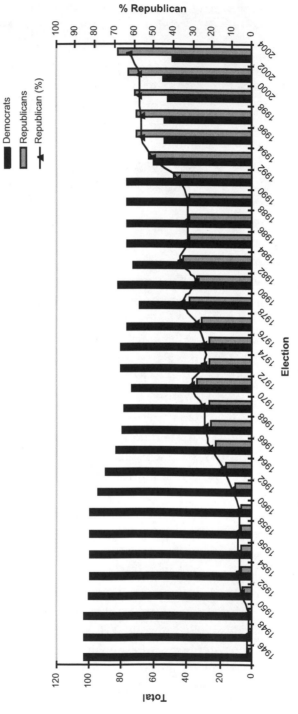

FIGURE 1.1 Partisan Composition of U.S. House Districts in the Postwar South, 1946–2004

the economic conservatism pushed by the GOP prior to the civil rights movement (Bartley and Graham 1975; Lublin 2004; Shafer and Johnston 2006) was eventually wedded to a growing racial conservatism that the party emphasized with the reinstatement of African American suffrage (Carmines and Stimson 1989). Then, in the late 1970s religious/cultural conservatism began to align with the Republican Party as Ronald Reagan expressed his opposition to *Roe v. Wade* in the 1980 presidential campaign. Thus, how Democratic and Republican politicians positioned themselves with regard to major social changes (i.e., economic development, increasing education, and northern in-migration; see Black and Black 1987) and period effects (e.g., the 1964 Civil Rights Act, the 1964 presidential election, the 1965 Voting Rights Act, and the 1980 presidential election) set in motion and eventually reinforced the path dependency of successive candidates and officeholders who adapted to, and adopted the positions of their national parties (Stimson 2004).

The progression of this transformation of the groups comprising the major party's coalitions primarily takes the form of top-down advancement (Aistrup 1996). Top-down advancement means that white southerners first align their electoral preferences at the presidential level because presidential candidates take opposing positions on highly salient issues that serve to differentiate the national parties (Carmines and Stimson 1989). Thus, the high visibility of presidential elections ensures that voters will be aware of the policy positions staked out by the party's nominees (e.g., the 1964 presidential election). The stands taken by Democratic and Republican politicians on salient issues are viewed by the electorate through an ideological lens, and consequently GOP affiliation among white southerners gradually increases, particularly through a generational replacement effect with younger cohorts showing greater Republican identification. And as the parties continue to diverge ideologically, the most politically aware voters are the most likely to adjust their party identification to fit with their own ideology (Abramowitz and Saunders 1998).

At first, advancement in lower-level contests like the U.S. House is minimal because Democratic officeholders maintain positions that are aligned with white southerners (see Black and Black 2002).[11] In fact, it was not until the late 1970s when most Democrats (representatives and candidates) began to realign according to the positions taken by their national party (Deep South Democrats were slower to adjust; see Black and Black 2002). The infusion of growing numbers of black voters (mainly due to the Voting Rights Act of 1965) into the southern electorate provides white Democratic representatives with a choice: (1) take positions that will gain the votes of a coalition of black and white voters or (2) take positions that are favorable to whites and opposed by blacks. The choice made is in part a function of the racial composition of the district, but clearly most African Americans have decided to support the Democratic party from 1964 forward, and white Democratic representatives in districts with large black populations could either be responsive to these voters or risk defeat.

Throughout the 1980s, biracial coalitions proved successful in defeating the challenges of Republican candidates who could only win in districts with a landslide share of the white vote (60 percent or higher; see Black and Black 2002). The success of Ronald Reagan in the 1980s was the shot in the arm needed for so many whites to break with the Democratic Party, at least in terms of party identification (to a lesser extent with respect to vote choice in House races). Yet even with the success Reagan had in moving whites toward the GOP, the large majority delegation of Democratic representatives managed to scare off challenges from quality Republican candidates, and hence there was the growing presence of split-result districts: Republican in presidential contests and Democratic in House elections (see Campbell 1997). Numerous white voters did not have a sufficient reason to vote Republican because they resided in districts that were contested by inferior GOP candidates (especially with regard to elective experience, Jacobson 1990). Under these conditions, a large segment of white voters continued to reward Democratic incumbents for a job well done.

Then, however, before the 1992 elections the political landscape changed dramatically when the Department of Justice refused to "preclear" districting plans under Section 5 of the Voting Rights Act in several southern states until the new boundaries were drawn in order to further maximize the number of majority-minority districts (Cunningham 2001). Pursuing their own narrow objective of winning seats under the new congressional geography, white Republicans and black Democratic leaders formed partnerships to advocate for the maximization of newly created majority-minority districts (Black and Black 2002; Lamis 1999). The structural change brought about through redistricting was indeed a windfall for Republicans and black Democrats, whereas white Democrats were disproportionately harmed because the creation of majority-minority districts tore asunder the biracial coalitions that for so long proved their successful electoral strategy (Black 1998; Black and Black 2002; Lamis 1988; Shafer and Johnston 2006).

The structural change of redistricting fostered greater strategic behavior on the part of Republican challengers/candidates, who then targeted those districts that were now proportionally whiter and, consequently, more Republican—based on the presidential vote.[12] By drawing more politically homogeneous districts, the new congressional boundaries had the effect of increasing partisan polarization among candidates and the electorate. Concentrating African Americans and Hispanics in majority-minority districts made surrounding districts whiter, more Republican, and more conservative, and as a result Democratic candidates were no longer able to win contests based on center-left appeals that had worked in the past in more racially diverse districts.

These so-called "bleached" districts, with overwhelming white populations, consisted of loyal Republican voters and a good deal of redrawn constituents who were placed into districts with a different incumbent as a consequence of racial redistricting. With the bond of incumbency severed by being placed in a new district, most of these redrawn voters were in fact latent Republicans, at least based on their voting behavior in presidential elections (Bullock et al. 2005). Then, with the emergence of strong Republican challengers who contested these districts, redrawn voters finally had a compelling reason to vote Republican in House elections—and most of them did (McKee 2008; Petrocik and Desposato 1998).

Redistricting in the 1990s hastened the ascendancy of Republicans in the South because it was the single factor that could weaken the Democratic incumbency advantage (through the infusion of new voters) and at the same time reconfigure districts in a way that made them

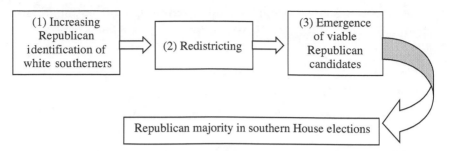

FIGURE 1.2 A Model of Partisan Change in Southern U.S. House Elections

competitive enough for viable Republican candidates to risk contest-ing.[13] The acceleration of Republican advancement in House elections due to redistricting in 1992 was a short-term effect that in turn com-plemented a long-term trend in favor of southern Republicanism. By the time of the 2002 redistricting, Republican advances registered in the 1990s were reinforced by the implementation of districting plans that generally maintained the electoral status quo. In short, partisan change in southern House elections from 1988 to 2004 is mainly a function of a secular realignment of whites into the Republican party, redistricting, and the emergence of viable Republican candidates. Fig-ure 1.2 restates the point graphically.

At the macro-level, this explanation for the rise of southern Repub-licans is conceptualized by a punctuated equilibrium/change model.

Edward Carmines and James Stimson (1989) and Walter Dean Burnham (1991) suggest that an improvement on the critical election concept (e.g., Key 1955) is a punctuated equilibrium model. The main difference with the concept of punctuated equilibrium vis-à-vis a crit-ical election is that there is noticeable change occurring and evident before a flashpoint is reached (see Key 1959), and afterwards (in subse-quent elections) there is a receding of movement with the onset of a more or less stable state as electoral gains occur at a lower rate. Here is Carmines and Stimson's characterization of the punctuated equilib-rium model:

It is dynamic because it presumes that at some point the system moves from a fairly stationary steady state to a fairly dramatic rapid change; the change is manifested by a 'critical moment' in the time series—a point where change is large enough to be visible and, perhaps, the origin of a dynamic process. Significantly, however, the change—the dynamic growth—does not end with the critical moment; instead it continues over an extended period, albeit at [a] much slower pace. This continued growth after the initial shock defines the evolutionary character of the model. (1989, 13)

So essentially, the main difference between a critical election and punctuated equilibrium is the period before and after the moment of upheaval. One can consider the "critical moment" to be the critical election in a punctuated change model. Thought of in this way, there is strong evidence that the 1994 election was the critical moment in a model of punctuated equilibrium. In the South, the model fits political reality very well. Competition in House elections appears to be stable in 1988 and 1990, before the onset of change in 1992 and the critical moment in 1994, after which GOP gains continued at a lower rate through the 2004 elections. From 1996 to 2000, Republicans controlled the same majority of seats, 71 out of 125 (57 percent)—evidence of a new stable state with the GOP firmly in control.[14] In most southern states, congressional redistricting in 2002 served to maintain the partisan status quo because most maps were drawn to protect both party's incumbents. There was, however, a noticeable jump in the number of Republicans after the 2004 elections because of a successful Republican gerrymander enacted in Texas.

Republican advancement in southern House elections clearly reflects the S-curve pattern of punctuated equilibrium in an issue evolution theory. But what makes the case of southern House elections distinctive is the causal mechanism for this punctuated change. The ongoing secular realignment of white southerners in favor of the GOP provided the requisite foundation for the flip-over pattern to occur, but the rapid ascendancy of House Republicans in 1992 and 1994 was mainly due to the destabilizing effect of racial redistricting and the concomitant emergence of viable Republican candidates. The structural change induced by redistricting in 1992 set the stage for the critical moment in 1994 when southern Republicans won enough seats to become the majority party in the South for the first time since Reconstruction.

In *Agendas and Instability in American Politics*, Frank Baumgartner and Bryan Jones (1993) present a general theory of change that can be applied to an analysis of southern House elections.[15] Citing William Riker (1980), Baumgartner and Jones (1993) argue that instability is the common state of affairs in politics.[16] Stability or equilibrium is induced by political actors working through institutional arrangements. Stable arrangements are achieved by the implementation of rules that bias outcomes in favor of the ruling party and by their control of the issue/policy agenda: "Issue definition and institutional control combine to make possible the alternation between stability and rapid change that characterizes political systems" (Baumgartner and Jones 1993, 16).

Equilibrium is only temporary at best because it is contingent upon maintaining a set of conditions (the status quo) that political entrepreneurs can alter by appealing to another dimension where a different majority of preferences hold (see Riker 1982). Thus, there are generally two kinds of processes at work in politics: (1) incrementalism, which tends to reinforce the status quo through a negative feedback loop, and (2) periods of rapid change brought about by more infrequent periods of positive feedback. Like Burnham (1996) and Carmines and Stimson (1989), Baumgartner and Jones consider instances of rapid political change as adhering to an "S-shaped curve," a punctuated equilibrium model.

For the status quo to be drastically altered requires the emergence of a mobilized opposition, and an opposition will materialize if the prospects for change increase. What keeps the current system from unraveling is primarily inattentiveness or public apathy (Baumgartner and Jones 1993, 16–21). This means that so long as the public is not aroused by a countervailing agenda, the current state of affairs will persist. But Baumgartner and Jones point out that since "the possibility exists of mobilizing the previously indifferent through the redefinition of issues, no system based on the shared preferences of the interested is safe" (19). Expanding the scope of the conflict a la E. E. Schattschneider (1960), altering the dimensions of political discourse a la Riker (1986), or changing institutional parameters via redistricting can all lead to punctuated change. Furthermore, according to Baum-gartner and Jones, "If a social equilibrium is induced only by the struc-tures that determine participation in its choice, then altering the structures (or changing the rules) can cause the equilibrium to quickly disappear" (1993, 16).

In the case of southern House races, a combination of the incum-bency advantage and static congressional boundaries maintained a preference- and structure-induced electoral equilibrium that held from the mid-1980s through 1990. Southern Democrats' majority sta-tus was safe so long as the electorate remained inattentive and the GOP continued to run inferior candidates. Unfortunately for the Democratic Party, however, redistricting upset the electoral status quo by triggering the emergence of viable Republican candidates who then aroused the electorate with a winning campaign message that drasti-cally altered the voting behavior of white southerners in favor of the Republican Party. Thus, all the ingredients for punctuated change were present in the case of southern House contests in the 1990s, and they played out in the fashion posited by the aforementioned theory. Stabil-ity in party competition in southern House elections was shattered by the structural impact of redistricting, which directly weakened the in-cumbency advantage. Voters drawn into districts represented by a new Democratic incumbent were more receptive to and supportive of Re-publican challengers, who then captured voting majorities by convinc-ing white southerners that their short-and long-term interests were better served by aligning with the GOP.

Notes

1. In this book the South is defined as the eleven ex-Confederate states: Ala-bama, Arkansas, Florida, Georgia, Louisiana, Mississippi, North Carolina, South Carolina, Tennessee, Texas, and Virginia. Where necessary, the standard subregional distinction is used: Deep South—Alabama, Georgia, Louisiana, Mississippi, and South Carolina; Peripheral (Rim) South—Arkansas, Florida, North Carolina, Tennessee, Texas, and Virginia.

2. Author's analysis of National Election Studies (NES) data.

3. Speaking to the disadvantage of being the minority party, Cox and Katz (2002) contend that the value of a seat for a minority party candidate is worth

less, and therefore an ambitious candidate will run under the majority party label. According to Cox and Katz: "Truly hopeless minorities, such as the Republicans were for so long in the South, suffer much larger investment problems. Such parties see ambitious and talented politicians who might otherwise join their ranks seek instead to compete within the majority party" (215).

4. Based on author's calculation of NES data.

5. For a comprehensive review of the literature on race-based redistricting in congressional elections see McKee (2004).

6. Hill regressed the 1992 Democratic House vote on the presidential vote, incumbency, contestedness of the district, percent black, the change in percent black (from 1990), and a dummy for black majority district.

7. In none of Jacobson's work does he analyze the impact of racial redistricting on Republican gains. He favorably cites the work of Hill (1995) in his agreement that majority-minority districting led to Republican pickups (Jacobson 1996; 2001).

8. Abramowitz and Saunders (1998) also run a regression with party ID being a function of parental partisanship and ideology (controlling for age, gender, education, family income, race, and region). They run this model on the 1978 and 1994 data (separately) and find that the coefficient for ideology is noticeably larger in 1994 (although they do not say whether it is significantly larger than the ideology coefficient in 1978).

9. According to Jacobson (2001) the process of partisan polarization is dynamic and interactive, but the direction is primarily top-down.

10. These issues would have been acceptable as topics to bring up in the South, but the Contract with America was designed to be a national Republican agenda.

11. It is also the case that candidates (e.g., southern Democrats) take positions that make voters perceive them as ideologically acceptable (see Frymer et al. 1997).

12. There is ample evidence that "Republican presidential success in the 1980s was expanding the grassroots base needed to improve Republican competitiveness in congressional elections" (Black and Black 2002, 203).

13. Of course, there were also short-term factors before the 1994 elections that broke decidedly in favor of Republican candidates—who proved adept at "nationalizing the elections" in their local contests (see Burnham 1996; Fiorina 2005; Jacobson 1996; 2004).

14. Republicans controlled 63 percent (82 of 131 districts) of southern House seats after the 2004 elections.

15. Given its relevance to southern House elections, it is worth quoting at length a passage from Baumgartner and Jones:

Focusing on consequences directs our attention to institutional structures. All political institutions channel conflict in a particular way; all are related to the mobilization of bias. Noting the structure of bias inherent in any set of political institutions not only shows who is advantaged, however; it also shows what changes might come about from destruction or alteration of an existing arrangement. Those left out of the original system may not be heard there, but if the structures are changed, then dramatic changes in the mobilization of bias may result. Institutional structures in American politics are generally not easy to change, but when they do change, these changes often lead to dramatic and long-lasting changes in policy outcomes. So institutions play an important role in this analysis, since they make possible a system of periods of relative stability, where the mobilization of bias is structured by a set of institutions that remain stable for some period. However, these periods of stability may be linked by periods of rapid change during which the institutional framework is challenged. Because of this, incremental changes are less important than the dramatic alterations in the mobilization of bias during these critical periods. The result is that the American political system lurches from one point of apparent equilibrium to another, as policymakers establish new institutions to support the policies they favor or alter existing ones to give themselves greater advantage. (1993, 12)

16. Baumgartner and Jones (1993) present the following quote from Riker: "And what we have learned is simply this: Disequilibrium, or the potential that the status quo be upset, is the characteristic feature of politics" (1980, 443).

2

The Dynamics of
Party Identification

The transformation of Southern party attachments may
be explained from many theoretical vantage points.
(2002, 155)

—Donald Green, Bradley Palmquist, and Eric Schickler

Given its tremendous electoral influence, American politics scholars casually refer to party identification as the so-called 800-pound gorilla in studies of voter preferences. As such, it should come as no surprise that a substantial part of the explanation for the ascendancy of the Republican Party in southern House contests is the increase in the number of southern whites who identify with the GOP. The growth, then, in the proportion of southern Republican identifiers provided a critical mass of voters capable of ushering in a Republican House majority in the 1990s.

Party identification is one of the most written about subjects in American politics. There are several reasons why political affiliation receives so much attention, including the following: (1) scholars disagree on how to conceptualize party ID, (2) there is widespread disagreement on how stable party ID is, and (3) there is disagreement on what factors alter party ID. What is indisputable, however, and what makes party ID such a noteworthy topic, is its massive effect on vote choice. It is certainly the case that an increase in the proportion of Republican identifiers generally translates into the election of more

Republican candidates, and this makes an investigation of party ID essential to understanding the rise of the southern GOP in House elections.

Party Identification: Not Always the "Unmoved Mover"

There is considerable disagreement among scholars with respect to the concept of party identification.[1] For our purposes, the dispute boils down to a question of stability—how loyal and resilient are partisan attachments? The traditional view is that party ID is a stable, affective, and highly durable psychological attachment to a political party acquired through political socialization (i.e., transmitted from parent to offspring) and reinforced by a sense of belonging to a social group aligned with one's preferred political party (Campbell et al. 1960; Green et al. 2002). According to these scholars, the *traditionalists* (the "Michigan School" and their contemporary supporters like Green et al. 2002), only under exceptional circumstances like a partisan realignment is it thought that political affiliations are greatly altered.

The classic statement on party ID was made by the authors of *The American Voter* (Campbell et al. 1960). In this work, Campbell et al. argue that party ID is an enduring psychological attachment to one of the political parties. They state that, "Generally this tie is a psychological identification . . . most Americans have this sense of attachment with one party or the other. And for the individual who does, the strength and direction of party identification are facts of central importance in accounting for attitude and behavior" (121). Party ID is fundamental to understanding political behavior because it precedes and shapes the formation of other political attitudes (Bartels 2002). In addition, party ID is thought to be stable, durable, and resistant to change. According to *The American Voter* authors:

> When we examine the evidence on the manner in which party attachment develops and changes during the lifetime of the individual citizen, we find a picture characterized more by stability than by change—not by rigid, immutable fixation on one party rather than

the other, but by a persistent adherence and resistance to contrary influence. (Campbell et al. 1960, 146)

Likewise, Carsey and Layman (2006, 465) succinctly explain the traditional perspective on party identification:

[P]arty identification is an 'unmoved mover:' a deeply held psychological attachment that is (1) largely unchanging over time even as events change, and (2) a filter through which citizens view and interpret new political information. From this perspective, party identification shapes policy preferences and other political attitudes, but is largely unchanged by them.

This traditional view of party identification has been challenged by numerous scholars, often referred to as *revisionists*, who have marshaled evidence that party ID is not as stable as originally argued because it is influenced by short-term political factors (e.g., issue evaluations, candidate evaluations, economic evaluations, and presidential approval). Because party ID is affected by short-term events, revisionists contend that party ID may not be an enduring psychological attachment, but rather, according to one prominent scholar, a "running tally of retrospective evaluations" of party performance (Fiorina 1981, 255).

The traditional view of party identification, as espoused and promoted by the authors of *The American Voter*, came under attack by revisionist scholars in the mid-1970s. Perhaps it is fitting that one of the most cogent arguments against the traditionalist approach was made by the authors of *The Changing American Voter* (Nie et al. 1976). Amassing an enormous amount of evidence on voting behavior from the 1950s through the mid-1970s, Nie et al. claimed that, compared to the 1950s, voting behavior was significantly altered by the 1960s and into the 1970s because the political context was fundamentally altered during this time. Issues became more important as a cue in guiding the vote, especially in the presence of declining partisanship among the electorate, and thus party ID exhibited a reduced influence on vote choice.

According to Nie et al., because the parties did not take clear, opposing sides on various issues of political importance during the 1960s and 1970s, party ID was no longer a decisive shortcut for vote choice. Instead, candidates of both parties had an incentive to stake out their own positions on a range of issues since there was less guidance provided by the parties. In this political climate—characterized by an increase in candidate-centered campaigns, the emergence of a broad range of issues (e.g., the environment, the Vietnam War, women's rights, crime, social welfare, etc.) that the parties had yet to take definitive positions on (see Sundquist 1983), and a concomitant decline in partisanship (manifested by an increase in ticket-splitting)—it is no wonder that party ID did not exhibit the same level of stability that was apparent in the 1950s. According to Nie et al.:

> The presidential elections of 1952, 1956, and 1960 presented few burning issues to the public and the candidates went out of their way to emphasize the person or the party they represented. In contrast, polarizing issues were the stuff of the 1960s, and the candidates emphasized them. (1976, 386)

The work of Fiorina (1981) bolstered the revisionist argument that the stability of party ID was time-bound and hence highly dependent on political context. Given the susceptibility of party ID to short-term factors such as retrospective evaluations of party performance, Fiorina conceptualized party ID as a running tally, a scorecard that adjusts to changes in a party's electoral fortunes (see also Key 1966).

Fiorina's challenge of the traditional conception of party ID was undertaken at the individual level, but MacKuen et al. (1989, 1992) challenged the traditional view of party ID at the aggregate level. MacKuen et al. found that partisanship (based on quarterly measures of the Gallup Poll question)[2] in the aggregate, or what they term macropartisanship, was responsive to presidential approval and economic evaluations (consumer sentiment surveys administered by the University of Michigan). Contrary to the traditional view that party ID affects candidate evaluations and other political judgments, MacKuen et al. found, like other proponents of the revisionist perspective, that party ID is itself impacted by other political attitudes, and this accounts for why macropartisanship fluctuates in response to changes in public opinion of presidential performance and the state of the economy. When the electoral environment clearly shifts in favor of one party, macropartisanship responds by exhibiting an increase (decrease) in the party ID of the advantaged (disadvantaged) party. In short, aggregate-level data on political affiliation is a good barometer for gauging the "what have you done for me lately question" as it applies to party evaluations.

The revisionist view of party ID offers a refutation of the traditional argument that party ID is mainly antecedent to the formation of other political attitudes, is highly stable, and amounts to an enduring psychological attachment to a political party. Instead, revisionists contend that party ID and other political attitudes (e.g., candidate evaluations) exhibit a recursive relationship, and this explains why party ID is malleable and, as should be expected, more pliable when the political climate is in a state of flux (e.g., from the mid-1960s through the 1970s).

Although the revisionist model of party ID is arguably the prevailing position (see Franklin 1992; Miller 1991), it has received a formidable challenge by Green et al. (2002), who provide a case for defending the traditional view of party ID in *Partisan Hearts and Minds*.[3] Green et al. conceptualize party ID as a social identity. They defend the traditional view put forth in *The American Voter*, particularly with respect to the idea that party ID is a powerful and enduring psychological attachment to a party and consists of an affective component. Green et al. draw on a sports analogy to explain their conceptualization of party ID as a social identity: Similar to the way fans root for their teams, partisans cheer on their candidates. Social groups align with political parties, and thus voters develop perceptions of, and attachments to, the parties based on the social groups that comprise the parties' electoral coalitions.

It is very plausible that the conception of party ID offered by Green et al. is accurate, at least for a subset of partisans—most likely strong partisans. Further, Green et al. show that after controlling for measurement error, party ID exhibits a high degree of longitudinal stability (but see Franklin 1992). What appears less defensible is making the case that most partisans—or even the typical partisan—fit the conception of party ID put forth by Green et al. For instance, going back to the sports analogy, fans can be very fickle, especially when their teams experience a losing streak. At least for some fans, the attractiveness of remaining loyal to one's team can depreciate considerably, and hence it may be time to jump on another team's bandwagon. The evidence for macropartisanship provides strong support for this behavior in the realm of politics; many voters adjust their political affiliations on the basis of party performance.

Another criticism of Green et al. is that they severely discount the role that issues play in affecting party ID.[4] Echoing the sentiment of their Michigan School forebears, because party ID is deeply rooted, akin to religious identification, issues rarely cross the threshold necessary to affect party ID. This argument is hard to reconcile with evidence that, even during normal politics, issues can influence party ID (Carsey and Layman 2006; Layman and Carsey 2002a). And partisan change occurs when the parties take opposing positions on salient issues that have the effect of altering the social bases of the parties (Carmines 1991; Carmines and Stimson 1989; Petrocik 1981; Stimson 2004; Sundquist 1983). In fact, by conceding that party-system change can be of the magnitude to alter party ID, Green et al. appear to be admitting that the impetus for a party realignment originates from a marked shift in the positions of the parties on salient, "easy" (see Carmines and Stimson 1980) issues like civil rights (see Green et al. 2002, 22–23).

There are a bundle of issues on which the parties take opposing positions, and the positions candidates adopt clearly reflect each party's support of, or opposition to, a set of social groups. In this sense, position-taking by the parties is in part a response to the support given by social groups, and, thus, there is a strong correspondence between position-taking on issues and the social identities of voters aligned with the parties. Perhaps the traditional view usually holds and, at least among most voters who are not well informed on the issues, party ID is the primary shortcut for deciding how to vote (e.g., Converse 1964). On the other hand, it appears undeniable that the changing composition of the social groups aligned with the parties is a function of the positions the parties take on issues that are so consequential they cause voters to alter their political affiliations.

The main disagreement between traditionalists and revisionists centers on the relative stability of party ID and what affects it—and not defining it per se. Of course, disagreement over the stability of party ID is tied to defining the concept—i.e., how stable is it? If we admit that party ID is greatly affected by political context, as the revisionists argue, then the stability of party ID depends on the political setting. As Franklin (1992, 308) states: "So long as preferences and identification agree, the revisionist model predicts a reinforcement and strengthening of partisanship."

In the case of the American South, starting in the 1960s, party system change was so great that no scholar would disagree that it had the effect of significantly altering the political affiliations of the southern electorate. The traditional and revisionist conceptualizations of party ID are both relevant to understanding the dynamic of partisan change when a realigning period commences. The long-term shift in the party identification of southern whites is the question we now examine.

Changing Political Affiliations of Southern Whites

The long-term trend exhibiting an increase in Republican partisanship among southern whites has its roots in the complex interaction between elected representatives/candidates and the electorate. Only the emergence of a major issue on which the political parties would take clear opposing sides was capable of putting in motion a long-term shift in favor of the GOP. Furthermore, the period that originally gave rise to a shift in political affiliations needs to be reinforced in a long series of elections if the minority party is going to have a chance to attain majority status. Party elites (officeholders and activists) are the agents who transform the old political system into a new one, as they clarify the positions of their respective parties on those issues that are important enough to alter, and then subsequently reinforce voter loyalties.

Before the civil rights movement gained steam in the early 1960s, the appeal of the GOP was limited to pockets of mountain Republicans and an emerging white middle class located in metropolitan areas of the peripheral South who were attracted to its pro-business philosophy (Bartley and Graham 1975; Black and Black 1987; Phillips 1969). At the national level, the pre-civil rights GOP was slightly more liberal on the race issue (Carmines and Stimson 1989), and among southern whites, despite the class-based arrangement of American politics stemming from the New Deal realignment, upper-income whites were slightly more likely to identify with the Democratic Party (Nadeau et al. 2004; Shafer and Johnston 2006).

Apart from those isolated areas in the South (mainly in Appalachia: eastern Tennessee, western North Carolina, western Virginia, and northern Alabama) with a Republican presence because of opposition to the Democratic Party dating back to the Civil War, and the modest inroads made among white, middle-class suburbanites who voted for Eisenhower, the GOP struggled in the 1950s to draw supporters away from the Democrats. Below the presidential level, the GOP amounted to little more than a nominal party whose primary function was to distribute patronage (Key 1949). Ideological disputes between conservative and moderate-to-liberal factions were settled within the confines of the Democratic Party, whose raison d'être since the end of Reconstruction was the establishment and subsequent maintenance of the Jim Crow system of white supremacy. The race issue was what held together the southern Democratic Party (Aldrich 2000; Black and Black 1987; Key 1949), and it was the single issue capable of splitting it apart.

By the 1960s, the southern Democracy could no longer bottle up the race issue. It exploded onto the national agenda with the growing momentum of the civil rights movement. The 1964 presidential election was a pivotal moment in the South. By voting against the 1964 Civil Rights Act and opposing federal intervention as a means to promote racial equality, the Republican Goldwater campaign sent a clear signal to southern whites who opposed integration. On the Democratic side, however, President Johnson's push for civil rights after the assassination of Kennedy revealed his 1964 presidential campaign strategy: win the election by abandoning the South in favor of a pro-civil rights agenda with broad appeal in the rest of the nation. The number of votes garnered by endorsing civil rights and promoting the issues of the New Deal coalition swamped the anti-civil rights, free market, and hard-line foreign policy positions of Barry Goldwater.

Yet despite President Johnson's landslide victory,[5] by providing the electorate with a clear alternative ("a choice, not an echo"), Goldwater's campaign planted the roots for contemporary southern Republicanism. His original "Southern Strategy," of cultivating the support of southern whites by taking a conservative approach on civil rights, has been repeated ad infinitum, although the appeals to racial conservatism have evolved in accordance with the growing sensitivity of the issue (e.g., the use of code words; see Bass and De Vries 1976; Carter 1996; Glaser 1996). And even though the focus of political scholars centers on Goldwater's position regarding civil rights because of the importance of the issue at that time, Goldwater espoused conservative positions on economics and foreign policy.

In fact, Goldwater and Reagan were practically ideological mirror images of one another.[6] In hindsight, we can see that the conservative views of Reagan were more popular when he was elected president because New Deal liberalism was under fire in the late 1970s (Stimson 2004). In addition, the gains of social liberals in the 1970s, particularly with *Roe v. Wade* (1973), mobilized the religious right, who found a home with the GOP as a result of the pro-life views of Reagan. In sum, apart from Reagan's engaging personality (a quality that one should not discount in electoral politics), he and Goldwater essentially stood for the same things. The main difference was that, compared to Goldwater, the political climate was much more favorable to Reagan. By serving two presidential terms, Reagan was a towering figure in the growth of southern Republicanism— he was its principal architect. His consistently conservative positions on economic, racial, social/religious, and military issues realigned conservative whites and dealigned moderate whites, who previously identified with the Democratic Party (see Black and Black 2002, 205–240).

Issue Evolution and Partisan Change

So how can this brief historical account shed light on the reasons why southern whites initially moved, and continue to move, in favor of identification with the GOP? This question is answered by providing a theoretical interpretation of the aforementioned political events.[7] The race issue, as it became embodied in the conflict over civil rights, underwent an issue evolution (see Carmines and Stimson 1989; Stimson 2004) that eventually contributed to the ascendancy of the Republican Party in southern House elections. It should be understood, however, that the race issue alone is not what grew the Republican Party (Abramowitz 1994; Lublin 2004). It is more complicated than that. By altering the positions of the national parties on the civil rights issue, racial issue evolution became the catalytic agent for exposing and enhancing old and new fault lines on economic, military, and cultural issues that all served to widen the ideological divide between the Democratic and Republican parties.

American politics scholars have put forth numerous theoretical variants to explain partisan change. Indeed, realignment theory has encompassed so many different incarnations and accompanying caveats that the whole enterprise has been called into question (see Mayhew 2002). Nevertheless, political change happens, and it is necessary to understand what factors account for it.

More than any other theory of partisan change, issue evolution presents the most plausible causal process for producing a long-term electoral realignment. Stripped to its essential elements, issue evolution begins when a high-profile party elite, most likely a presidential candidate, introduces a salient political issue into the electoral arena. The issue is divisive in the sense that the political parties, in the form of their candidates, take opposing positions on it. In addition, the substance and consequences of the issue are easily understood by voters (Carmines and Stimson 1980). Finally, for the issue to realign the parties, it must cut across the existing cleavage that heretofore separates them (Sundquist 1983). In this way, the original axis of party alignment rotates to the extent that the mass electorate re-sorts itself into opposing partisan camps based on the influence of the new cross-cutting issue.

The onset of an issue evolution is apparent when party elites mobilize on opposite sides of what once was either a dormant or settled issue (Stimson 2004). The new issue alignment is fostered and solidified by path dependency—the consistent position-taking of each party's present and future candidates on the new issue. The issue evolution runs its course as party activists bring increased attention to the new developing alignment, and the mass electorate responds in kind by maintaining or altering their party affiliations (Carmines and Woods 2002).

Although the initial evidence for an issue evolution might be easy to detect, its duration is lengthy because the mass public may be slow to realign on the issue. The pace of partisan change depends on political awareness, issue saliency, and the degree of elite resistance. First, those voters who are aware that elites have taken opposing sides on a new issue are more likely to change affiliations. Second, if the issue is very important to the voter—usually among those who view it in ideological terms—they are more likely to switch parties. Finally, voters will be slower to realign if a subset of elites, like U.S. House candidates, resist adopting the position staked out by their national party leaders (presidential nominees). Because party affiliation is durable and resistant to change, especially as individuals get older, generational replacement is often a fundamental component of the issue evolution life cycle (Carmines 1991). Depending on a voter's age, political awareness, and political ideology, both partisan dealignment and realignment will be relevant indicators of an issue evolution.

In the mid-twentieth century, a remarkable feature of the American South was the juxtaposition of large-scale societal transformation (i.e., economic development, increasing levels of education, and population change through northern in-migration; see Black and Black 1987), occurring alongside a highly static and resistant conservative political culture. There was no way to stem the tide of social change, but, given the region's history on the race issue (see Woodward 2002), a reactionary response to civil rights seemed only natural. Indeed, as President Johnson signed the 1964 Civil Rights Act, he anticipated that the white South would leave the Democratic Party. He was right, but unlike African Americans who moved swiftly and uniformly into the Democratic Party both in their voting behavior and party affiliation from 1964 onward, the general movement of southern whites away from the Democratic Party and toward the GOP has been gradual—spanning several generations of voters.

Elections narrow the number of issues that parties emphasize to those that are expected to win votes. The issues promoted by the parties and their respective positions on the issues depend on the current partisan alignment, the extant political context, and the probability of electoral success. In what is expected to be a close election, if we assume that public opinion on an ideological dimension is normally distributed, then the parties will move to the middle and will purposely avoid drawing clear contrasts in their issue positions (Downs 1957). Further, the issues emphasized are of course those that are consciously on the minds of the electorate and thus are relevant to the vote decision. Under these conditions, issue convergence rather than issue divergence is the dominant strategy for candidate positioning.

By contrast, in the context of a political setting that clearly favors one party, there will be a strong incentive for the party on the losing side to introduce a new issue and take a position on it that can alter the electoral status quo (Stimson 2004). The goal is to stake out a position on an issue that has the effect of adding a new dimension to the current electoral dimension (Riker 1986). The expectation is that more votes can be won on the new dimension than would be won in the absence of introducing the new issue. By adding a new dimension, the issue is assumed to be cross-cutting, drawing supporters and opponents across the original cleavage that divided the parties and their supporters. The partisan electoral balance and the composition of the voters aligned with the parties can be permanently altered when the introduction of a cross-cutting issue leads to a critical moment when the parties take opposing positions on the issue and thereby risk their immediate and long-term electoral prospects.

Figure 2.1 is a simplified illustration of the alignment of the national political parties.[8] We can think of the old line of political cleavage that divides the Democrats and Republicans as an economic cleavage. On the economic issue, the Democratic Party is dominant because it won the fight over New Deal policies. The Republican Party, losing on the New Deal issue, softens its free market positions, but clearly remains to the right of the Democratic Party on the economic cleavage that divides the parties. Given the political context before the civil rights movement, for national Republicans the economic issue is

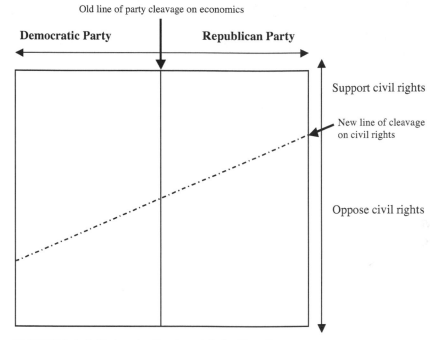

FIGURE 2.1 Splitting the Parties with the Race Issue

a loser; at least in the short-term it is settled and thus the Republican Party needs to present a "new"[9] issue with the hope that it can alter the electoral status quo by appealing to voters across the original economic cleavage.

Civil rights is just the sort of issue that can cross-cut and hence draw support across party lines. Figure 2.1 shows the civil rights issue cutting across the original economic cleavage that divides the Democrats and Republicans. Below the civil rights cleavage are those who oppose civil rights. Above the civil rights cleavage are the supporters of civil rights.

Figure 2.2 takes the analysis a step farther, illustrating how an issue evolution realigns the parties. It is important to stress that the process documented in Figure 2.2 does not play itself out immediately—especially with respect to changing party identifications and the relative balance of electoral power between the parties. Instead, it can take decades as the new electoral arrangement is reinforced and solidified by the advent of new generations of voters (Carmines 1991). We view the

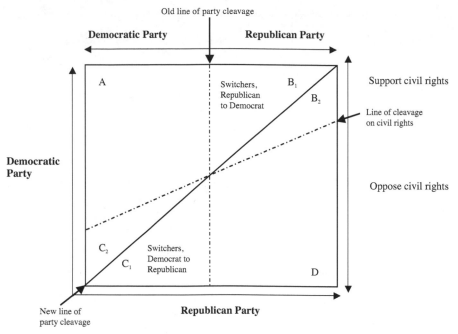

FIGURE 2.2 The Changing Composition of the Parties in Response to Civil Rights

spaces A, B1, B2, C1, C2, and D in Figure 2.2 as the location of voters and/or candidates. Although the introduction of the cross-cutting issue is the product of an elite calculation made by a candidate, the sorting process in response to the new issue is roughly the same for candidates, activists, and voters.[10] What varies is the pace of issue evolution, with candidates and activists[11] moving in response to the issue at a much faster rate than rank-and-file voters (Carmines and Woods 2002).

At this point in the discussion a caveat is definitely warranted in the case of the South. Below the presidential level, prior to the 1960s the region lacked an electorally viable Republican Party (Black and Black 2002). The reintroduction of the race issue in the 1964 presidential election amounted to an exogenous shock to the southern electorate since the presidential nominees decisively changed their respective parties' positions on the issue. Indeed, for a regional party that dominated the political landscape for well over seven decades because the electorate was purposely circumscribed to consist only of those southern whites who viewed the Democratic Party as the defender of white supremacy, the national partisan role reversal on civil rights was revolutionary. In presidential contests, now national Democrats look like erstwhile northern Republicans whereas national Republicans adopt the position of southern Democrats. Over time, white southern resistance to civil rights coupled with economic conservatism became the foundation upon which to build a competitive Republican Party below the Mason-Dixon Line (Aistrup 1996; Black and Black 2002; Lublin 2004).

Voters

As for the position of the voters, they will divide over the new civil rights issue according to how much importance they assign to it. A segment of voters are "New Deal" Democrats, and their liberal dispositions lead them to adopt the pro-civil rights position of the national party. In Figure 2.2, these voters reside in space A. Likewise, the civil rights issue does not affect the partisanship of Republican voters located in space D, who side with their party on the old economic cleavage and its opposition to civil rights.

The emergence of the civil rights issue has its greatest effect on the political affiliations of those voters who find themselves at odds with their party's position on this new issue. These cross-pressured voters occupy spaces B1, B2, C1, and C2. The civil rights issue is of such importance to voters B1 and C1 that these voters switch political parties in order to align with the party in closer agreement with them on this issue. Most likely, these voters are more politically aware, find the issue to be salient, and thus their political ideology drives them to change partisan allegiances (Abramowitz and Saunders 1998, 2006). Consequently, pro-civil rights Republicans become Democrats and anti-civil rights Democrats become Republicans. Voters occupying spaces B2 and C2, on the other hand, decide to stick with their parties even though initially they are in disagreement over their respective parties' positions on civil rights. As Carsey and Layman (2006) demonstrate, many voters may oppose their party on a specific issue, but if they do not assign it that much importance, then they will eventually change their issue preference so it aligns with their partisanship.

Again, this sorting process among voters does not occur all at once—it takes decades in some cases, and therefore in the aggregate, partisan change with respect to political affiliations is gradual (Key 1959).[12] Many of the voters who find themselves in spaces B2 and C2 will assign a lot of importance to the civil rights issue and yet only go so far as to dealign, cutting ties with their old party, but not going far enough to identify with the other party. It is the children of these voters who take the next step and switch parties in favor of the one that shares their views on civil rights and newer issues (e.g., abortion emerges as a partisan issue in the late 1970s; see Adams 1997) that align on the new cleavage that separates the parties.[13]

As Stimson (2004) points out, party primaries become a fundamental mechanism for recalibrating party identification according to voters' preferences concerning the new issue that splits the parties. Where candidates stand on the new issue becomes the basis for the primary vote decision, particularly in the absence of candidate differentiation on older, settled issues. According to Stimson:

> As the [issue] evolution proceeds, eventually it becomes nearly impossible to survive intra-party politics unless aligned with the dominant party position. The primary election mechanism ensures that once started, a new issue commitment will eventually run to completion. A party cannot cast itself in a new direction on an issue that matters and then later cast it off or ignore it. Once this process starts the alignment of voters with issue stands carries the parties along in the direction initially chosen. . . . This process is highly path-dependent. Early steps, that is, dictate later ones. (2004, 67–68)

Candidates

From the vantage point of a party's candidates, the stakes are higher, so ending up on the unpopular side of the issue can result in forced retirement at the ballot box. Democratic and Republican House candidates located in spaces A and D, respectively, are not cross-pressured by the introduction of the civil rights issue. These candidates maintain their political affiliations and adopt the position favored by majorities in their parties (and we can assume voter majorities) on the civil rights issue.

House candidates located in spaces B1 and C1 find it in their interests to switch parties on the basis of the civil rights issue. Democrats who oppose civil rights switch to the GOP and Republicans in favor of civil rights become Democrats. The last pair of candidate types, those located in spaces B2 and C2, are perhaps the most influential because they have the power to slow the pace of partisan change. For whatever reason, personal conviction or, most likely, electoral considerations, these candidates choose not to switch parties on the basis of their positions on civil rights.

There were not many southern Republican House candidates located in space B2. For one, when the civil rights issue came to the fore in the 1964 presidential election, the pool of Republican candidates was small, and second, what served to increase their numbers was campaigning in opposition to civil rights and against the social welfare positions advocated by New Deal/populist Democrats (Lublin 2004). In fact, the melding of economic and racial conservatism is what eventually revived the Republican Party in the South. By contrast, a clear majority of southern Democrats were located in space C2 when the civil rights issue was introduced.[14] These candidates slowed and thus prolonged the issue evolution of race for decades because in electoral terms their best strategy in the short-run was to remain Democrats. By remaining Democrats, these candidates held the balance of electoral power and delayed the white electorate's shift in party ID to the Republican Party, and this in turn stymied the emergence of competitive Republican candidates (Lublin 2004).

For the typical Democratic candidate located in space C2, immediately switching parties after the introduction of the civil rights issue would have amounted to electoral suicide since most southern whites were still Democrats and these voters recognized that below the presidential level most southern Democratic candidates had yet to move in favor of civil rights (Black and Black 2002). From the perspective of Democratic candidates then, the civil rights issue creates a classic prisoner's dilemma. In the short-term (the next election), because a majority of voters identify with the Democratic Party, the dominant strategy for each candidate is to remain a Democrat. But in the long-run, the more consistently conservative positioning of the Republican Party on economics and civil rights is the winning side,[15] and therefore Democratic candidates would be collectively better off if they switch to the Republican Party. Of course many incumbent southern Democrats eventually see the writing on the wall and, by switching parties, some incur a short-term electoral hit (see Grose and Yoshinaka 2003) that is necessary to save their political careers.

The Voting Rights Act, Its Reinforcement of Issue Evolution, and Conflict Extension

The electoral calculus of Democratic and Republican candidates becomes more complex with the passage of the 1965 Voting Rights Act (VRA). The infusion of large numbers of black voters as a consequence of the VRA complicates the short- and long-term decisions of House candidates. In those districts with sizable black populations (e.g., 15 percent or higher), the most important question for a House candidate is: Do I have a better chance of winning an electoral majority with a biracial coalition of voters or with a super-majority of white voters? If the chance for victory appears greater with a biracial coalition, then one should run as a Democrat if the latter option is more promising, one should run as a Republican.

As Black and Black (2002, chapters 5 and 6) meticulously document, in the 1960s and 1970s the reluctance to switch parties among those southern Democratic candidates and voters who opposed civil rights is a primary reason why Republican advancement moved at a snail's pace in House elections. Furthermore, in the 1980s, the longevity of Democratic dominance in House contests was prolonged another decade by the many Democrats who were able to secure electoral majorities by cobbling together biracial voter coalitions even as the number of white Democratic identifiers steadily declined.

From the mid-1960s through the 1980s, the success of the Democratic Party in House contests in the South led to a split-level realignment of the parties. In a split-level realignment, different parties have majority support given the particular level of election (Campbell 1997). Southern white voters shifted rather abruptly in favor of the Republican Party in presidential contests beginning in 1964, but their shift in favor of the GOP in lower contests like the U.S. House was much more gradual (Campbell 2006). A clean break in favor of identification with the GOP may have been likely if it were not for the strategic positioning of Democratic House candidates. Indeed, the persistence of Democratic strength in House contests and Republican dominance in presidential elections indicates that a portion of southerners reflected this arrangement by holding dual-party identifications—classifying themselves as Democrats in state contests and Republicans in national elections (see Hadley 1985).

The passage of the Voting Rights Act in 1965 enabled the Democratic Party to extend its majority status in the southern House delegation for another thirty years. The enfranchisement of southern blacks constituted a Democratic bloc vote that Democratic candidates could rely on as their shares of the white vote diminished. The national Democratic Party, under the leadership of President Johnson, spearheaded the passage of the 1964 Civil Rights Act, and in response to this action southern blacks shifted their identification to the Democratic Party virtually en masse. With African Americans typically voting over 90 percent in favor of Democratic House candidates, the Democratic Party only needed to draw on a sizable—but less than majority share—of the white vote in order to remain dominant in southern elections. Republican candidates, on the other hand, needed to secure white voting majorities generally on the order of 60 percent to carry a southern House district (see Black and Black 1987; 2002).[16]

Figure 2.3 presents a distribution of the southern white electorate on an ideological continuum after the passage of the 1964 Civil Rights Act, but prior to the passage of the VRA in 1965. Assuming a virtually all-white electorate in the South, Republican candidates are located to the right of Democratic House candidates. If the political context changes in favor of the GOP because of their more uniformly rightward position on civil rights and economics, then the distribution will shift right and Republican candidates should capture electoral majorities. But in

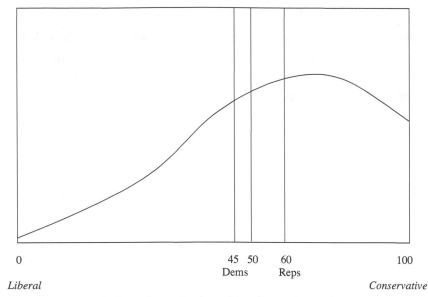

0		45 50	60		100
		Dems	Reps		

Liberal   *Conservative*

FIGURE 2.3 The Ideological Distribution of Southern Whites After Passage of the 1964 Civil Rights Act and Before the 1965 Voting Rights Act

the short run, Democratic candidates are favored because of the vast majority of Democratic identifiers who are not yet ready to vote Republican, and also because there is a dearth of experienced Republican candidates capable of exploiting the GOP's spatial advantage.

In other words, there is a lag effect, with a substantial share of southern whites, who, because of their enduring attachment to the Democratic Party, cannot bring themselves to vote for the party of Lincoln. Furthermore, in contrast to the clear partisan differentiation on civil rights at the presidential level, despite being generally to the left of the Republican Party, Democratic candidates are close enough to their Republican opponents that most voters fail to see any differentiation on the civil rights issue in House elections. And of course, in particular contests—especially in the Deep South—many Democratic candidates actually moved to the right of their Republican opponents with respect to the civil rights issue. As Black and Black (2002, 172) explain: "The possibility of partisan realignment based on racial cleavages was smothered by the conservative Democrats, many of whom continued to act as though blacks were not really part of their nomination or election constituencies."

Indeed, given the rightward shift of southern Democrats on the civil rights issue, the one promising avenue for Republican advancement was to accentuate partisan differences on the New Deal economic cleavage—a successful strategy for a small but growing number of Republicans running in majority urban districts with small black populations primarily in the Peripheral South (Black and Black 2002; Lublin 2004). So long as the southern Democracy remained unified in its opposition to civil rights, the economic issue could be handled among competing factions within the Democratic Party. There was in fact considerable diversity within the party regarding social welfare issues, with liberal and conservative factions vying for power across the region (e.g., Texas was known for its strong factional disputes between economic conservatives and economic populists, see Davidson 1990 and Key 1949).

But with federal intervention on civil rights, the emergence of a Republican opposition made it possible to exploit the economic issue. Since Republicans were more uniformly conservative on economic policy, the New Deal alignment that was firmly in place in the North finally presented itself in the South, and the region's growing middle class came to recognize the appeal of the GOP (Black and Black 1987). Racial issue evolution reinvigorated the economic issue because, with the advent of a legitimate Republican opposition, it could no longer be handled within the Democratic Party (Cowden 2001).

And for numerous Democrats, passage of the 1965 Voting Rights Act eventually made it much more difficult for them to minimize the electoral damage associated with being more liberal on the civil rights issue. With African Americans supporting the Democratic Party as a bloc, the more consistently conservative economic and civil rights positions of the GOP gained traction, especially in those congressional districts with low black populations and an expanding middle class (Black and Black 2002). As shown in Figure 2.4, the enfranchisement of African Americans shifted the overall ideological distribution of voters to the left[17] and also changes the shape of the distribution from what was a negatively skewed bell curve to a bimodal distribution. Under the new voter distribution created by the return of blacks to the southern electorate, the dominant strategy of Democratic House

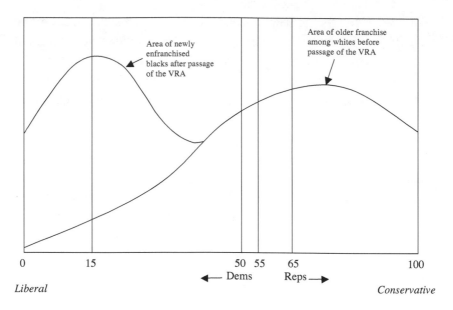

FIGURE 2.4 **The Ideological Distribution of Southern Whites and Blacks After Passage of the 1965 Voting Rights Act**

candidates was to make appeals to a majority of white voters that, when coupled with an African American bloc vote, amounts to a landslide electoral majority.

Again, for most southern Democrats, after passage of the VRA the immediate response was to resist the pro-civil rights position of their party. This essentially proved to be the best of both worlds for Democrats, since the black vote is monolithically Democratic and, by blurring the civil rights issue, white voters remained supportive. In the long run, however, this positioning of southern Democrats could not endure. With the growing participation of African American voters, there was increasing pressure for southern Democrats to move left on civil rights. In addition, institutional imperatives demanded that southern Democrats "nationalize" their voting as northern Democrats took control of the Democratic Caucus. In exchange for allowing southern Democrats with committee seniority to maintain their power, national Democrats expected greater party loyalty with regard to the House's legislative agenda. This necessarily led to more liberal voting records among influential southern Democrats (Black and Black 2002; Rohde 1991).[18]

Given their predicament, by the late 1970s biracial coalitions became the winning strategy for maintaining the Democrats' majority status in southern House contests (Black and Black 2002; Lamis 1988). The growing departure of racially conservative Democratic incumbents was compensated for with a new generation of southern Democrats, who proved adept at mixing liberal positions on civil rights with moderate-to-conservative stances on economic and social issues: "In district after district, as veteran Democrats retired or died, it would become much easier for white Democrats to capture nominations and win general elections by building biracial coalitions" (Black and Black 2002, 172).

Thus, the democratization of the American South via enforcement of the Voting Rights Act (Lublin 2004) greatly delayed Republican advancement in House elections. As explained by Black and Black:

> Reduced to fundamentals, when Republican activists transformed the party of Abraham Lincoln into the party of Barry Goldwater, they foolishly wrote off black southerners at the very time when black participation was dramatically increasing. In repudiating Lincoln and embracing Goldwater, southern Republicans implicitly narrowed their possible targets to those congressional districts in which Republican candidates could consistently attract sizable majorities of white voters. (2002, 138–139)

In the long run, however, the Republican strategy finally paid electoral dividends. With respect to policymaking, the growing influence of black voters on the direction of the Democratic Party highlighted the differences between most whites and blacks on a range of salient economic, racial, and cultural/religious issues. As time passed, it became much more difficult for Democratic House Representatives to make appeals to their black constituents without losing the support of white voters. The racial cleavage that constituted the new dimension dividing the parties also brought into greater prominence the old, underlying economic cleavage separating Democrats and Republicans.

African Americans put pressure on the Democratic Party to deliver on social welfare programs, and this severed the electoral support of middle- and upper-class whites who strongly opposed these policies. The racial cleavage that served as the impetus for the initial shift in favor of Republican identification was reinforced by the old economic cleavage that resurfaced because of the increasingly tight linkage between race and class (Carmines and Stimson 1982). In this way, as opposed to the traditional notion that realignments suppress or displace the original issue in favor of the latest one that cuts across the parties (Sundquist 1983), in the South it appears that racial conflict contributed to "conflict extension" (see Layman and Carsey 2002b). In other words, in the South the growing polarization of the parties, which was sparked by civil rights, has continued to expand because the parties have become more ideologically differentiable on economic, racial, and cultural issues (Layman and Carsey 2002a). Thus, for the subset of voters who are most politically aware, their loyalties will reside with the party that is ideologically closest to them across a range of political issues (Abramowitz and Saunders 2006). As Layman and Carsey point out:

> Southern whites tend to be relatively conservative on all three domestic issue agendas: racial, cultural, and social welfare. Thus, their movement out of the Democratic party and eventually into the Republican party made the Republican coalition more conservative, in the aggregate, on all three agendas, and left the Democratic coalition less conservative on all three agendas. (2002a, 231)

The issue evolution of race set in motion the long-term trend in Republican identification. Along the way, the racial issue was reinforced by economic and social issues as well as foreign policy—and, on all of these issues Republican candidates generally take the more conservative position. In this way, the Republican Party was consistent across a range of issues, and hence for many voters all of these issues fold into a single ideological dimension (Stimson 2004, 65; but see Carsey and Layman 2006) that placed the Republican Party clearly to the right of the Democratic Party.[19] With the gradual shift in the political affiliations of southern whites in favor of the Republican Party, the distribution of the southern electorate eventually moved in favor of the positions staked out by the GOP. Eventually, the presence of a plurality of white Republican identifiers provided a necessary electoral founda-

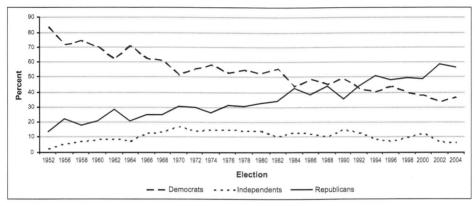

FIGURE 2.5 The Changing Political Affiliations of Southern Whites

tion for the GOP to win control of the southern House delegation. The next section and remainder of the chapter presents empirical evidence of the shifting political affiliations of southern whites.

Growing Republican Identification of Southern Whites

The pattern of growing Republicanism among southern whites has unfolded rather steadily over the course of the last fifty years. By presenting a variety of data on party identification, we can get a clear picture of the movement of southern whites in favor of the Republican Party. Figure 2.5 presents the percentage of southern whites who identified themselves as Democrats, Independents,[20] and Republicans in National Election Study surveys from 1952 to 2004. In 1952, the first year in the time series, 84 percent of southern whites were Democrats, 14 percent were Republicans, and only 2 percent claimed political independence. This electorate still resembled the one-party South that V. O. Key (1949) analyzed in *Southern Politics in State and Nation.*

But the racial issue evolution that commenced with the passage of the 1964 Civil Rights Act and the 1965 Voting Rights Act initiated a marked decline in Democratic identifiers and a corresponding rise in the percentage of Independents. There was a fairly swift move toward dealignment, as the percentage of Democrats in 1964 is 71 percent and was reduced to 52 percent by 1970. Over the same period, Independents went from 8 percent to 18 percent of white southerners. Finally, Republican identification expanded from 21 percent in 1964 to 31 percent in 1970. As expected, evidence of dealignment and realignment coexist (on this point see Stanley 1988) as some southern whites shed their Democratic attachments and others went a step farther by affiliating with the Republican Party.

As revisionist theory contends, poor party performance should affect voters' political affiliations even in the short term. Evidence from the 1972–1974 elections supports this claim. The disgrace of Watergate had a sharp negative effect on Republican fortunes, and this registers in the party identification data. Compared to 1970, in 1974 the percentage of Democrats increased to 58 percent, whereas the Republican percentage dropped to 26 percent. From 1976 to 1982, there was a fairly stable gap between Democrats and Republicans, with the former comprising somewhat over half the white electorate and the latter accounting for about a third.

Reagan's landslide reelection in 1984 brought Democrats and Republicans close to parity for the first time, with Democrats making up 44 percent of southern whites and Republicans 42 percent.[21] This closing of the gap between Democratic and Republican identifiers did not last, as seen when, in the off-year contests of 1986 and 1990, Republican identification dropped. But in 1992, southern white Republicans finally outnumbered Democrats—44 percent vs. 43 percent. As we will see in the next chapter, in 1992 the structural impact of redistricting proved electorally beneficial to the GOP, triggering the onset of Republican ascendancy in southern House elections. Since that time, Republican identifiers have outnumbered Democrats and, with the exception of 1996, the difference is considerable: 10 percentage points or more. In 2002 and 2004, a comfortable majority of southern whites identify themselves as Republicans. Perhaps less noticeable but still certainly important is the evidence that, as the partisan realignment of white southerners runs its course, dealignment comes to an end. In 2004, only 7 percent of southern whites were Independents, the lowest percentage since 1956 at 6 percent.

Thus far, the data presented encompass the southern white electorate at the regional, South-wide level. But what does the difference between

TABLE 2.1 The State-Level Partisan Balance Among Southern Whites
(Percentage of Democrats Minus Percentage of Republicans)

Year	AL	AR	FL	GA	MS	NC	SC	TN	TX	VA
1980	25.2									
1981	19.0				11.0					
1982	25.4			25.2	17.9					
1983	16.9									
1984	-0.8			21.3	8.8				1.1	
1985	3.7		-4.2	8.7		0.9			-5.0	-5.6
1986	-1.3		-10.7		-4.8	9.4			-5.0	-6.1
1987	6.3		-11.6			6.9			-6.3	-2.5
1988	-13.6		-2.4	-4.3	-10.9	-2.0			-9.4	-12.0
1989	5.6		-16.2			-8.1	-25.9	-13.1	-10.7	-24.6
1990	-6.3		-12.9		-2.3	-6.3	-24.8	-4.3	-16.4	-8.9
1991			-8.3	-7.2		-8.1	-21.7	-7.2		-8.0
1992	-6.9		-14.6	-1.9	-15.1	-7.5	-23.7	0.8		-13.9
1993	-6.4		-6.8	-3.6		-5.8		2.0		
1994	-7.6		-6.8	0.4		-16.1		-6.1		
1995	-15.6		-19.4	-12.5		-14.1		-7.4		
1996	-15.9		-14.1	-6.7		-16.2		12.9		
1997			-11.5	-7.3		-14.4				
1998				-0.7		-11.4				
1999		7.3				-11.5				
2000		8.3		-8.1		-11.6				
2001		-0.8		-25.0		-13.6				
2002		-1.3		-23.6		-11.4				
2003		9.9				-18.4				

Note: All state survey data are from the state poll data archive available through the Odum Institute at the University of North Carolina at Chapel Hill. In most of these polls party identification was measured in polls administered in the fall and spring. For each year, if there was a fall and spring poll, then the data are from the fall poll. The data were calculated by subtracting the percentage of Democrats from the percentage of Republicans. The percentage of Independents are accounted for, and thus the data are not the difference just among partisans. A positive number indicates more Democrats than Republicans and a negative number means there are more Republicans than Democrats. AL = Capstone Poll; AR = Arkansas Poll; FL = Florida Annual Policy Survey; GA = Georgia Poll; MS = Mississippi Poll; NC = Carolina Poll; SC = South Carolina State Policy Survey (1989 data), South Carolina State Omnibus Survey (1990–1992); TN = Tennessee Survey; TX = Texas Poll; VA = Commonwealth Poll.

Democratic and Republican identifiers look like if we examine state-level data? Perhaps it is not a surprise, but the general pattern of growing Republicanism is evident in every southern state. However, the rate of Republican growth varies considerably depending on the state. Table 2.1 presents the difference in the percentage of Democratic and Republican identifiers in every southern state except for Louisiana[22] from 1980 to

TABLE 2.2 The State-Level Partisan Balance Among Southern White Voters (Percentage of Democrats Minus Percentage of Republicans)

Election	AL	AR	FL	GA	LA	MS	NC	SC	TN	TX	VA
1982	33.3									21.2	3.9
1984	-4.6					-13.2	0.3			-8.5	
1986	20.1		-0.6	7.0	14.5		2.8			3.1	
1988			-12.7			-7.7	-12.5			-16.5	
1990	9.7	24.6	-8.4	-4.9			-6.4	-23.4	1.9	-11.2	
1992	-4.6	11.5	-1.5	-11.3	8.2	-24.9	-4.6	-28.0	2.8	-19.5	-16.6
1994	-3.2	16.2	-11.6	-8.8				-34.7	-10.7	-24.8	-21.0
1996	-17.4	15.6	-5.9	-17.7	1.7	-23.0	-12.9	-33.3	-8.8	-24.7	-9.8
1998	-1.4	23.8	-12.5	-27.8	3.1		-17.4	-28.8	-18.4	-24.6	
2000	-20.7	8.8	-14.3	-22.0	-9.7	-43.3	-16.7	-29.9	-16.0	-29.3	-14.1
2002			-8.6							-36.0	
2004	-48.5	-3.6	-13.2	-37.2	-25.2	-54.5	-30.9	-47.5	-21.7	-37.6	-26.4

Note: All data, with the exception of Florida and Texas in 2002, are from state exit polls. In 2002, the Florida and Texas data were extracted from the national exit poll because there were no state exit polls conducted by the Voter News Service for this year. Only Florida and Texas had sample sizes large enough (n > 700) to use data from these states for 2002. 1982 = ABC/Washington Post; 1984 = CBS; 1986–1988 = CBS/New York Times; 1990–1992 = Voter Research and Surveys; 1994–2002 = Voter News Service; 2004 = National Election Pool. The data were calculated by subtracting the percentage of Democrats from the percentage of Republicans. The percentage of Independents are accounted for, and thus the data are not the difference just among partisans. A positive number indicates more Democrats than Republicans and a negative number means there are more Republicans than Democrats. All data are weighted.

2003. Given a lack of consistency in administering these surveys, the time series vary substantially depending on the state. These data account for the percentage of Independents, but what is presented is the percentage difference between Democrats and Republicans in each state's southern white electorate. A positive number indicates a Democratic plurality and a negative number shows a Republican plurality. For each state, except for Arkansas in 2003, these survey data illustrate the increase in the percentage of Republican identifiers.

The growing partisan advantage for the GOP is even more pronounced if we look only at white voters in the southern states.[23] Table 2.2 presents the difference in the percentage of Democrats and Republicans with state-level exit poll data from 1982 to 2004. Regardless of the state, there is a uniform trend of increasing Republican identification. Clearly, by 2004 the number of white Republicans greatly outnumbered white Democrats. Even in Arkansas, Republicans outnumbered Democrats in 2004. And in the Deep South states of Alabama, Mississippi, and South Carolina, among southern whites, Republican voters comprised a majority in 2004. As Hayes and McKee (2008) show with the same exit poll data, younger voters were driving the increase in Republican identification among southern whites. The next section emphasizes the significance of age in driving the Republican realignment of white southerners.

Party Identification and Generational Replacement

All of the data on party identification presented thus far have been cross-sectional. Ideally, we would like to track the same respondents over a long span of years in order to assess the process of partisan change. Fortunately, this can be done with two sets of respondents who participated in the Youth-Parent Socialization Panel Study: 1965–1997 (ICPSR #9553 for 1965, 1973, and 1982, and ICPSR #4037 for 1997). This panel study was conducted primarily to assess changes in political behavior over a long time period. With regard to partisanship, the design of the study lends itself to evaluating generation effects, period effects, and life-cycle effects. All of these types of effects may contribute to partisan change (see Flanigan and Zingale 2007).

In the South, there is reason to anticipate evidence for all three types of aforementioned effects. First, since the passage of the Voting Rights Act, it is expected that younger white southerners are disproportionately responsible for the increase in the number of Republican identifiers. Generally speaking, younger voters are much less stable in their partisanship because many of them are just coming to understand what the parties stand for politically as well as the groups and issues they represent (Green et al. 2002). So in terms of a generation effect, younger voters should be more likely to identify with the Republican Party.

Second, there is the possibility of a period effect that shapes partisanship. It is expected that voters who came of age politically at the height of candidate-centered politics in the mid-1960s through the 1970s would exhibit strong evidence of political independence. A large share of Independents would reflect this period of dealignment in American politics (Beck 1977). Finally, is it the case that a life-cycle effect is present—meaning that as individuals age their partisanship strengthens?

Using data from the Youth-Parent Socialization Panel Study, we can track the partisanship of two groups of southern whites: (1) a panel of youths who were high school seniors in 1965 and (2) a panel comprised of the parents of these high school seniors.[24] Both sets of respondents were interviewed three times: in 1965, 1973, and 1982.[25] The youth panel was also interviewed again in 1997. There are a total of 136 southern youths who were interviewed in 1965, 1973, 1982, and 1997. There are a total of 171 southern parents who were interviewed in 1965, 1973, and 1982. The length of time between each follow-up survey allows one to assess the extent to which party identification changes among these two generations of southern whites. In addition, the timing of these surveys is particularly useful for examining partisan change in the South.

For the youth, their first opportunity to cast a vote in a general election is 1966, the first election after the passage of the Voting Rights Act. For both the youth and parent panels, 1973 is a year firmly tied to the period of electoral dealignment. And 1982 was a down year politically for the Republican Party, but it was after Ronald Reagan captured the White House and hastened the partisan realignment of southern whites, especially conservative whites (Black and Black 2002). Finally, 1997 rests firmly in the period of Republican ascendancy in southern House elections, and thus it is anticipated that most of these bygone southern youths have become Republicans.

Figure 2.6 presents the distribution of partisanship among southern whites in the youth panel as measured in 1965, 1973, 1982, and 1997. The data capture a remarkable transformation in the partisanship of southern whites who came of age in the South at the height of the civil rights movement. Among this generation of southern whites, the pattern of partisan dealignment and finally realignment is documented. To simplify the discussion of the findings, similar to Figure 2.5, inde-

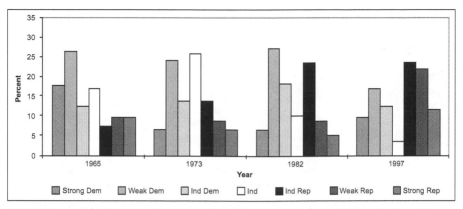

FIGURE 2.6 The Dynamic Partisanship of Younger Southern Whites, 1965–1997

pendent leaners will be considered partisans—a common classification scheme because Independents who admit to being closer to one of the parties behave similar to weak partisans (Keith et al. 1992).

In 1965, 57 percent of these respondents were Democrats, 17 percent were Independents, and 26 percent were Republicans. In 1973, dealignment is under way with a 23 percent reduction in Democrats at 45 percent and a 53 percent increase in Independents at 26 percent. The percentage of Republicans increases slightly to 29 percent. By 1982, a sharp decline in the percentage of Independents (from 26 percent to 10 percent) is offset by the large increase in the percentage of Republican leaners (from 14 percent to 24 percent). The massive reduction in the percentage of strong Democrats in 1973 holds steady in 1982 (a 61 percent decline, 18 percent in 1965 and 7 percent of all respondents in 1973 and 1982). With surveys conducted in 1973 and 1982, it is clear that the partisan distribution of these southern youths was shifting to the right in favor of the Republican Party.

Fifteen years later in 1997, it appears that the partisan life cycle of this cohort of white southerners was complete. Dealignment is over, with just 4 percent of these forty-nine- to fifty-year-olds classified as pure Independents. Three decades after their high school senior year, the percentage of Democrats is now 39 percent, down from 57 percent in 1965. Finally, the percentage of Republicans is now 57 percent, a 119 percent increase over the 1965 Republican total (26 percent).

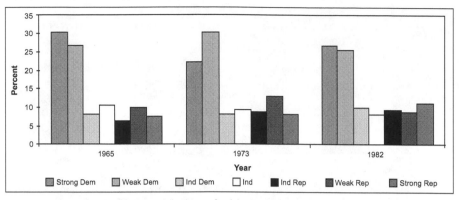

FIGURE 2.7 The Stable Partisanship of Older Southern Whites, 1965–1982

We can conclude from the data in Figure 2.6 that this generation of southern whites was anything but stable in terms of partisanship from 1965 through 1997. The pattern of partisan change supports the issue evolution theory. This generation of white southerners reached maturity just as the Voting Rights Act mandated the massive re-enfranchisement of African Americans. Indeed, these youth came of age at the start of the racial issue evolution, and it is evident from Figure 2.6 that, as a group, they were some of the prime movers in the Republican realignment. Lacking firm partisan attachments as seventeen- to eighteen-year-old high school seniors in 1965, political events and the positioning of Republican and Democratic candidates affected their party affiliations— with the GOP being the long-term beneficiary. In the mid-1960s, initial party identification with the dominant political party declined rapidly, and dealignment became a way station on the road to further movement toward identification with the ascending party.

Does the same pattern of partisan change exist among the parents of these southern whites? In Figure 2.7, we see that the answer is a resounding no. Among this generation of southern white parents there is no evidence of changing partisanship. The lack of partisan change points to the significance of age. Apparently, these respondents were essentially too old to have their partisanship affected by this period of substantial party system change. What is perhaps most remarkable is that there is hardly any evidence of dealignment. The general conclusion one can draw from the data on these parents is that the period effects that greatly influenced their children hardly dented their own partisanship.

It is very rare to have access to such a long-running panel survey that includes a large enough sample of southern whites to assess changes in party ID. With the most recent interview of the youth panel in 1997, these data confirm the claims of other scholars, who expected that the movement toward Republican identification among this cohort most likely persisted through the 1990s (e.g., Abramowitz and Saunders 1998; Green et al. 2002; Miller 1998). And it is safe to assume that the children of this generation should be even more likely to identify with the Republican Party (see Hayes and McKee 2008).[26] This analysis demonstrates the critical role that generational change plays in fostering a partisan realignment (Beck 1979).

Factors Affecting Party Identification

The effect of age on Republican identification can also be evaluated by segmenting the southern electorate into generational cohorts. However, a difficulty with assessing the impact of generational replacement on partisanship is the decision of where exactly to partition generations. The generational distinctions made in the South probably are separable from the classification scheme one would use outside the South. For example, Miller (2001) divides the voting electorate (those individuals old enough to vote) into Pre-New Deal (precedes the election of 1932), New Deal (1932–1964), and Post-New Deal (after 1964 to present, or up to 1988, in his article) cohorts.

With the passage of time since Miller's analysis, perhaps a more appropriate cohort scheme would reflect the pivotal events impacting the South since the advent of the civil rights movement. A sensible division of the southern voting electorate is a pre-Civil Rights cohort (up to the 1956 election), Civil Rights cohort (1957–1979), and Republican cohort (1980 to present). Ending with the 2004 election, the age breakdown for these three cohorts is: sixty-six years and older, between forty-three and sixty-five years old, and between eighteen and forty-two years old, respectively. The Republican generation should be the most likely to identify with the Republican Party because this cohort came of voting age during or after the Reagan realignment of 1980 (Black and Black 2002).

In addition to the significance of generational cohorts, this chapter has discussed at length several other factors that may influence party ID, including political ideology, race, vote choice, religion, income, education, and southern subregion. Ideology in particular should have a substantial impact on party identification. The political ideology of the southern electorate has been fairly stable for over thirty years, and as the parties have polarized across a range of issues, ideology has been a driving force in the southern Republican realignment (Abramowitz and Saunders 1998, 2006; Hayes and McKee 2008; Knuckey 2006; Valentino and Sears 2005).

The movement in favor of Republican identification of course is also due to other obvious considerations, like race and vote choice in House elections. Although the shift in favor of the GOP is almost completely due to the movement of whites, we can still measure the effect of race on Republican identification. And, in accordance with the revisionist approach, how one votes should affect their party affiliation (Fiorina 1981). Thus, individuals who vote Republican in House races are expected to be more likely to identify with the GOP.

As a very broad proxy for capturing the influence of cultural issues on party ID, because Protestants are the most supportive of the religious right agenda, it is expected that Protestants are more likely to classify themselves as Republicans.[27] In order to capture the class-based component of Republican identification, income and education should increase the likelihood of affiliating with the GOP. Finally, because the pace of Republican electoral gains vary and so has party identification, depending on subregion (Black and Black 2002; Valentino and Sears 2005), it is appropriate to control for whether individuals live in the Deep South or Peripheral South.

With the use of the National Election Studies cumulative file (1948–2004), we can evaluate the influence of the above-mentioned factors on the likelihood that a southerner will identify with the Republican Party.[28] The span of elections is 1992 through 2004—the period capturing Republican ascendancy in southern House elections.

To simplify the analysis, the variable for party identification is collapsed into those who identify with the Republican Party (strong and weak Republicans) and everyone else who either identifies with the Democratic Party or is a political Independent (including those who lean toward either the Republican or Democratic Party). Hence, the dependent variable for party ID is dichotomous (1 = Republican, 0 = otherwise), and this allows us to use logistic regression.

With logistic regression we can determine the likelihood of identifying with the Republican Party (1 = yes, 0 = no) as a function of generational cohort (Civil Rights, Republican, and pre-Civil Rights as the omitted category), political ideology (1 = extremely liberal to 7 = extremely conservative), race (1 = white, 0 = nonwhite), House vote (1 = Republican vote, 0 = Democratic vote), religion (1 = Protestant, 0 = otherwise), education (1 = less than high school, 2 = high school, 3 = some college, and 4 = college graduate), family income[29] (1–5 categories), subregion (1 = Deep South, 0 = Peripheral South), and a control for presidential year (1 = presidential year, 0 = midterm).[30]

Table 2.3 presents the results of two logistic regressions. The first model is confined to those southern respondents who either voted for a Republican or Democrat in the U.S. House election. The second model includes the entire southern electorate, voters and nonvoters alike. In addition to presenting the estimates for these two models, the maximum difference in the likelihood of identifying with the Republican Party is displayed for every statistically significant independent variable.

In both models, the Republican cohort, ideology, race, and education all have a significant and positive effect on Republican identification. Going from an extremely liberal respondent to an extremely conservative respondent increases the probability of identifying with the GOP by .69. And compared to minorities, whites are 27 to 28 percent more likely to identify with the Republican Party. Voting for a Republican for the U.S. House has the same impact on the likelihood of being a Republican (.27). In the voter and nonvoter models, there is a substantial difference in Republican identification for those with no high school education versus individuals with a college degree (a probability difference of .15 and .18 in the respective models). Finally, those

TABLE 2.3 Factors Affecting Republican Identification in the South, 1992–2004

Independent Variables	U.S. House Voters	Max Δ in Probability	All Southerners	Max Δ in Probability
Civil Rights cohort (1957–1979)	.196 (.260)	--	.055 (.200)	--
Republican cohort (1980–2004)	.837 (.256)***	+.18	.595 (.188)**	+.11
Ideology (7-point scale)	.776 (.082)***	+.69	.796 (.056)***	+.69
White	2.099 (.465)***	+.27	2.346 (.282)***	+.28
House vote (1 = Rep, 0 = Dem)	1.484 (.221)***	+.27	--	--
Protestant	.219 (.222)	--	.371 (.146)*	+.06
Education	.293 (.111)**	+.15	.352 (.078)***	+.18
Family income	-.086 (.089)	--	.120 (.059)*	+.09
Deep South	-.089 (.212)	--	.057 (.153)	--
Presidential year	.176 (.192)	--	-.091 (.130)	--
Constant	-8.488 (.745)***		-8.540 (.509)***	
Log Likelihood	-393.39		-782.54	
Pseudo R²	.33		.24	
N	896		1,642	

Note: Data are from the NES cumulative file 1948–2004. The dependent variable equals 1 if the respondent identifies with the Republican Party; Independent (including leaners) and Democratic identifiers equal 0. In the first model, individuals self-reported voting either Democratic or Republican in the U.S. House election. Coefficients are logistic regression estimates with standard errors in parentheses.

***p ≤ .001, **p ≤ .01, *p ≤ .05 (two-tailed).

House voters who came of voting age during the Reagan era or later were 18 percent more likely than the pre-Civil Rights cohort to be Republicans (11 percent more likely to identify with the GOP for the Republican cohort in the entire electorate).

In the model of the entire southern electorate, two additional variables attain statistical significance: family income and Protestantism. Protestants are 6 percent more likely to be Republicans, and those individuals in the highest income percentile are 9 percent more likely to identify with the GOP compared to those respondents in the lowest income percentile.

Conclusion

This chapter discussed competing conceptualizations of party identification and then presented a historical and theoretical account of the events that led to an increase in the Republican identification of southern whites. The issue evolution theory, as argued by Carmines and Stimson (1989) (see also Carmines 1991 and Stimson 2004), is used to explain the steady growth of southern Republicanism since the peak of the civil rights movement in the mid-1960s. A large array of survey data on southern whites was presented to support the theory of partisan change.

As argued, the increase in Republican identification is mainly a response to the positions that the political parties and their candidates take on the issues of greatest importance to white voters. Over time, as the percentage of Republicans has increased, a growing number of southern whites identify with the party through a socialization process just like the one that perpetuated Democratic hegemony during the days of the Democratic Solid South. The continual increase in the share of southern white Republicans is by no means inevitable; it has happened because Republican candidates have consistently positioned themselves in the political space favored by a majority of the white electorate (Hayes and McKee 2008).

Heading into the 1990s, despite Republican gains in party identification, the Democratic Party remained firmly in control of southern House contests. The incumbency advantage and biracial coalitions continued to register electoral dividends for southern Democrats. And even though it became apparent that southern Republicanism had finally produced enough adherents to elect a GOP House majority, the party seemed stuck—comprising a third of the southern congressional delegation for three straight elections. The GOP needed to find a way to overturn the current electoral equilibrium. Something that could weaken the Democratic incumbency advantage and concomitantly undermine biracial coalitions would do the trick. Fortunately for the Republican Party, congressional redistricting was a dream come true.

Notes

1. See Carsey and Layman (2006) and Fiorina (2002) for excellent reviews of this literature.

2. Unlike the party ID question asked by the National Election Studies, which has a built-in long-term component to it by prefacing the question of party ID with the phrase "Generally speaking," the Gallup Poll question for party ID states, "In politics, as of today, do you consider yourself a . . . "

3. The one clear disagreement between Green et al. (2002) and Campbell et al. (1960) concerns the extent to which partisanship acts as a biased filter of political information. Green et al. claim that party ID has a modest impact on biasing political information, whereas Campbell et al. (1960) (see also Bartels 2002) contend that it has a strong effect on how partisans view politics.

4. Consider this passage from Green et al.:

Although the expression of group attachment may be augmented by instrumental motives such as desired policy outcomes, party attachments have been expressed historically by large segments of the population who would seem to be out of step with the party's stated policy ambitions. (2002, 220)

5. Johnson won every state but Goldwater's home state of Arizona and all five Deep South states, which contained the most racially militant southern whites.

6. Goldwater was one of Reagan's political heroes. Reagan's famous political endorsement of Goldwater occurred on October 27, 1964, in his speech "A Time for Choosing." Goldwater and Reagan were at odds on social issues like abortion, because Goldwater was a civil libertarian. Of course the abortion issue was not injected into electoral politics until the 1970s (Carmines and Woods 2002).

7. This account draws heavily on the issue evolution theory presented by Carmines (1991), Carmines and Stimson (1989), and Stimson (2004).

8. Figures 2.1 and 2.2 are adaptations of the figures presented in Sundquist (1983, 23–27).

9. As Stimson remarks, "Of course, no issue is ever new in the stronger sense of never having been thought of before. If it were, it would not be a question in a survey. Racial controversies, for example, are older than the country. But race was new as a partisan issue in 1964, the first time in modern America that the two parties squared off on opposite sides of the question" (2004, 70).

10. Stimson (2004) points out that the main difference between the candidates and voters regarding the sorting process over a cross-cutting issue is the intensity of preferences: "Voters, too, will divide into pro, con, or neutral. But most will have far less intense preferences than do the professional politicians, and few will have a *public* [emphasis original] commitment to a prior position" (66).

11. Without rigidly defining the term *activists*, suffice it to say that they are more involved in the political process in terms of participatory behavior (e.g., actively campaigning on behalf of candidates, voting in primaries, holding minor party office, representing the party as a national convention delegate, etc.).

12. In House elections, the initial resistance of southern congressional Democrats on the civil rights issue made it very difficult for white southerners to move away from their Democratic affiliation since in these contests the parties were often indistinguishable with respect to the race issue.

13. Of course, many of the children of these cross-pressured voters start out as Independents because their parents have moved to the Independent position, and thus these children then move from political independence to identification with a party.

14. Given the meager presence of the southern GOP at the onset of the civil rights issue evolution, there is no effort to capture the proper scale for Figures 2.1 and 2.2. These are hypothetical graphical representations of partisan change.

15. Of course future prospects are dependent on current decisions, and no one could foresee what the electoral future would hold—thus, this discussion is based on hindsight.

16. In the South, the black population is roughly 20 percent and the white population accounts for most of the difference except in Texas and Florida, which have substantial Hispanic populations. As Black and Black (1987) demonstrate, if we assume that 90 percent of African Americans vote Democratic, then based on the racial composition of the average southern electorate, a Republican candidate will need about 60 percent of the white vote in order to win the election.

17. Notice that the ideological median "50" moves to the left from Figure 2.3 to Figure 2.4.

18. In the mid-1970s, the Democratic Caucus made committee seniority subject to a secret ballot vote and several southern Democrats who were notoriously resistant to the liberal direction of the party lost their chairmanships (Rohde 1991).

19. There is evidence that for the mass electorate, economic/social welfare, racial, and cultural issues are separable ideological dimensions (see Layman et al. 2006). Nonetheless, for those voters who do not exhibit a high degree of ideological constraint across these different issues (Converse 1964), any of the three has promoted conflict extension because they are salient, "easy" issues (Carmines and Stimson 1980) that strongly affect party preferences. Thus, voters concerned with race will adjust their political affiliation accordingly, and likewise for voters who place a high importance on economic or cultural issues. So the party coalitions have re-sorted themselves due to the behavior of voters who are either liberal or conservative on any or all of these issues.

20. Independents that lean toward a party are classified as partisans.

21. Based on exit poll data of southern white voters, Black and Black (2002) find a surge in Republican identification among conservatives between 1980 and 1988 (going from 40 percent to 60 percent), whereas moderates dealigned with 52 percent Democratic in 1980 declining to 35 percent Democratic in 1988.

22. These data come from state surveys available through the Odum Institute at the University of North Carolina at Chapel Hill. There were no state surveys for Louisiana.

23. Unlike the NES, these data use a three-point scale to measure party identification. A respondent is merely a Democrat, Independent, or Republican. Strength and direction of identification—the definition of partisanship, which is captured by the seven-point scale—does not register with a three-point scale.

24. The sample consists only of those white southerners who lived in the South during all of the interviews.

25. Rice (1994) has also analyzed the Youth-Parent data specifically to assess the changing partisanship of white southerners. Of course, given the publication date, Rice did not have the opportunity to examine the 1997 youth data. According to Rice (1994, 249), for the full panel survey "[a]ll of the children were ages 17 to 18 in 1965, 25 to 26 in 1973, and 34 to 35 in 1982. The average age of the parents was 46 in 1965, 54 in 1973, and 63 in 1982."

26. Green et al. estimate that about "half of the Southern realignment is due to cohort replacement, not individual-level change" (2002, 141).

27. It would be easy to include more specific variables that tap into the culturally conservative agenda such as abortion, but the attempt here is to rely on a

very broad set of factors. Undoubtedly abortion is an issue that has served to re-align partisans (see Carmines and Woods 2002; Carsey and Layman 1999; Knuckey 2006; Layman and Carsey 1998). It is apparent, however, that the percentage of southern Protestants affiliated with the Democratic Party has steadily declined, and this simple dummy variable roughly approximates a secular versus religious divide, since Protestantism dominates the religious preferences of southerners.

28. For more sophisticated multivariate analyses of party identification that are limited to only white southerners, see Knuckey (2006) and Valentino and Sears (2005).

29. For family income, 1 = 0–16 percentile, 2 = 17–33 percentile, 3 = 34–67 percentile, 4 = 68–95 percentile, and 5 = 96–100 percentile.

30. Given the evidence of a gender gap in party support and affiliation (Black 2004), one might suspect that this is a variable that affects party ID. In analyses that included a control for gender, the variable was not significant (results not shown).

3

Electoral Effects of Redistricting

Given the unrealized Republican potential in many districts based on improved presidential Republicanism, reapportionment and redistricting might well accelerate a southern congressional realignment significantly benefiting white Republicans as well as black Democrats. (2002, 204)

—Earl and Merle Black

The redistricting that occurred for the 1992 U.S. House elections disrupted the electoral status quo. The drastically altered district lines throughout the South destabilized the white electorate, making voting behavior less predictable and, consequently, weakening the incumbency advantage of Democrats. The Department of Justice (DOJ) demanded that southern states maximize wherever possible their number of majority-minority districts. The direct and indirect effects of racial redistricting resulted in a substantial increase in the election of black Democrats and especially more Republicans. The big losers in this process were white Democrats and, by extension, the Democratic Party because the overall number of House Democrats was sharply reduced.

In the South, from 1986 to 1990, the number of Democratic and Republican House Representatives did not change; after each of these elections there were seventy-seven Democrats and thirty-nine Republicans. This equilibrium was shattered after the 1992 and 1994 elections.

71

The South gained nine seats through reapportionment for the 1992 elections, and Republicans netted nine seats in 1992, and then won another sixteen seats after the 1994 elections. So in a span of just two elections, southern Republicans went from being the perennial minority party to the majority party (sixty-four Republicans and sixty-one Democrats) by increasing their ranks by 20 percent. In 1996, Republicans added another seven seats to their delegation. After 1996, the partisan balance remained fairly steady until 2004, when a Republican gerrymander in Texas accounted for five of the six seats the GOP picked up in this election (eighty-two Republicans and forty-nine Democrats).[1]

This chapter highlights the role that redistricting has played in furthering the rapid advancement of southern Republicans in U.S. House elections. First, I discuss the redistricting literature[2] that seeks to explain its electoral effects. Next, several maps are presented to provide the reader with an illustrative view of how congressional redistricting has altered the southern political landscape. I then proceed in chronological order with analyses of the partisan impact of redistricting in southern U.S. House elections for 1992–1994, 2002, and Texas in 2004. I analyze data at the district and individual level to illustrate how redistricting has disproportionately favored southern Republicans.

The Partisan Impact of Redistricting

In *The Rise of Southern Republicans*, Earl and Merle Black (2002) meticulously document GOP growth in U.S. House and Senate contests from the 1950s through 2000. In the 1950s, southern Republicans had a trivial presence in the House delegation. For the next thirty years, from the 1960s until the end of the 1980s, Democratic hegemony was taken for granted—primarily because of southern Democrats' stranglehold on the incumbency advantage.

As summarized by Black and Black (2002, Table 6.1 on p. 188), Democratic dominance in the 1960s and 1970s was indiscriminate. As witnessed by their congressional voting, regardless of whether a southern Democratic House member was in step or completely out of touch with the positions taken by national Democrats, the Democratic incumbency advantage proved impenetrable. For these two decades, 67 percent of southern House elections contained a Democratic incumbent seeking reelection, and they were victorious 97 percent of the time (Black and Black 2002). As stated in Black and Black: "In the 1960s and 1970s the Solid Democratic South could perpetuate itself even without winning open seats or defeating Republican incumbents" (2002, 156).

Despite a necessary change in electoral strategy—the cultivation of biracial coalitions and a tempering of congressional voting so that it was more in line with the national party—the 1980s prolonged Democratic dominance in southern House contests. For this decade, 59 percent of southern House races involved a Democratic incumbent and, like the last twenty years, their success rate remained at 97 percent (Black and Black 2002). In short, there were just too many Democratic incumbents who were adept at holding on to their seats. To be sure, Republican incumbents also experienced very high victory rates (93 percent in the 1960s–1980s, Black and Black 2002), but there were not enough of them (20 percent of the southern delegation in the 1960s–1970s, and 30 percent in the 1980s, Black and Black 2002)[3] to wrest away the seats of their partisan counterparts who were even more successful at securing reelection.

The Democratic grip in southern congressional elections could only be pried apart by a major shock to the political system. Redistricting proved the Republican remedy. It swiftly loosened the Democratic hold on southern House seats by prompting a host of both voluntary and involuntary Democratic retirements due to the voting behavior of constituents drawn into districts with a new Democratic incumbent.

Redistricting was the main factor that interacted with the ongoing partisan realignment of southern whites to push Republicans into majority status in the southern House delegation after the 1994 elections. Altering congressional boundaries severed the incumbency bond for thousands of voters who were primed to vote Republican, especially given the presence of a viable GOP candidate. With respect to redistricting, there are two main partisan effects that disproportionately benefited southern Republicans.[4] The first effect is the direct impact of the creation of majority-minority districts. The second effect concerns the change in the voting behavior of constituents assigned to a different incumbent as a result of redistricting.

The First Partisan Effect: Racial Redistricting

During the 1992 round of redistricting, the Department of Justice pressured most of the southern states to maximize their number of majority-minority districts wherever possible (see Bullock 1995b; Butler 2002; Cunningham 2001). African Americans were packed into fewer districts with the result being large increases in the white percentages of surrounding districts. Because blacks are the most reliable Democratic voters, the optimal strategy for southern Democrats is to spread fairly evenly the district percentage of African Americans in order to maximize the number of districts that can be won by cobbling together biracial voting majorities.

At least in theory it is possible to create districts with large minority populations and not alter the partisan balance of a congressional delegation (Shotts 2001). But in the South, reality has told a very different story. If it were the case that almost all southern whites identified with the Republican Party then the creation of majority-minority districts would place an upper limit on the number of Republican districts. It is of course not true that nearly all southern whites are Republicans, and this helps explain why racial redistricting benefited the GOP.

As discussed in the last chapter, after passage of the 1965 Voting Rights Act, biracial coalitions eventually became the path to victory for most white Democrats. When upward of 90 percent of African Americans vote Democratic, a white Democratic candidate only needs to secure a respectable share of the white vote to win. This is why racial redistricting in the 1990s negatively impacted the Democratic Party: It compromised the biracial coalitions that proved so effective in electing southern Democrats.

In 1992, the most loyal Democrats—African Americans—were concentrated into a relatively small number of districts. As scholars have shown (Hill 1995), black voters were "packed" into these newly created majority-minority districts. This essentially means that there was a substantial surplus of minority votes that were wasted in these districts because these votes were not needed to elect a Democrat (Cameron et al. 1996; Epstein and O'Halloran 1999a, 1999b, 2000). From the vantage of the Democratic Party, these votes and thus these voters may have been pivotal in denying the election of Republicans who ran in neighboring districts that had increased white populations because of the creation of majority-minority districts (Lublin and Voss 2000).

We can use the state of Alabama to illustrate how racial redistricting favors Republicans in U.S. House elections. According to the 1990 Census, the black voting age population (BVAP) of Alabama was 23 percent and, given the miniscule population of other minorities (e.g., Hispanics), we can consider the white voting age population (WVAP) to be the remaining 77 percent. Alabama has a total of seven congressional districts. We calculate the necessary white share of the vote needed for a Democrat to win election in Alabama based on an equation presented by Black and Black (1987). The equation is:

$$wx = 50.1 - bp1$$

where 50.1 is the minimum share of the two-party vote needed to win; b is the BVAP in the district (the black vote); $p1$ is the percentage of the black vote cast for the Democrat; w is the WVAP (the white vote) in the district; and we solve for x, which is the minimum share of the white vote needed for a Democrat to win.

If we assume that 90 percent of African Americans vote for the Democrat, then we can solve the equation since we know the size of the BVAP and WVAP in each Alabama district. But instead of calculating the white shares necessary for a Democrat to win in each Alabama district based on the actual black and white voting age populations, three hypothetical scenarios are presented to illustrate the effect of racial redistricting on party competition in Alabama congressional races.

In the first scenario, we assume that 60 percent of white Alabamians vote Republican and the remaining 40 percent vote Democratic. Under the first redistricting plan, the BVAP is divided equally among all seven Alabama districts. Thus, the equation to solve for the minimum share of the white vote needed for a Democratic victory is: $77x = 50.1 - 23(.90)$; and therefore the minimum white share equals 38.2 percent. Since 40 percent of whites vote Democratic, under this redistricting plan Democrats win all seven districts.

In the second redistricting scenario, one district is a newly drawn black majority district with a BVAP of 64 percent—the actual BVAP of Alabama 7 in 1992. With a 64 percent BVAP in Alabama 7, we distribute the rest of the state's BVAP equally, and this means that the other six districts each have a BVAP of 16 percent. Alabama 7 is a guaranteed Democratic seat because no white votes are necessary for a Democrat to be elected given the size of the black vote. The equation for districts 1 through 6 then is: $84x = 50.1-16(.90)$, and solving for x gives us a minimum white share of 42.5 percent for a Democrat to win. Maintaining the assumption that 40 percent of whites vote Democratic, the consequence of creating a 64 percent BVAP district is that Republicans win the remaining six seats.

Under the second scenario, it is clear how racial redistricting advantages Republicans. Note, however, that if the GOP were to increase its voter loyalty among white southerners, racial redistricting can then place a ceiling on the number of Republican-won districts. For instance, if we return to the first scenario where the BVAP is equally distributed (23 percent BVAP for each district), and now 65 percent of whites vote Republican and 35 percent vote Democratic, then Republicans win every district since the minimum white share for a Democrat to win is 38.2 percent. Hence, if 65 percent of whites vote Republican, then racial redistricting actually benefits Democrats because otherwise the GOP would sweep all seven districts (on this point see Shotts 2001).

Hypothetical scenarios aside, the racial redistricting plans implemented in the South for the 1992 House elections worked to the benefit of Republican candidates in heavily white districts and African American Democrats who ran in black majority districts. White Democrats, however, were crowded out because of the large reduction in the number of districts with high minority populations. There were fewer districts where white Democrats could assemble biracial coalitions comprised of large black vote shares coupled with smaller white vote shares that amounted to 50.1 percent of the two-party vote. The flip side is that racial redistricting made it easier for Republicans to construct voting majorities by relying almost entirely on the support of southern whites.

In 1992, racial redistricting reduced the number of districts with 20 to 40 percent African American district populations (forty-seven districts in 1990 versus just twenty-four districts in 1992, Handley et al. 1998), precisely those districts where white Democrats can put together biracial voting majorities. By comparison, racial redistricting increased the number of districts with over 40 percent black district populations from six to eighteen (Handley et al. 1998), and only one of these districts was represented by a white Democrat, Mike Parker in Mississippi 4 (the remaining districts were all won by African American Democrats).[5] The number of districts with less than 10 percent black district populations increased from thirty-two in 1990 to fifty-one in 1992. Democrats represented 53.1 percent of under-10 percent black districts in 1990 and just 39.2 percent in 1992 (Handley et al. 1998).[6] These super-white majority districts are of course the ones where we would expect the GOP to be most competitive.

The Second Partisan Effect: The Behavior of Redrawn Voters

We should not, however, overstate the direct impact of racial redistricting. In many districts, a reduction in the minority population cannot wholly explain Republican victories. In addition to reduced minority populations, a percentage of white voters who previously voted Democratic would have to vote Republican for the GOP to win many of their seats. This brings us to the second main effect of redistricting.

In many of these districts, there was an increase in Republican voting beyond a simple reduction in the minority percentage of the district population. This observation was pointed out by Petrocik and Desposato (1998), who provide an explanation for what they call the second-order effect of redistricting: the behavior of redrawn voters. The redrawing of district boundaries done to satisfy the equal population requirement and the majority-minority maximization order issued by the DOJ resulted in a plethora of voters who were represented by a new incumbent before the 1992 House elections. According to

Petrocik and Desposato, these so-called "new" voters,[7] "defined as individuals who were in a different incumbent's district prior to the redistricting" (1998, 616), were much more likely to vote Republican in the 1992 and 1994 southern U.S. House elections.

Petrocik and Desposato contend that a combination of GOP tides (in 1992 and especially 1994) and the effect of unhinging voters from their old incumbents explains the short-term success of southern House Republicans. The bond of incumbency is severed when a voter is drawn into a district with a different incumbent. In other words, the non-partisan electoral benefits that accrue to incumbents based on things like name recognition, constituency service, and pork-barrel spending can be greatly discounted with regard to redrawn voters. Redrawn constituents have not resided in the district long enough to be impacted by these kinds of incumbent activities that serve to increase the personal vote (Cain et al. 1987).

In addition to the fact that the incumbency advantage is severely discounted among redrawn voters, the early to mid-1990s was a time when House Democrats were unusually vulnerable because of political missteps (especially the House Banking Scandal, see Dimock and Jacobson 1995; Abramson et al. 1994) and the unpopular actions of President Clinton (Campbell and Rockman 1996). There was an anti-incumbent mood in the electorate and, given the Democratic Party's majority status, this translated into an anti-Democratic incumbent mood. By cutting the incumbency bond, redistricting created a large population of redrawn voters who were already predisposed to vote Republican because public opinion was moving against the Democratic Party (McKee 2008).

Also, these redrawn voters should be expected to vote Republican because many of them were already voting Republican in presidential contests. This point is crucial because redistricting not only reinforced but actually accelerated the secular realignment of southern whites into the Republican Party (Hill and Rae 2000). Outside the South, the short-term factors that benefited the GOP—a historically low approval rating of (the Democratic majority) Congress (Stimson 2004) and the low approval of President Clinton—accounts for the reason why these redrawn voters swung Republican in 1992 and 1994. But in the South, these short-term factors were magnified by the fact that southern whites have been trending Republican for at least the last thirty years.

The Political Geography of Southern Congressional Elections

It is perhaps surprising that so much of the recent scholarship on southern congressional elections and even the redistricting literature in general rarely presents maps. The visual representation of U.S. House districts provides invaluable evidence of the tremendous alteration of the southern congressional electorate after the 1990 and 2000 censuses. In this section, a series of six congressional maps of the South are displayed. Maps are presented in tandems to illustrate the changing U.S. House geography as it relates to a specific district-level variable. There are a total of three variables displayed in the following congressional maps: (1) the district percentage of the black voting age population (BVAP), (2) the district percentage of redrawn constituents, and (3) the number of Democratic and Republican U.S. House Representatives in the South.

As discussed above, the 1992 redistricting played a pivotal role in the rise of southern Republicans because of the way it impacted district racial compositions with the attendant effect of vastly increasing the district portion of redrawn constituents. Both of these effects served to increase the number of elected black Democrats and white Republicans—with the overall result being the reduction of Democrats in the southern congressional delegation. The first set of maps, 3.1a and 3.1b, show the percentage BVAP in southern U.S. House districts in the 1990 and 1992 elections, respectively. The maps are given three shades depending on the percentage BVAP, taking on a darker hue for higher black district populations: (1) 0 to 20 percent BVAP, (2) 20 to 40 percent BVAP, and (3) 40 percent BVAP and higher.

The change in the racial compositions of southern congressional districts between the 1990 and 1992 House contests is nothing short of revolutionary. In 1990, there were four districts (3 percent) that had

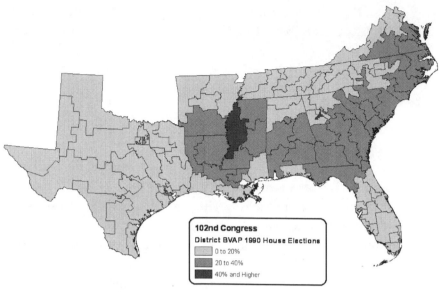

Map created by Pete Reehling – GIS Librarian, Univ. of South Florida

MAP 3.1a Percentage of the Black Voting Age Population (BVAP) in 1990 Southern U.S. House Elections

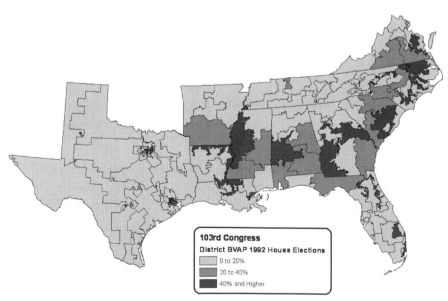

Map created by Pete Reehling – GIS Librarian, Univ. of South Florida

MAP 3.1b Percentage of the Black Voting Age Population (BVAP) in 1992 Southern U.S. House Elections

BVAPs at 40 percent or higher, thirty-nine districts (34 percent) with a BVAP between 20 and 40 percent, and seventy-three districts (63 percent) with BVAPs less than 20 percent. By comparison, after the redistricting that was enacted for the 1992 elections, seventeen districts (14 percent) had BVAPs at 40 percent or higher, sixteen districts (13 percent) with BVAPs between 20 and 40 percent, and ninety-two districts (74 percent) with BVAPs less than 20 percent.

A 40 percent BVAP or higher appears to be close to the minimum threshold for electing a black Democrat in the South (see Epstein and O'Halloran 1999a, 1999b).[8] With this in mind, for the 1990 and 1992 southern House contests, every single district with at least a 40 percent BVAP elected an African American Democrat. A quick check of the district shapes in 1990 vis-à-vis 1992 makes it apparent that it took some very creative cartography to create a total of seventeen southern U.S. districts with at least a 40 percent BVAP. Due to Supreme Court rulings, several of these districts were altered in order to reduce the black populations because it was deemed unconstitutional to make race the driving factor in drawing congressional districts (see Butler 2002).

Nonetheless, most of these districts essentially remained intact, and this obviously had the direct effect of severely cutting the number of districts with 20 to 40 percent BVAPs—those districts where white southern Democratic House candidates thrived from the end of Reconstruction through the 1980s. Of course the reduction in the number of 20 to 40 percent BVAP districts also increased the number of districts with BVAPs of 20 percent and less—those districts where southern Republicans have their greatest electoral success, since these candidates win with super-white majorities (Black 1998).

This large redistribution of the African American population in southern congressional districts in 1992 also resulted in a very large percentage of constituents being redrawn into districts represented by a different incumbent. Maps 3.2a and 3.2b document the percentage of redrawn constituents in the 1992 and 2002 southern congressional elections, respectively. In addition, both maps indicate those districts with open seat contests. From the vantage of an incumbent running for reelection, redrawn constituents comprise those residents whom the incumbent did not represent prior to redistricting. As mentioned above, these constituents proved to be the main reason why so many Democratic incumbents lost vote share or even their reelection bids.

There are two primary differences that show up in these maps. First, in 1992 the much vaster changes in congressional geography resulted in a higher number of districts with substantial redrawn populations. Second, because of such a massive transformation of the southern congressional map, there were a lot more incumbent retirements in 1992—this is evident in terms of the number of open seats. The 31 open seats in 1992 constituted 25 percent of southern House districts (31 out of 125 districts). By comparison, there were 23 open seats in 2002, and this accounted for 18 percent of southern congressional districts (23 out of 131 districts). Because many southern states opted in favor of incumbent gerrymanders for the 2002 elections, it is no wonder that fewer Representatives chose to retire.

In Map 3.2a, valid for the 1992 elections, in twenty-seven districts (22 percent) the redrawn percent was less than 10 percent, twenty-one districts (17 percent) had a redrawn percent between 10 and 20 percent, twenty-three districts (18 percent) were between 20 and 40 percent redrawn, and twenty-three districts (18 percent) had redrawn populations of 40 percent and higher. Map 3.2b, valid for the 2002 elections, displays thirty-eight districts (29 percent) with a redrawn percent less than 10 percent, twenty-eight districts (21 percent) with a redrawn percent between 10 and 20 percent, thirty-three districts (25 percent) were between 20 and 40 percent redrawn, and just nine districts (7 percent) had redrawn populations of 40 percent and higher. For so many southern Democrats who decided against retirement in 1992 and 2002, we will see that their redrawn constituents' voting behavior indicated that involuntary retirement was a suitable choice.

Finally, in the last pair of maps the number of districts represented by Democrats and Republicans is shown for the 1990 and 2004 elections. Map 3.3a shows that in 1990 there were seventy-seven Democratic-held districts (66 percent) versus thirty-nine districts represented by Republicans (34 percent) (n = 116 districts). In the span of just fourteen years, or seven elections, the southern congressional landscape was fundamentally altered. After the 2004 U.S. House contests, as displayed in Map 3.3b, in the South there were now eighty-two Republican Representatives

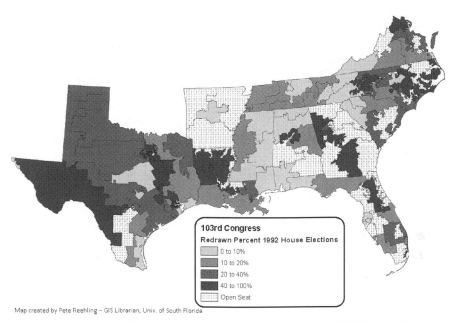

MAP 3.2a Percentage Redrawn Constituents in 1992 Southern U.S. House Elections

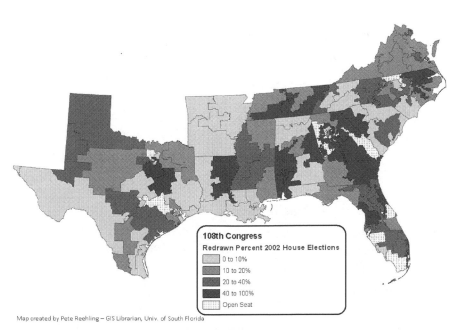

MAP 3.2b Percentage Redrawn Constituents in 2002 Southern U.S. House Elections

(63 percent) versus forty-nine Democratic House members (37 percent) (n = 131 districts). Large-scale changes to congressional boundaries and their subsequent influence on voting behavior and candidate strategies proved the keystone to Republican ascendancy in southern House races.

The next three sections of the chapter provide empirical evidence for the electoral effects of redistricting in 1992–1994, 2002, and Texas in 2004, respectively. For the 1992–1994 elections, we see the substantial effect that racial redistricting had on upsetting the partisan status quo by greatly increasing the number of presidentially Republican districts and thus the percentage of redrawn voters. As mentioned, the 2002 redistricting generally reinforced the new Republican status quo as most southern states implemented incumbent-protection plans. The 2004 U.S. House elections in Texas were more reminiscent of the conditions that were present in 1992 and 1994 because the Texas GOP understood that drastically altering district lines would create a large population of redrawn voters poised to vote Republican.

Partisan Impact of Redistricting in the 1992–1994 U.S. House Elections

Table 3.1 shows data for the average percentage of the black voting age population according to the type of representative before and after the 1992 redistricting. The creation of black majority districts increases the number of black Democrats from five to seventeen, and yet the average BVAP for these representatives is increased by 4 points. The direct consequence of the increase in the number of black Democrats is a large reduction in the average district BVAP assigned to white Democrats and white Republicans. In addition, we see that the number of white Democrats declines from sixty-eight to fifty-six, whereas the number of white Republicans increases from thirty-eight to forty-five.[9]

As Black and Black (2002) contend, the changing racial foundations of southern House districts benefited Republicans because they "improved the southern Republicans' presidential foundations" (337). We can take

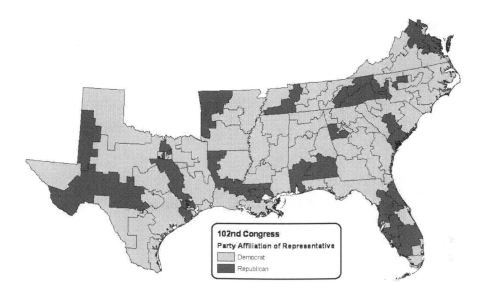

MAP 3.3a Party Affiliation of Southern U.S. House Representatives in 1990

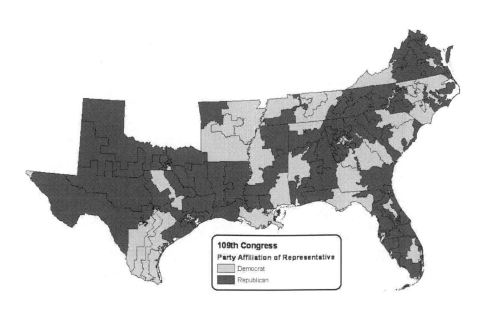

MAP 3.3b Party Affiliation of Southern U.S. House Representatives in 2004

TABLE 3.1 **Weakening the Democratic Biracial Coalition, 1990 and 1992**

Representative	Black Dem 1990	Black Dem 1992	White Dem 1990	White Dem 1992	White Rep 1990	White Rep 1992
Mean BVAP (%)	51.0%	55.1%	18.3%	14.6%	13.5%	9.1%
N	5	17	68	56	38	45

TABLE 3.2 **Percentage of Redrawn Constituents for Incumbents Seeking Reelection in 1992**

Incumbent Type	Mean Redrawn (%)	Median Redrawn (%)	N
All Incumbents	25.6	19.5	92
Democratic Incumbents	20.5	14.8	61
Republican Incumbents	35.6	28.6	31

Note: Data include uncontested races (uncontested = 10, contested = 82). Data exclude two districts in Louisiana where in each district two incumbents faced each other in 1992 (LA 5 and LA 6).

this argument to the logical end by demonstrating that improved presidential foundations meant improved U.S. House foundations.

If we consider 60 percent or more of the two-party vote to be a landslide victory, then based on the 1988 Republican presidential vote, after the 1992 redistricting "[t]he number of Republican presidential landslide districts increased from fifty-three to sixty-five" (Black and Black 2002, 335). A highly revealing way to get a sense of the partisan impact of the 1992 redistricting is to present graphically the distribution of the 1988 Republican presidential vote in districts before and after the 1992 redistricting (see Kousser 1996). Figure 3.1 displays a substantial difference in the distribution of the 1988 Republican presidential vote for 1992 districts vis-à-vis 1990 districts. Again, not surprisingly it is among the large number of districts where the 1988 Republican presidential vote was increased in 1992 that we find the vast majority of seats won by Republicans.[10]

Another way to assess the impact of redistricting on the 1992–1994 U.S. House elections is by focusing on the behavior of redrawn voters/constituents. Racial redistricting resulted in a large percentage of constituents with new incumbents. Table 3.2 provides the average and median percentage of redrawn constituents for: (1) all incumbents, (2)

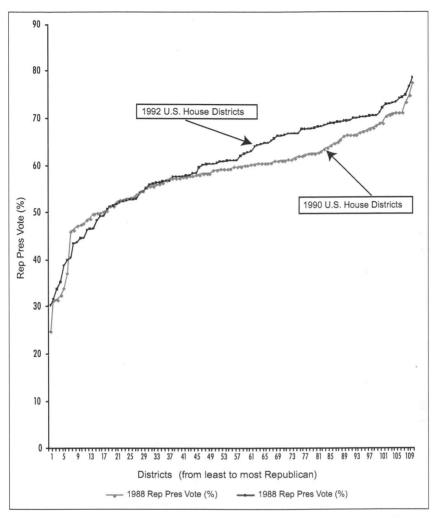

FIGURE 3.1 Redistricting and the Change in the Distribution of the Republican Presidential Vote in Southern House Districts, 1990 and 1992

Note: Data are the 1988 Republican share (two-party) of the district presidential vote for districts in 1990 and 1992. There are a total of 125 districts in the South in 1992, but only for 110 districts is it possible to record the 1988 Republican presidential vote in 1990 and 1992.

incumbent Democrats, and (3) incumbent Republicans. The mean percentage of redrawn constituents for an incumbent seeking reelection in 1992 was over a quarter of the district population. And for Republicans, well over a third of their constituents resided in different districts before the 1992 redistricting.

One may suspect that the Democratic Party (i.e., Democratic state legislators charged with redistricting) understood that in order to limit their electoral risks, they would have to limit their incumbents' share of redrawn constituents. After all, in the absence of a short-term factor that advantages one party over the other, we would expect that incumbents will earn a greater percentage of the vote from those constituents whom they represented before and after redistricting (Ansolabehere et al. 2000; Desposato and Petrocik 2003).[11] We will refer to these district residents as "same" voters/constituents. They are more likely to vote for the incumbent because many of them support the incumbent on a non-partisan basis. Essentially, the incumbent retains a substantial personal vote from these constituents because of name recognition and/or the incumbent's devotion to serving the district (Jacobson 2004).

The problem the Democratic Party faced in 1992—and especially before the 1994 elections—was that the GOP put forth a national agenda that emphasized the need for a new party majority in Congress. Under the leadership of Newt Gingrich, Republicans capitalized on the vulnerabilities of Democrats by offering a unified message to the American people embodied in their Contract with America (Gimpel 1996; Rae 1998). The GOP placed an emphasis on electoral accountability by harping on the transgressions committed by the Democratic majority. Republicans pledged to be the answer to the public's demand for political change. For instance, southern whites (particularly white males) registered abysmally low approval of President Clinton before the 1994 elections (see Jacobson 1996). Furthermore, by unhinging the bond of incumbency through the redrawing of district lines, these voters were especially primed to respond to the message of viable Republican candidates who targeted districts made more competitive through redistricting.

At the district level, we can test the impact of redistricting on partisan outcomes by examining whether or not redrawn constituents affect the two-party U.S. House vote. To be more precise, the hypothesis is: After controlling for other factors, the district percentage of redrawn constituents positively affects the Republican share of the U.S. House vote (two-party). To isolate the effect of redrawn constituents, it is important to include other explanatory factors we would expect to affect the vote. Therefore, the following variables are included: whether the incumbent running for reelection in the district was a Democrat or a Republican, the district percentage of the Republican presidential vote (two-party), the district percentage of the black voting age population (BVAP), the median family income in the district (in thousands), southern subregion (Deep South = 1, Peripheral South = 0), and a 1994-year dummy for the models that pool the 1992 and 1994 elections.

Because of the power of incumbency, it is expected that a Democratic incumbent negatively impacts the Republican share of the U.S. House vote. The Republican presidential vote serves as a proxy for district partisanship,[12] thus the higher the GOP presidential vote, the greater the Republican House vote. The BVAP is expected to negatively impact the Republican share of the U.S. House vote. Median income should serve as a rough measure of class, and therefore it should have a positive effect on the Republican share of the House vote. Even in the early 1990s, it is possible that the lag in Republican growth by southern subregion may show that the Deep South indicator negatively impacts the Republican House vote. And for the pooled models, there is a strong expectation that the 1994 election exhibits a highly significant and positive effect on the Republican congressional vote.

I estimate two regressions to evaluate the effect of redrawn constituents on the Republican percentage of the U.S. House vote in 1992, 1994,[13] and both elections pooled. The first regression, the additive model, includes the previously mentioned variables. The second regression, the interactive model, includes an interaction between the percentage redrawn constituents and incumbent type (Democratic incumbent = 1, Republican incumbent = 0). In the second model, it is expected that the interaction is positive and significant, which means that the higher the percentage of redrawn constituents, the higher the Republican share of the vote in districts with incumbent Democrats running for reelection. In other words, an increase in the percentage of redrawn constituents lowers the share of the vote for Democratic incumbents. By comparison, this means that the percentage of redrawn constituents should have no effect on the Republican two-party vote share.

It is important to point out that in both models the only districts included are those that were contested by Democrats and Republicans. Further, these districts must include an incumbent running for reelection because redrawn constituents can only be understood with respect to incumbents (see Desposato and Petrocik 2003; McKee 2008; Petrocik and Desposato 1998). In other words, in open seat contests, by definition, all of these districts contain the equivalent of 100 percent redrawn voters since neither candidate represented these residents in the U.S. House before the election. In short, the percentage of redrawn constituents is an appropriate way to operationalize the possible impact of redistricting on incumbents' electoral fates.

Table 3.3 displays the results for the additive and interactive models for 1992, 1994, and both elections pooled. As expected, in all three additive models, controlling for the other variables, the percentage of redrawn constituents has a positive and significant effect on the Republican share of the U.S. House vote. Even controlling for incumbent party affiliation, an increase in the portion of redrawn constituents positively influences the GOP House vote. These results indicate that in the South, short-term electoral conditions favored the Republican Party, reinforcing the long-term movement of whites in favor of the GOP. In these three models, a 10 percent increase in the district percentage of redrawn constituents raises the Republican House vote by eight- to nine-tenths of a percentage point.

With the exception of the 1994 election, the interaction for redrawn constituents and incumbent type is significant. For a Democratic incumbent, a 10 percent increase in their percentage of redrawn constituents raises the Republican House vote by almost 2 percentage points in 1992 and by 1.4 percentage points for the pooled 1992 and 1994 elections. In sum, analyses of the 1992 and 1994 southern House contests support the expectation that redrawn constituents threatened the reelection bids of Democratic incumbents. Going back to Table 3.2, which shows the percentage of redrawn constituents according to the type of incumbent, it is evident that in many districts, the impact of redrawn constituents on the House vote was substantial.[14]

TABLE 3.3 The Partisan Impact of Redistricting: District-Level Models of the 1992, 1994, and 1992–1994 Southern U.S. House Elections

DEP VAR: Republican House vote (%)	1992 Additive	1992 Interactive	1994 Additive	1994 Interactive	1992–1994 Additive	1992–1994 Interactive
Variables of Interest						
Incumbent (1 = Dem, 0 = Rep)	-.206 (.022)***	-.255 (.028)***	-.224 (.025)***	-.252 (.034)***	-.218 (.016)***	-.257 (.021)***
Redrawn constituents (%)	.090 (.038)**	-.024 (.056)	.082 (.041)*	.032 (.057)	.091 (.027)***	.012 (.039)
Redrawn * Incumbent	--	.192 (.072)**	--	.095 (.078)	--	.141 (.052)**
Control Variables						
Republican pres vote (%)	.361 (.112)***	.391 (.108)***	.403 (.127)***	.407 (.126)***	.375 (.083)***	.388 (.081)***
Black voting age population (%)	-.141 (.084)*	-.153 (.081)*	-.067 (.092)	-.072 (.091)	-.098 (.061)	-.107 (.059)*
Median income (in thousands)	.000 (.001)	.001 (.001)	.000 (.001)	.000 (.001)	.000 (.001)	.000 (.001)
Deep South	-.046 (.021)*	-.043 (.021)*	-.011 (.025)	-.010 (.025)	-.028 (.016)*	-.026 (.016)
1994 Election	--	--	--	--	.060 (.012)***	.062 (.012)***
Constant	.433 (.078)***	.423 (.075)***	.473 (.082)***	.481 (.081)***	.430 (.056)***	.433 (.055)***
Adjusted R²	.79	.81	.79	.79	.80	.81
N	82	82	64	64	146	146

NOTE: Estimates are ordinary least squares (OLS) coefficients with standard errors in parentheses. Dependent variable is the Republican district share of the two-party U.S. House vote. The models only include contested districts (Democrat vs. Republican) with incumbents seeking reelection. The variable of interest, "Redrawn constituents," is the district percentage of constituents an incumbent inherited after redistricting. The variable was calculated based on data from the following link: http://oseda.missouri.edu/plue/geocorr/.

***p ≤ .001, **p ≤ .01, *p ≤ .05 (one-tailed tests)

Partisan Impact of Redistricting in
the 2002 U.S. House Elections

The 2002 congressional redistricting contrasts sharply with the one implemented in 1992. Generally speaking, states drew incumbent-protection plans for the 2002 U.S. House elections (Schweers 2003).[15] With the increase in two-party competition throughout the 1990s, which was in no small part a consequence of the 1992 redistricting, both parties were wary of overextending and thus resorted to incumbent gerrymanders in 2002. Of course there were states that proved exceptions to the rule. For instance, Republicans controlled redistricting in Pennsylvania, and they proved to be quite adept at crafting a partisan gerrymander.

Figure 3.2 displays the distribution of the 2000 Republican presidential vote (two-party) for southern U.S. House districts in 2000 and 2002. Eyeballing the two distributions makes it clear that the 2002 redistricting only marginally affected the district partisanship in southern congressional districts. If we compare Figure 3.2 with Figure 3.1, the substantial differences that occurred to districts in 1992 are even more noticeable. In the South, the 2002 redistricting protected incumbents and therefore protected the Republican status quo that emerged during the 1990s. An obvious indicator of incumbent protection is that of the 107 districts with an incumbent seeking reelection in 2002, 39 percent (42 out of 107) of these districts were uncontested. By contrast, in 1992, of the 92 districts where incumbents ran for reelection, only 10 percent (9 out of 92) of these districts went unchallenged.

Compared to the 1992 redistricting (see Table 3.2), the percentage of redrawn constituents in 2002 was considerably reduced. Table 3.4 presents the average and median percentage of redrawn constituents in 2002 for (1) all incumbents, (2) Democratic incumbents, and (3) Republican incumbents. Table 3.4 shows that for all incumbents seeking another term in 2002, just under a fifth of their district populations were comprised of redrawn constituents (compared to over 25 percent in 1992). Democrats averaged 15 percent redrawn constituents and the median redrawn is just 11 percent. Again, compared to Democrats, we see that Republicans inherit a much larger share of redrawn

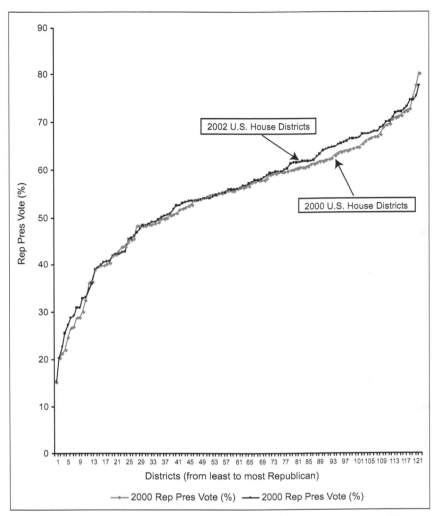

FIGURE 3.2 Redistricting and the Change in the Distribution of the Republican Presidential Vote in Southern House Districts, 2000 and 2002

Note: Data are the 2000 Republican share (two-party) of the district presidential vote for districts in 2000 and 2002. There are a total of 131 districts in the South in 2002, but only for 122 districts is it possible to record the 2000 Republican presidential vote in 2000 and 2002.

constituents. Nonetheless, the share of redrawn constituents for Republicans in 2002 is much lower than their share of redrawn constituents in 1992.

Despite relatively modest changes in the southern congressional map in 2002, there is still reason to expect that redrawn constituents exhibited

TABLE 3.4 **Percentage of Redrawn Constituents for Incumbents Seeking Reelection in 2002**

Incumbent Type	Mean Redrawn (%)	Median Redrawn (%)	N
All Incumbents	19.3	14.6	107
Democratic Incumbents	14.7	10.9	45
Republican Incumbents	22.7	19.6	62

Note: Data include uncontested races (uncontested = 42, contested = 65). Data exclude one district in Mississippi where two incumbents faced each other in 2002 (MS 3).

a partisan effect on the 2002 U.S. House vote. The primary reason why redrawn constituents are still expected to increase the Republican U.S. House vote in 2002 is because of the continuing growth of southern Republicanism (see Chapter 2). Also, in the 2002 midterm elections, a short-term factor like terrorism aided the GOP because after 9/11 the Republican Party "owned" the terrorism issue (see Jacobson 2003).

Like the models presented in Table 3.3, we can run similar regressions with data for 2002. After controlling for incumbent party affiliation, Republican presidential vote,[16] district racial composition (BVAP), median family income, and southern subregion, does the percentage of redrawn constituents have a significant and positive effect on the Republican share of the 2002 U.S. House vote? Table 3.5 shows that the answer is yes, but only in the case of the interactive model, where an increase in the percentage of redrawn constituents in districts represented by Democrats positively influences the Republican House vote. A 10 percent increase in the district percentage of redrawn constituents for Democratic incumbents boosts the 2002 Republican House vote by 2.4 percentage points.

Despite a much tamer redistricting cycle in the 2002 southern House elections, the extant trend in favor of the Republican Party still manifests itself in the district-level effects of redrawn constituents. Up to this point, the consistent finding that the percentage of redrawn constituents positively affects the GOP vote in southern congressional contests is impressive, but it is not appropriate to infer individual-level voting behavior from these results. Fortunately, the next two sections highlight the partisan impact of redistricting in the 2004 Texas U.S. House elections—employing both district- and individual-level (survey) data.

TABLE 3.5 **The Partisan Impact of Redistricting: District-Level Models of the 2002 Southern U.S. House Elections**

DEP VAR: Republican House vote (%)	2002 Additive	2002 Interactive
Variables of Interest		
Incumbent (1 = Dem, 0 = Rep)	-.277 (.021)***	-.315 (.027)***
Redrawn constituents (%)	.062 (.045)	.012 (.049)
Redrawn * Incumbent	--	.237 (.109)*
Control Variables		
Republican pres vote (%)	.421 (.095)***	.445 (.093)***
Black voting age population (%)	.077 (.089)	.043 (.087)
Median income (in thousands)	.001 (.001)	.001 (.001)
Deep South	.007 (.024)	.009 (.023)
Constant	.346 (.076)***	.350 (.073)***
Adjusted R^2	.89	.89
N	65	65

NOTE: Estimates are ordinary least squares (OLS) coefficients with standard errors in parentheses. Dependent variable is the Republican district share of the two-party U.S. House vote. The models only include contested districts (Democrat vs. Republican) with incumbents seeking reelection. The variable of interest, "Redrawn constituents," is the district percentage of constituents an incumbent inherited after redistricting. The variable was calculated based on data from the following link: http://mcdc2.missouri.edu/websas/geocorr2k.html.
***$p \le .001$, **$p \le .01$, *$p \le .05$ (one-tailed tests)

Partisan Impact of Redistricting in Texas' 2004 U.S. House Elections

After the 2002 elections, Texas Republicans took control of the governorship and both houses of the Texas Legislature. Before the 2002 elections, Republicans had a majority in the Texas Senate and held the governorship, but Democrats were the majority in the Texas House. This changed in 2002 because of a favorable Republican political climate and the enactment of a Texas House map that constituted a Republican gerrymander, yielding a GOP majority in the lower state house for the first time in 130 years (Arbour and McKee 2006).

With their control of the Texas Legislature and the governorship, U.S. House Majority Leader Tom DeLay (TX 22) steered Republican legislators to successful passage of a congressional map in 2003. The map was drawn for the sole purpose of increasing the number of

Republican U.S. House members.[17] Thus, with a slim Republican majority in the U.S. House, a new Texas congressional map became a prime opportunity to at least provide some extra cushion for the GOP's narrow margin (McKee et al. 2006). The Texas redistricting plan was designed specifically to capitalize on the expectation that redrawn voters would be the linchpin to Republican gains in the 2004 U.S. House elections.

Texas Republicans did not use race as the primary factor for redrawing districts. In fact, there was hardly any difference in the average Anglo and majority-minority voting age populations for Texas congressional districts in 2002 and 2004 (before and after the 2003 redistricting).[18] This explains why attempts by Texas Democrats (and other opponents) to overturn the map on the grounds that it violated the Voting Rights Act were not immediately successful.[19]

Figure 3.3 shows that, at least with respect to the distribution of the 2000 Republican presidential vote for Texas U.S. House districts in 2002 and 2004, there is not a marked difference. This is additional evidence that Texas Republicans were careful not to tinker with majority-minority districts. Instead, they banked on the expectation that redrawn voters would foster Republican gains, and thus they targeted Anglo Democrats by saddling these incumbents with very high percentages of redrawn constituents.

Prior to the 2004 elections, based on the presidential vote, most Anglo Democrats represented Republican landslide districts. These were the districts in the Republicans' crosshairs. Before 2004, Anglo Democrats managed to win reelection by exploiting the advantages that accrue through incumbency. It was apparent that if these Anglo Democrats did not stand for reelection, then the GOP could easily win these seats. After all, there is no southern state that rivals the rapid growth in Republicanism experienced in Texas during the latter half of the 1990s (McKee and Shaw 2005).

But short of retirement, the best chance to defeat these incumbents was to drastically alter their district lines. Redrawn voters would not consider their new Anglo Democratic House Representative to be their incumbent, and hence these voters would behave as though they were voting in an open seat contest. The recipe for de-

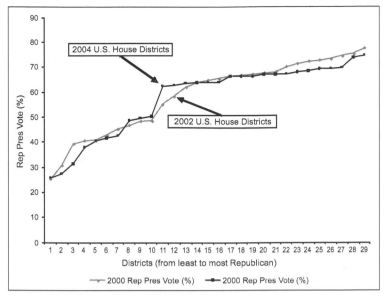

FIGURE 3.3 Redistricting and the Change in the Distribution of the Republican Presidential Vote in Texas U.S. House Districts, 2002 and 2004

Note: Data are from the Texas Legislative Council. Data are the 2000 Republican share (two-party) of the district presidential vote for districts in 2002 and 2004. There are a total of 32 U.S. House districts in Texas in 2004, but only for 29 districts is it possible to record the 2000 Republican presidential vote in 2002 and 2004.

feating Anglo Democrats amounted to a one-two punch: (1) utilizing the presence of redrawn constituents to nullify the incumbency advantage of Anglo Democrats, and (2) fielding competitive Republican challengers who could capitalize on the built-in Republican proclivities of these voters (as evidenced by the Republican presidential vote in these districts).

Table 3.6 presents the average and median percentage of redrawn constituents in Texas U.S. House districts in 2004 for: (1) all incumbents, (2) Democratic incumbents, (3) Republican incumbents, (4) minority Democratic incumbents, and (5) Anglo Democratic incumbents. There is no variation in the percentage of redrawn constituents if we confine our comparison to all Democrats and Republicans. This of course belies the great disparity in the percentage of redrawn constituents observed when we narrow our focus to subgroups of representatives like minority Democrats and Anglo Democrats. Now we see

TABLE 3.6 **Percentage of Redrawn Constituents for Texas Incumbents Seeking Reelection in 2004**

Incumbent Type	Mean Redrawn (%)	Median Redrawn (%)	N
All Incumbents	40.2	40.0	29
Democratic Incumbents	40.2	40.0	13
Republican Incumbents	40.3	40.0	16
Minority Democrats	19.3	18.0	6
Anglo Democrats	58.0	61.1	7

Note: Data include uncontested races (uncontested = 6, contested = 21). Data include a total of twenty-seven districts with incumbents seeking reelection. There are twenty-nine incumbents because in two districts Republican and Democratic incumbents faced each other (TX 19—Neugebauer-R vs. Stenholm-D; and TX 32—Sessions-R vs. Frost-D). Data are from the Texas Legislative Council.

that the Republican strategy for capturing the districts of Anglo Democrats was to swamp them with redrawn constituents.

Before the 2003 Texas congressional redistricting, the Texas U.S. House delegation was comprised of seventeen Democrats and fifteen Republicans. After the map for the 2004 elections was drawn, long-time veteran Anglo Democrat Ralph Hall switched in favor of the Republican Party—a wise move since his district was drastically altered.[20] So, prior to the 2004 elections, the Texas delegation was split evenly with sixteen Democrats and sixteen Republicans. After the 2004 elections, the Texas delegation included eleven Democrats and twenty-one Republicans. Of the five seats netted by Republicans, four of them were won at the expense of Anglo Democratic incumbents. Republicans had targeted five Anglo Democrats for defeat, and they only failed to unseat one: Chet Edwards (TX 17).

Two of the defeated Anglo Democrats (Martin Frost and Charles Stenholm) were doubly doomed. In addition to inheriting large shares of redrawn constituents, each faced a Republican incumbent who inherited a much lower percentage of redrawn constituents. Figure 3.4 presents the percentage of redrawn and same constituents for the five Anglo Democrats targeted for defeat under the 2004 congressional map. In addition, Figure 3.4 displays the Democratic percentage of the 2004 U.S. House vote cast by redrawn and same constituents.[21]

The vertical axis on the left measures the percent redrawn/same constituents, and the vertical axis on the right is the percent of the

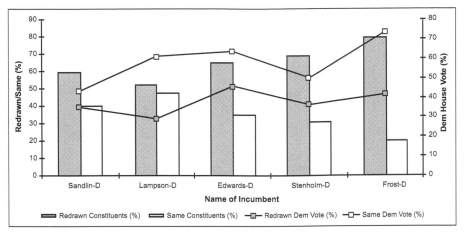

FIGURE 3.4 Targeted Anglo Democrats in the 2004 Texas U.S. House Elections
Note: Data were provided by the Texas Legislative Council.

2004 Democratic U.S. House vote. For each of these targeted Anglo Democrats, a majority of their constituents were redrawn (average and median = 65 percent redrawn constituents). Two of the five incumbents, Max Sandlin and Charles Stenholm, did not even secure a Democratic vote majority among their same constituents. The other three incumbents won over 60 percent of the vote among their same constituents.

The Democratic share of the vote cast by the redrawn constituencies of these Anglo Democrats is below 50.1 percent in every district (average = 37 percent, and median = 36 percent). In these five districts, the highest share of the Democratic vote among redrawn constituents was 46 percent, and this was won by Chet Edwards, the only targeted Anglo Democrat to win reelection in 2004. In every district, the percentage of the Democratic vote registered by same constituents exceeds that of redrawn constituents. The average difference in the Democratic percentage of the U.S. House vote among same constituents and redrawn constituents is 21 points. The data in Figure 3.4 reveal the effectiveness of weakening the incumbency advantage of Anglo Democrats by infusing their districts with high percentages of redrawn voters who proved to be substantially more supportive of Republican candidates.

A Case Study of Texas 19 in the 2004 U.S. House Election

As the high watermark for Republican success in contemporary southern U.S. House elections, 2004 provided two very intriguing matchups in the Lone Star State. In Texas 19 and Texas 32, Democratic and Republican incumbents faced off in the general contests. Employing a very effective redistricting technique, Texas Republicans "displaced" Democratic Representatives Charles Stenholm and Martin Frost. As explained by Cain (1984, 1985), under a partisan gerrymander one way to eliminate an incumbent is to dismantle their district to the point where there are no good options when they seek reelection. Some incumbents, upon seeing that their core constituency has been severely fragmented into several newly drawn districts, will opt for retirement. This was true for Democratic Representative Jim Turner, whose district in 2002 was Texas 2. In 2004, 61 percent of Turner's constituency became the redrawn Texas 8, and he decided to call it a career rather than oppose fellow incumbent Republican Kevin Brady, who sought and easily won reelection.

Unlike Turner, Representatives Charles Stenholm and Martin Frost chose to seek reelection even though their alternatives were considerably less promising (for details see McKee and Shaw 2005). Frost, who was the architect of a highly successful Democratic gerrymander implemented for the 1992 Texas U.S. House elections (see Barone and Ujifusa 1993; Black and Black 2002), found Republican retribution to be extremely harsh. He ended up seeking reelection in Texas 32 against Republican incumbent Pete Sessions. In a very ugly race, Frost did not stand a chance against Sessions, who retained 52 percent of his old constituency versus 20 percent of constituents represented by Frost prior to redistricting.

Unlike Frost, who was much more ideologically vulnerable to a strong Republican opponent, in 2004 Stenholm remained a conservative Democrat (based on his Democratic Party unity scores, see Black and Black 2002, 177–180), and this at least provided a dint of hope that he could survive what would be his toughest but, ultimately, last election. As was the case for three of his Anglo Democratic colleagues displayed above in Figure 3.4, the reconfiguration of his congressional district proved fatal to Stenholm's congressional career.

First elected in 1978, Charles Stenholm's district prior to 2004 abuts the outskirts of Fort Worth and sprawls west toward the New Mexico border (see Barone and Cohen 2003). In a brief account of four southern Democratic Representatives (Jamie Whitten-MS 1, Jim Wright-TX 12, Butler Derrick-SC 3, and Charles Stenholm-TX 17) who were cross-pressured due to their representation of conservative constituencies and the institutional imperatives placed on them by an increasingly liberal Democratic House leadership, Black and Black (2002) provide an insightful and remarkably prescient discussion of Stenholm:

> In the early 1980s he was a leader of the Democratic 'Boll Weevils' who supported much of President Reagan's tax and budgetary cuts. . . . Stenholm was far too conservative to win a major leadership position. His best bet for achieving power was to rise within the committee system, and by the late 1990s Stenholm was the ranking Democrat on the Agriculture Committee. Agriculture is the sort of second-tier committee that northern liberal Democrats are willing to cede to their party's few conservatives.
>
> All of these Democrats accommodated constituency opinion and institutional demands in ways that allowed them to have lengthy congressional careers. Whitten, Wright, Derrick, and Stenholm all knew how to leverage their incumbency back in their districts. Although none of these skilled Democrats were defeated by Republican challengers, they were nevertheless all operating to some extent on borrowed time. Each served in a district that was trending Republican in presidential politics. Derrick and Stenholm especially had to devote considerable time and energy to raising money to defend their seats. . . . Stenholm's district is a probable Republican pickup if and when he retires or *his district is significantly reconfigured* [emphasis added]. (Black and Black 2002, 180)

Unfortunately for Stenholm, in 2004 his district was significantly reconfigured. Prior to the 2004 redistricting, Stenholm already represented a very conservative, heavily Republican electorate. The Republican two-party percentage of the 2000 presidential vote was 72 percent, and in four out of his last five elections Stenholm won with under 55 percent of the vote (Barone and Cohen 2003). For the 2004 election, the newly drawn 19th congressional district would prove even less hospitable to Stenholm. At 75 percent (Barone and Cohen 2005), the Republican two-party percentage of the 2000 presidential vote in this new district was the highest in the South.

Map 3.4 shows Texas 19 in the 2004 U.S. House election and the remainder of the state delineated by congressional districts. As illustrated by the shading, Texas 19 was created from three congressional districts valid for the 2002 elections: (1) Texas 13, represented by Republican Mac Thornberry in 2002, (2) Texas 17, represented by Democrat Charles Stenholm in 2002, and (3) Texas 19, represented by Randy Neugebauer since 2003, when he won a special election to replace longtime incumbent Republican Larry Combest, who decided to retire shortly after winning reelection in 2002. With regard to the constituency population in the newly drawn Texas 19, 12 percent came from Texas 13, 31 percent from Texas 17, and the remaining 57 percent of the district population resided in the old Texas 19. Thus, Republican Randy Neugebauer had a substantial advantage over Democrat Charles Stenholm because he retained 57 percent of his constituents, versus 31 percent for Stenholm, and the remaining 12 percent of the district population used to be represented by Republican Mac Thornberry in what was a Republican stronghold.

In a sure sign that Neugebauer's original district was a Republican fortress[22]—he had to fend off sixteen other candidates, including nine Republicans—in a special election for the chance to finish out the rest of Combest's term. With 22 percent of the vote, Neugebauer earned a slim plurality, giving him the opportunity to compete in the runoff against the second place finisher, Republican Mike Conaway (21 percent of the vote). In the June 2003 runoff, Neugebauer prevailed in a nail biter (capturing 50.5 percent to Conaway's 49.5 percent) against the future Representative of the reconfigured Texas 11 after the 2004 U.S. House elections.[23]

Despite a short tenure as the Representative of the old Texas 19, in addition to retaining more of his constituency than Stenholm, Neugebauer had prior elective experience from his years as a Lubbock city councilman—the most populous city and the locus of the new Texas 19 (Barone and Cohen 2005). And, of course, the short-term political cli-

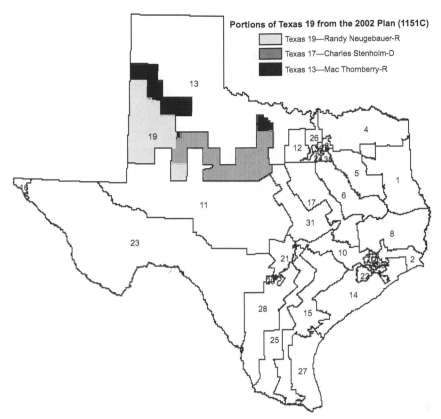

MAP 3.4 The Composition of Texas 19 in the 2004 U.S. House Election

mate in 2004 greatly favored a Republican in an election cycle that included the reelection bid of Republican President George W. Bush,
Texas' favorite son. In the 2004 election, Neugebauer defeated Stenholm, winning 59 percent of the two-party vote.[24]

Thanks to a survey conducted by former Texas Tech University political science professor Susan Banducci and former Texas Tech University graduate student Nathan Mitchell (Banducci and Mitchell
2004), it is possible to analyze political behavior in Texas 19.[25] This is a
rare opportunity to determine whether the aforementioned district-
level redistricting hypotheses are supported with individual-level data.

Although it is possible to evaluate the effects of redistricting on voting behavior with NES data (see McKee 2008), the subsample for the

South is too small and unrepresentative for confining an analysis to the voter preferences of southerners. Texas 19 contains a district population that certainly is not representative of the southern electorate writ large (e.g., it has a small African American population, 5.3 percent, and an above average Hispanic population, 29.0 percent, Barone and Cohen 2005, 1631), but the Banducci and Mitchell sample for Texas 19 is representative of the district population. In addition, the data contain an indicator for the ZIP code where each respondent lives. This makes it possible to determine which district each respondent resided in prior to the 2003 redistricting.[26]

What makes this individual-level analysis of redistricting different from the district-level analyses is that this particular race includes two incumbents—a scenario purposely omitted in all of the previous multivariate models. Fortunately, the sample does not entirely consist of respondents who were either represented by Neugebauer or Stenholm. A third group of respondents used to be represented by Mac Thornberry (TX 13 in 2002). This is crucial because it is expected that, compared to voters who resided in Stenholm's district, erstwhile Thornberry residents will be much more likely to vote for Neugebauer in the 2004 election. And viewed with respect to voters represented by Neugebauer before and after redistricting, redrawn Thornberry voters should be just as supportive. In other words, without the anchor of incumbency and with a short-term political climate favoring the GOP in Texas (see Petrocik and Desposato 2004), the preferences of redrawn Thornberry voters will be indistinguishable from Neugebauer's residents. Finally, because of the pull of incumbency, voters who were represented by Stenholm will be much less likely to vote for Neugebauer.

Out of a sample of 1,399 respondents in Texas 19 for the 2004 election, 9 percent used to reside in Texas 13 (Thornberry-R), 34 percent were from Texas 17 (Stenholm-D), and 57 percent were represented by Neugebauer in the old Texas 19. From the perspective of the Republican incumbent Randy Neugebauer, voters who used to be represented by Thornberry in Texas 13 or Stenholm in Texas 17 are both classified as "redrawn," whereas voters who remain in Texas 19 are considered "same-incumbent" voters. In Texas 19, the Republican two-party percentage of the 2004 U.S. House vote (Neugebauer's share) for redrawn

Stenholm voters was 46 percent, for redrawn Thornberry voters it was 66 percent, and for same-incumbent Neugebauer voters it was 69 percent (n = 1,051). Overall, Neugebauer's share of the two-party vote was 60.6 percent and Stenholm's was 39.4 percent—very close to the true percentage of the district vote in 2004 (59.3 percent vs. 40.7 percent).

A final check on the effect of redistricting on Republican success in Texas 19 can be done with three logistic regression models. In each of these models, the variables of interest are dummy variables that indicate in which district a respondent resided prior to the 2003 redistricting. The first model includes all voters in Texas 19, with a dummy for redrawn voters from Stenholm's district (1 = represented by Stenholm in Texas 17 in 2002, 0 = otherwise) and a dummy for redrawn voters from Thornberry's district (1 = represented by Thornberry in Texas 13 in 2002, 0 = otherwise). Hence, the base (omitted) category is same-incumbent Neugebauer voters (those respondents who Neugebauer represented in Texas 19 before and after redistricting). In the second model, the sample is confined to voters who were represented by either Stenholm or Thornberry before 2004. In the last model, the sample includes just redrawn voters from Thornberry's district and same-incumbent Neugebauer voters.

In all three models, the dependent variable is 1 = a vote for Republican Randy Neugebauer, 0 = a vote for Democrat Charles Stenholm. Finally, in all the regressions there are control variables for party identification (1 = Democrat, 2 = Independent, 3 = Republican), political ideology (1 = very liberal, 2 = liberal, 3 = moderate, 4 = conservative, 5 = very conservative), presidential vote (1 = Republican George W. Bush, 0 = Democrat John Kerry), and African American (1 = black voter, 0 = otherwise).[27] Stating the hypotheses specifically for each model:

- Model 1 (All voters in Texas 19)

    H1—Redrawn Stenholm voters will be significantly less likely to vote Republican in the 2004 U.S. House election in Texas 19.

    H2—Redrawn Thornberry voters will be indistinguishable from same-incumbent Neugebauer voters in their vote choice in the 2004 U.S. House election.

- Model 2 (Stenholm and Thornberry voters)
  H1–Compared to Stenholm voters, redrawn Thornberry voters will be significantly more likely to vote Republican in the 2004 U.S. House election in Texas 19.
- Model 3 (Neugebauer and Thornberry voters)
  H1–Redrawn Thornberry voters will be indistinguishable from same-incumbent Neugebauer voters in their vote choice in the 2004 U.S. House election.

The results for all three models are displayed in Table 3.7. As can be seen from the coefficients and their corresponding standard errors, all of the aforementioned hypotheses are confirmed. Beginning with the first model that includes all voters, redrawn voters from Stenholm's district were significantly less likely to vote Republican compared to same-incumbent Neugebauer voters. Redrawn voters from Thornberry's district were just as supportive of Neugebauer as were Neugebauer's old constituents. Holding the control variables at their mean values, the likelihood of voting Republican in Texas 19 in the 2004 U.S. House election was .52 for redrawn voters from Stenholm's district, .74 for redrawn voters from Thornberry's district, and .73 for voters represented by Neugebauer before redistricting.

The pull of incumbency is clearly evident with respect to voters who used to be represented by Stenholm, registering a twenty-point reduction in the likelihood of voting for Neugebauer in comparison to voters who used to be represented by either Thornberry or Neugebauer. In the case of Thornberry voters, without the pull of incumbency in the 2004 election, these voters shift in favor of Neugebauer, making their support for the Republican indistinguishable from the support Neugebauer obtained from the voters he represented before redistricting.

In the second model, which only includes voters who used to be represented by either Stenholm or Thornberry, the latter are much more likely to vote for the Republican Randy Neugebauer. In this model, after setting the control variables at their mean values, the probability of voting for Neugebauer was .49 for voters who used to be represented by Stenholm and .72 for voters who used to reside in Thornberry's district.

TABLE 3.7 Redistricting and Vote Choice in Texas U.S. House District 19 in the 2004 Election

Explanatory variables	All voters in Texas 19	Stenholm and Thornberry voters	Neugebauer and Thornberry voters
Redrawn Voter – Stenholm's District	-.921 (.186)**	--	--
Redrawn Voter – Thornberry's District	.062 (.337)	1.003 (.349)*	.019 (.333)
Party Identification (3-point scale)	1.349 (.124)**	1.415 (.194)**	1.223 (.149)**
Political Ideology (5-point scale)	.449 (.105)**	.467 (.157)*	.444 (.133)**
Presidential Vote (1 = Rep, 0 = Dem)	.695 (.199)**	.458 (.319)	.839 (.239)**
African American	.245 (.574)	1.328 (1.161)	.243 (.617)
Constant	-4.355 (.432)**	-5.331 (.695)**	-4.136 (.512)**
Log Likelihood	-410.66	-187.43	-262.10
Pseudo R^2	.29	.26	.27
N	883	369	585

Note: Dependent variable is 2004 U.S. House vote in Texas 19; 1 = Republican Randy Neugebauer, 0 = Democrat Charles Stenholm.

**p ≤ .001; *p ≤ .01 (two-tailed test)

Finally, in the last model that excludes voters who used to live in Stenholm's old district, there is no difference in the likelihood of voting Republican for same-incumbent Neugebauer residents (Republican vote probability = .75) and redrawn voters from Thornberry's district (Republican vote probability = .74). Like the district-level analyses, these individual-level models capture the independent electoral effects of redistricting in a southern U.S. House election. Depending on the political context, dislocating voters from their old incumbents can have a substantial effect on their preferences in U.S. House contests.

Conclusion

As demonstrated in this chapter, redistricting has had a significant impact on the outcomes of southern U.S. House elections—in 1992, 1994, 2002, and in Texas in 2004.[28] Data evaluated at the district-level support the expectation that redrawn constituencies boosted the Republican vote in southern congressional races. Although the individual-level data rely on a representative sample of voters in one congressional district, the findings jibe with the district-level analyses. The use of individual-level survey data to examine the voting behavior of redrawn respondents is an important contribution to the redistricting literature (see also Hood and McKee 2008; McKee 2008). The findings are consistent with the proposed hypotheses, and they remain robust even after controlling for those factors that we know have the greatest impact on voter preferences in U.S. House elections: party affiliation, ideology, presidential vote, and race.

Redistricting played a fundamental role in contributing to the rapid ascent of the Republican Party in southern U.S. House elections in 1992 and 1994. The gains made over these two elections established a new electoral equilibrium, with the GOP firmly in control. The 2002 redistricting served to reinforce the new Republican status quo, and yet we still find evidence for more GOP growth because redrawn constituencies in Democratic-held districts continued to trend Republican. And in Texas, which proved the exception to the rule of Republican success through redistricting in the 1990s (Black and Black 2002; McKee and Shaw 2005), we see that when the GOP controlled the redistricting process in 2003, redrawn voters were the key to Republican gains in the 2004 elections.

There is one factor that was purposely ignored in this chapter, but without accounting for it, redistricting would not have proven pivotal to Republican success in southern U.S. House elections. That factor is the presence of viable Republican candidates. Redistricting is crucial because it prompts the emergence of Republican candidates who possess the resources to wage competitive campaigns. Redistricting presented the opportunity for seats to be challenged by strong GOP candidates, but these candidates must emerge to realize the electoral potential provided by redrawn districts. In the context of southern congressional races, we can modify a line from the movie *Field of Dreams*: If you reconfigure the district boundaries, they will come. In the next chapter, the role of Republican candidate emergence is examined in detail.

Notes

1. The South gained seven more seats through reapportionment after the 2000 Census.

2. See McKee (2004) for a comprehensive review of the literature on 1990s congressional redistricting.

3. In the 1960s and 1970s, open seats accounted for 13 percent of southern House elections and 11 percent of contests in the 1980s (Black and Black 2002).

4. To be sure, redistricting was directly responsible for numerous Democratic retirements, but this chapter assesses its impact on southern Democrats' reelection bids. See Gaddie and Bullock (2000) for an in-depth analysis of open seat contests.

5. It should be noted that these data are for the percentage of the entire black district population as opposed to the black voting age population (BVAP). The district percentage BVAP is almost always a couple of points lower because of a higher portion of African American residents under the age of eighteen.

6. Democrats did gain ground in districts with between 10 and 20 percent black populations from 1990 to 1992, but there was only one district added in 1992 with a black population between 10 and 20 percent. There were thirty-one districts with 10 to 20 percent black populations in 1990, and the number was

thirty-two in 1992. Democrats represented 64.5 percent (twenty out of thirty-one) of these districts in 1990 and 68.8 percent (twenty-two out of thirty-two) in 1992 (Handley et al. 1998).

7. Petrocik and Desposato (1998; see also Desposato and Petrocik 2003) use the term "new" voters to describe voters who have a different incumbent seeking reelection as a result of redistricting. I use the term "redrawn" voters because it is more descriptive in the sense that these voters reside in districts with a different incumbent seeking reelection because of redistricting. Also, the term "new" voters is easily mistaken for its most common usage, which refers to those individuals who have never voted prior to the election under study.

8. Although the break point for the highest category is 40 percent BVAP or higher, the actual lowest BVAP in this category in 1992 was 45.8 percent (the newly created FL 23).

9. Please note that these data do not sum up to the total number of southern House Representatives because of a handful of newly created districts in 1992 that do not allow for a before and after comparison of district racial compositions.

10. See Black and Black (2002, 335–338) for a detailed breakdown of the GOP's success rate in districts based on the share of the Republican presidential vote.

11. Also, given the ticket-splitting behavior of a large segment of southern whites who voted Republican in presidential contests and Democratic in House elections, it is common knowledge that many of these voters were Republicans who previously voted Democratic for the House because of the efforts made by their Democratic Representative and/or the presence of an uncompetitive Republican challenger.

12. For the 1994 U.S. House elections, the district Republican presidential vote is based on the 1992 elections.

13. As discussed in McKee (2008, footnote 14 on p. 131), there were several states that redrew their congressional boundaries for the 1994 elections. In the South, this affected the calculation of the "Redrawn constituents" variable in Georgia, Louisiana, South Carolina, and Virginia. Through a GIS analysis, I was able to recalculate the "Redrawn constituents" variable so that "the 1994 redrawn percentages in these . . . districts were added to the 1992 redrawn percentages in these districts" (McKee 2008, 131). For the 1994 elections, there is an implicit assumption that for those incumbents who sought reelection, the percentage of redrawn constituents had an effect that lasted beyond the 1992 contests.

14. With respect to the control variables, incumbent type, Republican presidential vote, and the 1994 election dummy in the pooled models are all highly significant and signed in the hypothesized direction.

15. California epitomized the move in favor of incumbent-protection plans. In the 2002 U.S. House elections, none of California's fifty-three congressional districts experienced a change in partisan control (see Jacobson 2005).

16. For the 2002 U.S. House elections, the district Republican presidential vote is based on the 2000 elections.

17. See McKee and Shaw (2005) for a detailed account of the 2003 Texas congressional redistricting.

18. There are thirty-two U.S. House districts in Texas. Under the 2002 Texas U.S. House map, there were twenty-one Anglo majority districts with an average Anglo voting age population of 70 percent and eleven majority-minority (black plus Hispanic) districts with an average majority-minority voting age population of 68.1 percent. For the map enacted for the 2004 Texas U.S. House elections, there were twenty-one Anglo majority districts with an average voting age population of 70.2 percent and eleven majority-minority districts with an average majority-minority voting age population of 68.5 percent. Hence, with respect to racial composition, the new map was virtually indistinguishable from the old map (McKee and Shaw 2005). Again, the strategy was to sever the bond of incumbency by creating a large population of redrawn voters, the bulk of whom now resided in districts represented by Anglo Democrats.

19. There were, however, court-ordered boundary changes to five Texas congressional districts (TX 15, TX 21, TX 23, TX 25, and TX 28) prior to the 2006 elections (*LULAC v. Perry* 2006).

20. In 2004, Hall ran for reelection in a district comprised of 66 percent redrawn constituents.

21. Unlike the district-level data for the percentage redrawn constituents presented in previous sections of this chapter, these data account for the actual share of the aggregated district vote cast by same and redrawn voters.

22. Out of the seventeen total candidates, ten were Republicans and two were Democrats. In 2000, Bush won 76 percent of the two-party presidential vote in Texas 19, as configured for the 2002 elections (Barone and Cohen 2003).

23. These data are from the Texas Secretary of State website: http://elections .sos.state.tx.us/elchist.exe.

24. In accordance with the data presented in Figure 3.4, Stenholm won 49.7 percent of the vote among the constituents he represented prior to redistricting and just 36.1 percent of the vote cast by redrawn constituents.

25. I am extremely grateful that Susan Banducci provided me with these data because they confirm my expectations regarding the political behavior of voters affected by redistricting in this political environment. Karp and Garland (2007) analyzed these data for a different purpose.

26. A ZIP code indicator would not be a fine enough level of aggregation for determining the previous district residences of myriad voters living in more urban districts located in the Dallas-Fort Worth Metroplex, the Houston area, or San Antonio. Texas 19, however, is a very spacious district with low residential density that generally confines its borders to county boundaries. For this reason, every respondent was correctly matched with their previous district of residence based on the zip code indicator.

27. There is not a large number of African American respondents in Texas 19 (n = 50), but they are the most supportive of Democrat Charles Stenholm. It is interesting to note that Hispanics are the most likely to vote for Republican Randy Neugebauer, and the inclusion of a dummy for Hispanic voters would be positive and statistically significant.

28. See the table in Appendix B, which estimates the partisan impact of redistricting with pooled district-level data on the 1992, 1994, 2002, and 2004 (Texas only) southern U.S. House elections.

4

Republican Candidate Emergence

*Politicians do not follow normal career paths in periods
of dramatic electoral change. (1992, 349)*

—David T. Canon and David J. Sousa

As the aforementioned quote argues, during a period of rapid electoral change, the typical pattern of candidate emergence is considerably altered. Specifically, during those rare times when a perennial minority party ascends to majority status at an unusually swift pace, the proportion and success of amateur candidates (no previous elective experience) will be greater than it would be under the condition of normal politics. Amateurs play a critical role during a time of party system change because they are less risk averse than career politicians, and thus more will emerge under conditions that are advantageous and yet uncertain. In addition, because the southern GOP was for decades confined to the political wilderness, the pool of candidates with elective experience is just too thin to contest the large number of promising seats. Irrespective of whether a candidate is an amateur, however, is the reality that partisan change occurs because the ascending party runs more viable candidates who target those districts where the party is most competitive.

In this chapter, the changing political opportunity structure for Republican candidates is examined in detail. First, evidence is presented to illustrate the growth in the competitiveness of southern

House districts, which began with the redistricting that occurred for the 1992 elections. An increase in the number of competitive districts is one-sided in the sense that Republicans disproportionately benefit from the redrawn congressional map.[1] From the vantage of Republicans, the distinction is made between so-called normal-opportunity elections (1988–1990 and 1998–2004) and high-opportunity elections (1992–1996). By definition, GOP success rates are noticeably greater under the more favorable condition of a high-opportunity election.

Given more electorally promising districts for the GOP, data are presented to highlight evidence that reflects the greater viability of Republican candidates during high-opportunity elections. For instance, since candidate expenditures are an accurate measure of candidate viability, the role of money is analyzed to examine the relationship between spending and electoral success.

The chapter concludes with an in-depth look at the emergence patterns of amateur and experienced Republican candidates during normal- and high-opportunity elections. It is found that amateurs are more prominent and more successful during a period of dramatic electoral change. Under normal elections, when competition stabilizes, experienced candidates crowd out amateurs. From 1992 to 1996, punctuated party system change in southern House elections fostered the emergence of an unusually successful cadre of amateurs who were in the vanguard of the "Republican revolution." But as Republican control of the southern House delegation solidified, more established politicians emerged to entertain careers under the label of the dominant party. The pattern of candidate emergence observed in contemporary southern House elections exhibits many of the features present during earlier periods in American history that witnessed dramatic electoral change.

Competitiveness

A look back at Figure 1.1, which displays the partisan makeup of the southern U.S. House delegation from 1946–2004, shows that Republicans made their greatest gains in southern House elections from 1992 to 1996. In these three consecutive elections, the GOP netted thirty-two seats (nine in 1992, sixteen in 1994, and seven in 1996) to expand their share of the southern House delegation by 25 percent. These three elections are certainly atypical because Republicans did exceptionally well. By comparison, after the 1986, 1988, and 1990 elections, the partisan makeup of the southern House delegation remained exactly the same: seventy-seven Democrats and thirty-nine Republicans. Likewise, after the 1996 elections, we see evidence of a return to electoral stability with seventy-one Republicans and fifty-four Democrats following the 1996 and 1998 elections. The partisan balance was the same after the 2000 elections save for one incumbent (Virgil Goode VA 5), who switched from Democrat to Independent (seventy-one Republicans, fifty-three Democrats, one Independent). Republicans picked up seats in the 2002 midterm (seventy-six Republicans and fifty-five Democrats) and got a boost in 2004 because of a Republican gerrymander in Texas (eighty-two Republicans and forty-nine Democrats).

From 1986 through 2000, we see remarkable evidence of stability and change in southern House elections. Specifically, we see a period of dramatic electoral change (1992–1996) book-ended by two periods of electoral stability (1986–1990 and 1998–2000). Thus, the pattern is one of stability, change, and a return to stability. We see an electoral equilibrium (1986–1990), with Democrats in the majority disrupted by a period of punctuated change (1992–1996), which results in a new electoral equilibrium (1998–2000) with Republicans in the majority. Redistricting in the 2002 elections further solidifies the Republican majority, and the 2004 elections are noteworthy because redistricting in Texas almost single-handedly accounts for the GOP's gain of six seats (five out of six were netted in Texas U.S. House districts).[2]

It is important to revisit the pattern of Republican advancement in contemporary southern House elections because the rapid ascendancy of the GOP from 1992–1996 affected the electoral opportunity structure for House candidates. The increase in the number of competitive districts in the redistricting year of 1992 persisted through 1996, and viable Republican candidates emerged to contest districts during this exceptionally promising span of elections. Figure 4.1 presents *Congressional Quarterly*'s competitiveness rankings for southern House

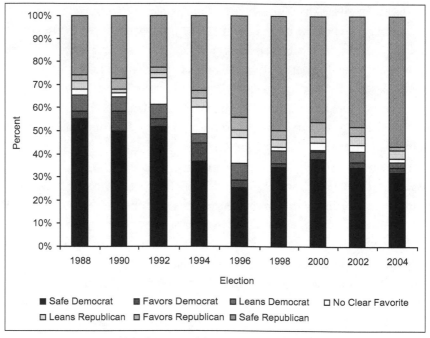

FIGURE 4.1 *Congressional Quarterly*'s Competitiveness Rankings for Southern U.S. House Districts, 1988–2004

districts from 1988 to 2004. These rankings are informative because they are not post hoc, but instead are published before the general elections. As expected, the 1992–1996 elections are exceptional because they entail a much greater percentage of competitive districts.

Based on the likelihood of Republican success, we can categorize the elections in Figure 4.1 as normal-opportunity elections and high-opportunity elections. Normal-opportunity elections consist of those years where the percentage of competitive districts is relatively low: 1988, 1990, 1998, 2000, 2002, and 2004. Based on *CQ*'s competitiveness classification, the most competitive districts are those with "no clear favorite." Among normal-opportunity elections, the 2000 elections had the highest percentage of "no clear favorite" districts at 3.2 percent (N = 4). If we add leaning districts (Leans Democrat, Leans Republican—the second most competitive category) to "no clear favorite" districts, the 1988 elections contained the greatest share of competitive districts (12.9 percent, N = 15) among normal-opportunity elections.

High-opportunity elections consist of those years where the percentage of competitive districts is unusually high: 1992, 1994, and 1996. For each of these elections the percentage of districts classified as "no clear favorite" was 11.2 percent (N = 14). If we add leaning districts, then the percentage of competitive districts for these elections was 20 percent (N = 25), 19.2 percent (N = 24), and 21.6 percent (N = 27), respectively. It is worth noting that *CQ* considered the 1994 elections to contain a slightly lower percentage of competitive districts compared to the 1992 and 1996 elections.[3]

The Changing Political Opportunity Structure

What sort of evidence should we expect to observe if greater competitiveness commencing with the 1992 elections essentially means more favorable districts for Republican candidates? For one, we should expect that Republican candidates contest a greater percentage of districts because more are projected to be competitive. Figure 4.2 presents the percentage of congressional districts contested by Democrats and Republicans from 1988 to 2004. From 1992 onward, compared to Democrats, Republicans contest a greater percentage of districts. In addition, the highest percentage of districts contested by Republicans occurs during high-opportunity elections.[4] The adage that you can't beat somebody with nobody constitutes the bottom line for elections, and clearly we see that the GOP ran more candidates when their prospects improved.

Another expectation is that elections are more competitive for Republicans because of a decline in the percentage of Democratic incumbents who run for reelection. Ceteris paribus, incumbents are always more difficult to defeat than candidates in open seat contests. Since the opportunity for Republican seat gains is a function of the electoral vulnerability of incumbent Democrats and the seats vacated by Democrats, Table 4.1 presents the number of political opportunities for Republicans.

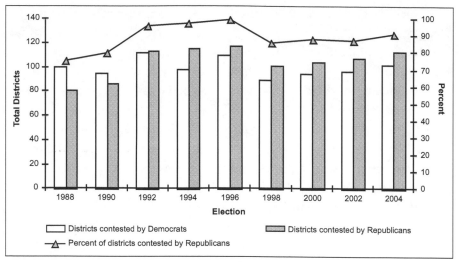

FIGURE 4.2 Districts Contested by Party, 1988–2004

Note: Data exclude Louisiana districts.

Table 4.1 shows the number of Democrats seeking reelection as a percentage of all southern House districts. The number of Democratic open
seats is equivalent to the number of Democrats who retired or were defeated in the primary for that particular election. As expected, compared
to 1990, there is a decline in the number of Democrats seeking reelection
from 1992–1996.[5] In 1996, the number of Democrats seeking reelection
amounts to only 30 percent of southern House districts. This constitutes
a sea change away from the status quo that prevailed from the end of Reconstruction until the 1990s—when the number and reelection rates of
Democratic incumbents guaranteed the party's unshakable dominance
(Black and Black 2002). Between 1992 and 1996, Democrats left thirty-
nine districts open, and Republicans won a total of twenty of these seats
(51.3 percent). By comparison, for the six elections designated normal
opportunity, Democrats left twenty-two districts open, and Republicans
captured only four of these seats (18.2 percent).

With the exception of the 1998 and 2000 elections, Republican opportunities, defined as the percentage of districts either left open by
Democrats or open as a result of redistricting, are substantially greater
after the 1988 and 1990 elections. This of course is a conservative defi-

TABLE 4.1 **The Changing Political Opportunity Structure for Southern Republicans**

	1988	*1990*	*1992*	*1994*	*1996*	*1998*	*2000*	*2002*	*2004*
Democrats seeking reelection	72	71	61	65	38	52	52	45	45
(Percent of all districts)	(62)	(61)	(49)	(52)	(30)	(42)	(42)	(34)	(34)
Democratic open seats	4	4	10	12	17	2	1	6	5
(Percent of all districts)	(3)	(3)	(8)	(10)	(14)	(2)	(1)	(5)	(4)
Open seats (redistricting)	—	—	16	—	1	—	—	8	3
(Percent of all districts)			(13)		(1)			(6)	(2)
Republican opportunities	5.3%	5.3%	29.9%	15.6%	32.1%	3.7%	1.9%	23.7%	15.1%
(Ratio: open seats/ total seats)	(4/76)	(4/75)	(26/87)	(12/77)	(18/56)	(2/54)	(1/53)	(14/59)	(8/53)

Note: Louisiana redistricting in 1996 created a new open seat (LA 5, which was won by Republican John Cooksey). In reality, ten of the sixteen open seats created by redistricting in 1992 were guaranteed Democratic pickups because of their high black voting age populations (> 45% BVAP). In 2002 all of the newly created open seats were possible Republican pickups (BVAP < 40%).

nition of what constitutes Republican opportunities because many Democrats who sought reelection were made vulnerable by the 1992 redistricting, as demonstrated in the previous chapter.

Another telling statistic is the increase in Republican presidential landslide districts as a result of the 1992 redistricting. Based on the district-level 1988 Republican presidential vote, the 1992 congressional redistricting increased the number of Republican presidential landslide districts from fifty-two to sixty-six. Using the definition of a landslide district as a Republican presidential vote of 60 percent or higher (Black and Black 2002), Table 4.2 presents the success rates for Republican candidates for 1988–1990 and 1992–1994. Compared with the 1988–1990 elections, from 1992 to 1994, Republicans contested all landslide districts, and their winning percentages were considerably higher in all districts (73.5 percent vs. 61.5 percent) and contested districts (66.7 percent vs. 55.7 percent). Among the seventeen districts

TABLE 4.2 **Republican Success Rates in Republican Presidential Landslide Districts and Non-Landslide Districts**

Elections	Districts	Districts contested by Republicans	Republican winners % (all districts)	Republican winners % (contested districts)
Landslide districts				
(Rep Pres vote ≥ 60%)				
1988–1990	104	99	61.5%	55.7%
1992–1994	132	132	73.5%	66.7%
Non-Landslide districts				
(Rep Pres vote < 60%)				
1988–1990	128	80	10.9%	13.2%
1992–1994	118	106	12.7%	13.2%

Note: Data are based on the 1988 Republican presidential vote (two-party) in districts. There were fifty-two Republican landslide districts in 1988 and 1990. As a consequence of redistricting, there were sixty-six Republican landslide districts in 1992 and 1994.

that *became* landslide districts as a result of redistricting,[6] the winning percentage for Republicans in these districts went from 14.7 percent (five out of thirty-four) in 1988–1990 to 58.8 percent (twenty out of thirty-four) for 1992–1994.

Despite contesting a greater percentage of non-landslide districts after redistricting (89.9 percent vs. 62.5 percent), Republican winning percentages were only marginally higher (12.7 percent versus 10.9 percent). And if we restrict the analysis to contested districts, then Republicans register the exact same percentage of victories—13.2 percent before and after redistricting. Reinforcing the findings of Black and Black (2002), these data demonstrate that the improved presidential foundations created through redistricting increased the number of landslide districts where Republican victories were overwhelmingly concentrated.

Money and Candidate Viability

For nonincumbent candidates, the most important indicator of candidate viability is the capacity to raise and spend a large sum of money. Referring to nonincumbents, Gary Jacobson states:

TABLE 4.3 Narrowing the Spending Advantage of Incumbent Democrats

Election Type	Democratic Incumbent Median ($)	Republican Challenger Median ($)	Dem/Rep Spending Ratio	Cases
Normal Opportunity	698,064	65,795	10.6/1	220
High Opportunity	612,253	130,313	4.7/1	154

Note: Campaign expenditures are adjusted for inflation, using 2004 dollars with 1982–1984 as the base period for the consumer price index (CPI). The CPI for all urban consumers was used to adjust for inflation. Normal opportunity elections = 1988–1990, 1998–2004. High opportunity elections = 1992–1996. Contested districts only (Democrat vs. Republican).

Most are largely unknown before the campaign, and the extent to which they penetrate the awareness of voters—which is crucial to winning votes—is directly related to how extensively they campaign. The money spent on nonincumbents' campaigns buys the attention and recognition that incumbents already enjoy at the outset of the campaign. . . . It comes down to this: Regardless of their potential, if challengers cannot raise lots of money, they can forget about winning. (2004, 46–47)

In this section, candidate expenditures are analyzed to show that: (1) competitiveness impacts the level of spending, and (2) electoral success is a function of spending. Again, if we make the distinction between high-opportunity and normal-opportunity elections, we can see that in the former, Republican challengers raise and spend more money. In addition, Republican candidates get more "bang for their buck" in high-opportunity elections. Finally, factors like redistricting affect the amount of money raised by Republican challengers.

Focusing on contested districts with Democratic incumbents seeking reelection, Table 4.3 illustrates the increase in spending among Republican challengers in high-opportunity elections. The median spending for Republican challengers is almost twice as large in high-opportunity elections ($130,313) compared to normal-opportunity elections ($65,795). In addition, the ratio of Democratic spending to Republican spending narrows considerably in high-opportunity years. Finally, incumbent Democrats do not raise as much money in high-opportunity elections. Apparently, the relatively greater vulnerability of incumbent Democrats

TABLE 4.4 Candidate Expenditures (in Thousands) and Republican Challenger Success in Normal- and High-Opportunity Elections

	Normal Opportunity Elections				High Opportunity Elections			
Landslide Districts	Dem Inc	Rep Chall	Ratio	Rep Winners (%)	Dem Inc	Rep Chall	Ratio	Rep Winners (%)
Mean	$867	$343	2.5/1	5.7	$563	$259	2.2/1	22.2
Median	$695	$169	4.1/1		$469	$225	2.1/1	
N	53				9			
Non-Landslide Districts	Dem Inc	Rep Chall	Ratio	Rep Winners (%)	Dem Inc	Rep Chall	Ratio	Rep Winners (%)
Mean	$797	$238	3.3/1	1.2	$731	$241	3.0/1	6.2
Median	$716	$48	15.0/1		$620	$117	5.3/1	
N	167				145			

Note: Campaign expenditures are adjusted for inflation, using 2004 dollars with 1982–1984 as the base period for the consumer price index (CPI). The CPI for all urban consumers was used to adjust for inflation. Normal opportunity elections = 1988–1990, 1998–2004. High opportunity elections = 1992–1996. Contested districts only (Democrat vs. Republican). Landslide districts = Republican presidential vote ≥ 60%; Non-Landslide districts = Republican presidential vote < 60%.

(of course the vast majority still win) makes it more difficult to raise money during those elections that advantage Republicans.

Table 4.4 presents a more detailed view of candidate spending. The expenditure data are divided between landslide and non-landslide districts and normal- and high-opportunity elections. In high-opportunity elections, the median spending for Republican challengers is higher, the ratio of Democratic incumbent to Republican challenger spending is reduced, and Republican challengers have a higher winning percentage. It is particularly surprising to see that in high-opportunity elections and non-landslide districts, the Republican winning percentage exceeds the percentage in landslide districts for normal-opportunity elections (6.2 percent vs. 5.7 percent).

Figure 4.3 shows that for all nonincumbent Republican candidates, in all but one expenditure category (400–499), the percentage of Republican winners is greater under high-opportunity elections. Further, in high-opportunity elections, Republican candidates manage to win seats in very low spending categories: 8.3 percent (two out of twenty-

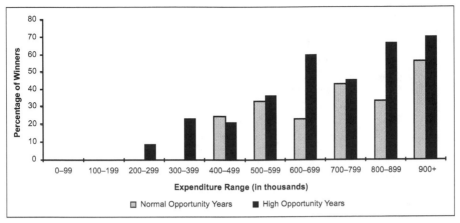

FIGURE 4.3 Republican Winners by Expenditure Levels in Normal-Opportunity and High-Opportunity Years

Note: Campaign expenditures are adjusted for inflation, using 2004 dollars with 1982–1984 as the base period for the consumer price index (CPI). The CPI for all urban consumers was used to adjust for inflation. Data only include Republican challengers and Republican candidates in open seat contests (no Republican incumbents). Normal opportunity elections = 1988–1990, 1998–2004; N = 283. High opportunity elections = 1992–1996; N = 219. Contested districts only (Democrat vs. Republican).

four) of Republicans win in the 200–299 expenditure range and 23.1 percent (three out of thirteen) of Republicans win in the 300–399 expenditure range. Evidently, a Republican partisan tide lifts all Republican boats.

Finally, the amount of money Republican challengers spend is affected by redistricting. If we confine the analysis to contested elections (Democrat versus Republican) with Democratic incumbents seeking reelection, in 1992 the correlation between redrawn constituents and Republican challenger spending is .44 (p < .001, two-tailed; n = 57). A multivariate regression (see Table 4.5) controlling for factors that shape the competitiveness of congressional districts reaffirms the relationship between redistricting and Republican challenger spending. After controlling for district partisanship (Republican presidential vote), district racial composition (black voting age population), and median district income (in thousands), the percentage of redrawn constituents has a large and positive effect on Republican challenger expenditures. A 10 percent increase in the district percentage of redrawn constituents raises Republican expenditures by $45,000.

TABLE 4.5 **Effect of Redistricting on Republican Challenger Spending in 1992 Elections**

	Republican Challenger Spending
Redrawn constituents (%)	449.013 (121.910)*
Republican presidential vote (%)	248.093 (283.144)
Black voting age population (%)	-281.495 (196.774)#
Median income (in thousands)	6.534 (3.925)#
Constant	-179.307 (196.847)
Adjusted R^2	.25
N	57

Note: Ordinary Least Squares (OLS) regression coefficients with standard errors in parentheses. The dependent variable Republican challenger spending is in thousands and adjusted for 2004 dollars.
#p < .10, *p < .001 (one-tailed test).

Emergence Patterns in Normal- and High-Opportunity Elections

Generally, experienced candidates are more successful in House elections because the fact that they have held an elective office is strong evidence that they want to make a career of politics. According to Jacobson:

> Other things being equal, the strongest congressional candidates are those for whom politics is a career. They have the most powerful motive and the greatest opportunity to master the craft of electoral politics. They are most likely to have experience in running campaigns and in holding elective office. (2004, 38)

Jacobson and Kernell (1983) point out that experienced candidates also behave more strategically in the sense that they are more likely to emerge to contest those districts where the likelihood of winning is greatest (e.g., open seat contests). Jacobson and Kernell conclude that "Politicians do act strategically. Their career decisions are influenced by their assessment of a variable political environment" (1983, 34).

There is ample evidence that shows experienced candidates are more likely to emerge and win elections when political conditions are most favorable (Abramowitz 1995; Carson 2005; Carson et al. 2006;

Carson and Roberts 2005; Hetherington et al. 2003; Hogan 2003, 2004; Jacobson 2004, 1996; Jacobson and Kernell 1983). Nonetheless, it is also the case that the emergence of experienced candidates is conditioned by the level of electoral uncertainty in the political environment. In other words, even if political conditions clearly favor one party, experienced candidates may not be any more likely to emerge if the political environment is unstable.

Consider the following quotes from Jacobson (2004, 38) and Jacobson and Kernell (1983, 23), respectively:

> An experienced politician will have acquired valuable political assets—most typically, a lower elective office—that increase the probability of moving to a higher office. But these assets are at risk and may be lost if the attempt to advance fails. Thus the potentially strongest congressional aspirants will also make the most considered and cautious judgments about when to try for a congressional seat.
>
> The political neophyte wishing to go straight to Congress risks little more than the personal cost of the campaign; even a low likelihood of success may not deter the attempt. The seasoned state senator whose district represents a large chunk of the congressional district, however, will await optimal political conditions before cashing in his investment.

The period designated as high-opportunity elections, 1992 to 1996, constitutes a highly unstable political environment (especially 1994), and, as such, experienced candidates may not have been positioned to emerge at a higher rate than they would during normal-opportunity elections. And in addition to being more risk averse than amateurs, because of the remarkably rapid ascendancy of the GOP in southern House elections, there may not have been an adequate supply of experienced candidates who found themselves in a position to run for Congress (Canon and Sousa 1992; Gaddie and Bullock 2000). Finally, in some instances, viable amateur candidates may have been just as competitive as experienced candidates because the electorate viewed them as more credible agents of change (see Canon 1990; Gaddie and Bullock 2000).

TABLE 4.6 **Republican Primary Candidates, 1988–1998**

Candidates	1988	1990	1992	1994	1996	1998
Total Candidates	95	86	205	168	167	78
Amateurs	80	72	164	147	151	65
Experienced	15	14	41	21	16	13
Experienced (%)	15.8	16.3	20.0	12.5	9.6	16.7

Note: Republican incumbents are not included.

Using data on Republican candidates in primary and general contests, the next two sections show the variable pattern of candidate emergence according to candidate type: amateur (never won elective office) or experienced (has won elective office), under normal-opportunity and high-opportunity elections.

Primary Elections

With data on candidates at the primary level from 1988 to 1998,[7] we will see that the likelihood of emergence and success for Republican amateurs is greater during high-opportunity elections. Table 4.6 shows the number of amateur and experienced Republican candidates in primary elections from 1988 to 1998.

Notice the marked increase in the number of Republican candidates for high-opportunity elections (N = 540 in 1992–1996; N = 259 in 1988–1990 and 1998). Also, in 1992 we find the largest percentage of experienced candidates at 20 percent. Because of a favorable redistricting, according to the strategic politicians hypothesis (see Hetherington et al. 2003; Jacobson and Kernell 1983), we should expect to see an increase in the number of experienced Republican candidates in 1992. But notice that in 1994 and 1996, the percentage of experienced Republicans (12.5 percent and 9.6 percent, respectively) is the lowest over the entire span of elections. This is support for the argument that the GOP did not have enough experienced candidates positioned to emerge after the 1992 elections.

We can separate primaries into three types: (1) experienced only, (2) amateurs only, and (3) experienced versus amateurs. In addition,

TABLE 4.7 Contested Republican Primaries by Candidate Type, 1988–1998

Candidate	1988	1990	1992	1994	1996	1998	Total
Experienced	1	2	1	0	0	0	4
only (%)	(5)	(14)	(2)	(0)	(0)	(0)	(2)
Amateurs vs.							
Experienced	5	4	18	12	6	5	50
(%)	(24)	(29)	(34)	(31)	(21)	(29)	(29)
Amateurs only	15	8	34	27	23	12	119
(%)	(71)	(57)	(64)	(69)	(79)	(71)	(69)
Total	21	14	53	39	29	17	173

Note: Data include primaries with only Republican candidates. Republican incumbents are not included.

we can distinguish between contested and uncontested primaries. Table 4.7 presents data on the number of contested primaries that fall into the above mentioned three categories from 1988 to 1998. It is hardly ever the case that we see experienced only primaries (4 out of 173 primaries = 2 percent). Most primaries are amateurs only, at 69 percent. The remaining 29 percent of primaries include amateur versus experienced candidates. We see the clear distinction between high-opportunity elections and normal-opportunity elections by the fact that seven out of ten contested primaries occurred in high-opportunity years (1992–1996): a total of 121 contested primaries in high-opportunity years versus 52 contested primaries in normal-opportunity years.

Contrary to contested primaries, with regard to uncontested primaries the data indicate no variability on the basis of normal- and high-opportunity elections. As a percentage of all Republican primaries (excluding incumbents), 36.9 percent (86 out of 233) went uncontested in high-opportunity elections (1992–1996) and 36.8 percent (78 out of 212) went uncontested in normal-opportunity elections (1988–1990, 1998). Likewise, there is hardly a distinction between normal- and high-opportunity elections, respectively, if we look at the distribution according to uncontested amateur primaries (88.5 percent versus 89.5 percent) and uncontested experienced primaries (11.5 percent versus 10.5 percent).

TABLE 4.8 Success Rate for Amateurs Who Ran in Contested Primaries with Experienced Opponents, 1988–1998

Amateurs	1988	1990	1992	1994	1996	1998
Success Rate	40%	25%	50%	58%	50%	80%
N = contests	5	4	18	12	6	5

Note: Data include primaries with only Republican candidates. Republican incumbents are not included.

In the case of contested primaries where amateurs and experienced candidates faced each other, we can see if the success rate for amateurs differs according to normal- and high-opportunity elections. Table 4.8 presents the percentage of amateur primary winners who faced experienced opponents from 1988 to 1998. In 1988 and 1990, experienced candidates won two-thirds of these contests. In 1998, however, it was an unusually good year for amateurs, as they won four out of five primaries (80 percent). Overall, amateurs win 53 percent (nineteen out of thirty-six) of primaries held in high-opportunity years and 50 percent (seven out of fourteen) in normal-opportunity elections.

General Elections

What was the general election success rate of Republican candidates who emerged from the three aforementioned contested primary categories? Also, what was the general election success rate for Republican candidates who ran in uncontested primaries? Table 4.9 answers both of these questions. Clearly, "amateur versus experienced" primaries include the most viable Republican candidates based on their general election success rates. The 100 percent success rate in the "experienced only" contested primary category in 1992 is misleading because there was just one case. Overall, in contested primaries Republican candidates were almost twice as likely to win a House seat in high-opportunity elections versus normal-opportunity elections (26.4 percent vs. 13.5 percent).

With respect to uncontested primaries, victory in the general election was rare. In fact, in 1988 and 1990, a total of sixty-three Republican can-

TABLE 4.9 General Election Success Rates (Percentage) According to
Primary Type, 1988–1998

Contested Primaries	1988	1990	1992	1994	1996	1998	Normal	High
Experienced only	0.0	0.0	100.0	NA	NA	NA	0.0	100.0
Amateurs only	13.3	0.0	5.9	25.9	0.0	0.0	5.7	10.7
Amateur vs. Experienced	60.0	25.0	44.4	75.0	83.3	20.0	35.7	61.1
Contested Total	23.8	7.1	20.8	41.0	17.2	5.9	13.5	26.4
N	21	14	53	39	29	17	52	121

Uncontested Primaries	1988	1990	1992	1994	1996	1998	Normal	High
Experienced	0.0	0.0	28.6	100.0	NA	33.3	11.1	44.4
Amateur	0.0	0.0	8.3	6.1	5.0	0.0	0.0	6.5
Uncontested Total	0.0	0.0	12.9	12.1	5.0	6.7	1.3	10.5
N	27	36	31	35	20	15	78	86
Overall Total	10.4	2.0	17.9	17.6	12.2	6.3	6.2	16.4
N	(48)	(50)	(84)	(74)	(49)	(32)	(130)	(207)

Note: Data exclude primaries with Republican incumbents. NA means there are no cases in the category. Normal = 1988–1990, 1998; and High = 1992–1996 elections.

didates ran in uncontested primaries, and not one of them won office. In normal-opportunity elections, the success rate was a meager 1.3 percent (one out of seventy-eight primaries), whereas it was 10.5 percent (nine out of eighty-six) in high-opportunity elections. Compared to uncontested amateur primaries, uncontested experienced primaries yield substantially more successful candidates. But no matter which type of primary we look at, as expected, the general election success rate is greater under the condition of high-opportunity elections.

Table 4.10 shows the proportion and success rate of experienced and amateur Republican candidates in general elections designated normal- and high-opportunity from 1988 to 2004. This analysis is a modification of the one found in Canon (1990). Similar to Canon, the point of the analysis is to demonstrate that in high-opportunity years, amateurs are relatively more prominent and successful in winning House elections.

In high-opportunity elections, experienced candidates constituted a smaller portion of the total number of Republican candidates, going from

TABLE 4.10 **Candidate Emergence in Southern U.S. House Races, 1988–2004**

Republicans		High opportunity	Normal opportunity	Total
Candidates	Experienced	16.3%	25.9%	21.7%
	Total n	(215)	(278)	(493)
Winners	Experienced	44.4%	78.0%	60.5%
	Total n	(45)	(41)	(86)
Winners as	Amateurs	13.9%	4.4%	8.8%
proportion	Total n	(180)	(206)	(386)
of candidate	Experienced	57.1%	44.4%	48.6%
pool	Total n	(35)	(72)	(107)

Note: Table includes all contests (open and incumbent) except those with Republican incumbents. Normal election years are 1988–1990, 1998–2004. Years 1992–1996 are high opportunity elections for Republicans. Observations include only Republican candidates. Entries are the percentage in each category. Number of cases is in parentheses.

25.9 percent in normal elections to 16.3 percent in high-opportunity elections. Even more noteworthy is that the share of experienced winners among all winners drops from 78.0 percent in normal years to 44.4 percent in the high-opportunity years.

The winning percentage confined to the pool of amateur candidates and experienced candidates, respectively, makes it evident that both amateur and experienced candidates are much more successful in high-opportunity elections. Note, however, that amateurs are relatively more successful, with their winning rate increasing by over 200 percent (from 4.4 percent to 13.9 percent) in high-opportunity elections, whereas the success rate for experienced Republicans increases by 29 percent (from 44.4 percent to 57.1 percent) in high-opportunity elections.

The data in Table 4.10 illustrate that it is not always the case that experienced candidates are more likely to emerge during promising electoral times. Canon and Sousa (1992) have noted that periods of party system change are the exceptional case when it is more likely for amateurs to compete successfully. They found this was true in the 1850s and 1930s, two realigning episodes where the emerging party lacked a supply of experienced candidates commensurate to the electorate's demand for partisan change. Commenting on the American South (from

1930 to 1988), Canon and Sousa note a similar pattern of Republican amateurs having unusual success because there was a shortage of experienced candidates. Because of its significance to this work, it is worth quoting a lengthy passage from Canon and Sousa:

> [I]n periods of electoral change many newly elected representatives are inexperienced amateurs. Amateurs are not usually strong candidates, and normally only weak parties rely on large numbers of them to stand for major offices. But in the 1850s, the 1930s, and the recent period in the South, amateurs played an important role in the emergent party's rise to power. In an important amendment to accepted theory, we found an inverse relationship between the political experience of a party's winning candidates and political opportunities in realigning periods and other periods of extraordinarily high political opportunity. The reason seems simple: emerging parties may lack a large pool of experienced candidates positioned to take advantage of new opportunities. The problems confronted by the Republican party in the South in the 1960s, 1970s, and 1980s illustrate this problem. (1992, 358–359)

We can add the 1990s to the statement made by Canon and Sousa—in southern House elections, Republican amateurs were especially abundant as a proportion of elected candidates in high-opportunity years. We can assess four hypotheses offered by Canon and Sousa (1992) since they remain relevant to southern House elections.

1. A greater share of winning Republican candidates will be amateurs in a period of electoral change (1992, 349, 353, 355);
2. Experienced candidates will comprise a greater proportion of winners when the ascending party has made substantial gains (or when the electoral environment has stabilized) (1992, 349, 353, 355);[8]
3. During a period of dramatic electoral change, experienced candidates who have been out of politics "are drawn back into electoral politics by the proliferation of opportunities" (1992, 352);[9]
4. Party switching in favor of the ascending party should be a more common occurrence (1992, 356).

TABLE 4.11 **Republican Amateurs Elected to the U.S. House in the South,
1988–2004**

Election Type	Amateur Republicans (%)
Normal Opportunity (1988–1990, 1998–2004)	24.5
(N)	(49)
High Opportunity (1992–1996)	55.6
(N)	(45)
Total	39.4
(N)	(94)

From 1988 to 2004, there were ninety-four newly elected Republicans in the southern House delegation (see Appendix C for a detailed accounting of newly elected southern House Republicans over this span of elections). Seventy-five Republicans were elected from contested primaries, and the remaining nineteen elected Republicans ran in unopposed primaries immediately preceding their first successful general election. Table 4.11 examines the first and second hypotheses by presenting the percentage of amateur Republicans elected to the House in normal- and high-opportunity elections.

The difference in the percentage of Republican amateurs elected under normal- and high-opportunity elections is striking. When the electoral environment was stable, 25 percent of elected Republicans lacked previous elective experience, whereas 56 percent of newly elected Republicans were amateurs during high-opportunity elections. Speaking even more clearly to the expectation that experienced candidates will crowd out amateurs when the political system has stabilized, the percentage of amateur Republicans out of all newly elected Republicans from 1998 to 2004 was just 16.3 percent (seven out of the forty-three newly elected Republicans).[10]

There is evidence to support the third hypothesis that many former elected officeholders will return to electoral politics in a period of substantial party system change. From 1988 to 2004, 18 percent (seventeen out of ninety-four) of newly elected Republicans were experienced politicians who were not currently holding elective office when they won seats in the U.S. House. These out of the "woodwork" Republicans comprised 20 percent (nine out of forty-five) of the elected Republi-

TABLE 4.12 U.S. House Party Switchers in the South, 1965–2004

Name	State/ District	Years Served	Date of Last Switch	Switch	No. of Elections
Alexander, Rodney	LA 5	2003–present	8/2004	D to R	4
Deal, Nathan	GA 9	1993–present	4/1995	D to R	9
Hall, Ralph	TX 4	1981–present	1/2004	D to R	15
Goode, Virgil	VA 5	1997–2009	2/2002	D to I to R	7
Gramm, Phil	TX 6	1979–85	1/1983	D to R	4
Grant, Bill	FL 2	1987–91	2/1989	D to R	3
Ireland, Andy	FL 8/FL 10	1977–93	7/1984	D to R	8
Laughlin, Greg	TX 14	1989–97	6/1995	D to R	5
Parker, Mike	MS 4	1989–99	11/1995	D to R	5
Tauzin, Billy	LA 3	1981–2005	8/1995	D to R	12
Watson, Albert	SC 2	1963–71	1/1965	D to R	5

Note: Except for the data on Rodney Alexander and Ralph Hall (Barone et al. 2005), the data are reproduced from Grose and Yoshinaka (2003, Table 1). With the exception of Greg Laughlin, these data include only those representatives who switched parties and then subsequently won reelection to the U.S. House.

cans in high-opportunity years and 16 percent (eight out of forty-nine) of elected Republicans in normal-opportunity elections.

Finally, with respect to the fourth hypothesis, we can consider the entire span of elections in the post–World War II American South to illustrate the unusually large number of party switchers who switched after they were elected to the U.S. House of Representatives. Table 4.12 shows that since the end of the Second World War, there have been eleven southern U.S. House Representatives who switched parties while in office and then won reelection under their new party label. All of these members switched from Democratic to Republican. Sixty-four percent (seven out of eleven) of these party switchers became Republicans after the 1994 elections—strong evidence that changing their political affiliation was considered a matter of electoral survival.

These data support the expectation that during a period of rapid partisan change, candidates will switch their political affiliation to that of the rising party. But at the same time, these data do not capture the total number of southern politicians who at some point in their careers made the switch to the Republican Party before running for the House.[11] With an increase in the pool of experienced Republican candidates in lower offices (especially state legislatures) and the majority status of the Republican Party in the southern House established, party switching should be a much less frequent occurrence.

Conclusion

In a period of rapid party system change, the electoral opportunity structure is drastically altered to favor the aspirations of candidates who run under the label of the ascending party. Because those candidates who have the most to lose in electoral politics act strategically, a more promising electoral environment for Republicans was partly a function of Democratic incumbents who chose to retire instead of facing a difficult reelection during high-opportunity years.

With a more favorable political climate initially created through redistricting, viable Republican candidates emerged to take advantage of the situation. With an understanding that the new congressional map would disproportionately favor Republicans, we see that there is an increase in the percentage of experienced candidates who emerged in the 1992 elections. But after the 1992 elections (1994–1996), the supply of experienced Republican candidates could not meet the demand, and amateurs emerged to win an exceptionally large share of Republican seats during high-opportunity years.[12] But when the electoral environment is stable (in normal-opportunity years), both before (1988–1990) and after (1998–2004) the episode of punctuated change (1992–1996), and especially after the GOP had solidified its dominant position, the vast majority of victorious Republicans had elective office-holding experience. Thus, similar to the findings of Canon and Sousa (1992), who examined candidate emergence patterns in previous periods of dramatic party system change (1850s, 1930s, and the American South from the 1930s to 1988), in contemporary southern House elections, there is indeed "an inverse relationship between the political experience of a party's winning candidates and political opportunities in realigning periods and other periods of extraordinarily high political opportunity" (358).

This chapter and those preceding it end with data that goes up through the 2004 congressional elections—the apex of southern Republican ascendancy. So what about the 2006 and 2008 contests? Considering the Democratic Party's strong performance—especially outside the South—it appears that these were definitely not "normal" elections. And even in Dixie, Republicans experienced some electoral slippage in these years. In the next chapter, we consider the national implications of Republican ascendancy in southern U.S. House elections.

Notes

1. Racial redistricting for the 1992 elections created many safe (noncompetitive) Democratic districts for African American candidates.

2. Outside of Texas, the remaining Republican pickup was by Louisiana Representative Rodney Alexander, who switched to the Republican Party shortly before the 2004 elections.

3. This perhaps is revealing of the unanticipated level of success the GOP had in the 1994 elections. No one expected the GOP to win as many seats as they did in 1994, and this unexpected outcome casts light on the type of candidates we should expect to emerge when the electoral environment is unstable. This question is addressed at length later in the chapter.

4. Percentage of districts contested by Republicans in high-opportunity elections = 95.8 percent in 1992, 97.5 percent in 1994, and 99.2 percent in 1996. Percentage of districts contested by Republicans in normal opportunity elections occurring after 1992 redistricting = 85.6 percent in 1998, 88.1 percent in 2000, 87.1 percent in 2002, and 91.1 percent in 2004.

5. From 1988 to 2004, as a percentage of all Democratic incumbents, the lowest percentage of Democrats ran for reelection from 1992–1996 at 80.8 percent (164 out of 203): 85.9 percent (61 out of 71) in 1992, 84.4 percent (65 out of 77) in 1994, and 69.1 percent (38 out of 55) in 1996. For normal opportunity years, the percentage of Democrats who sought reelection was 93.9 percent (337 out of 359): 94.7 percent in 1988–1990 (72 out of 76; 71 out of 75, respectively), 96.3 percent (52 out of 54) in 1998, 98.1 percent (52 out of 53) in 2000, 88.2 percent (45 out of 51) in 2002, and 90.0 percent (45 out of 50) in 2004. These data exclude Louisiana because of the complication of open primaries.

6. There were seventeen districts that were not landslide districts until after the 1992 redistricting, but the net total of landslide districts went from fifty-two before 1992 to sixty-six after the 1992 redistricting. Thus three districts that

were landslide districts before redistricting were no longer such after the 1992 redistricting.

7. These data are from *Congressional Quarterly Weekly Report*, various issues. After 1998, *CQ* no longer provided detailed data on the occupational backgrounds of all candidates competing in House primaries.

8. Most experienced candidates who win House seats have previously served in state legislatures (Jacobson 2004). There is a pronounced increase in the percentage of southern Republican state legislators between 1991 and 1995. For southern state houses, the proportion of Republicans goes from 27.7 percent in 1991 to 37.5 percent in 1995. For southern state senates, the proportion of Republicans goes from 24.3 percent in 1991 to 37.6 percent in 1995. I thank Jeremy M. Teigen for these data.

9. This is referred to as a "'woodwork theory' of critical elections, in which aspiring candidates come out of the woodwork when new opportunities become available" (Canon and Sousa 1992, 352).

10. The tables in Appendix C also point to two other interesting findings. First, compared to normal-opportunity elections, in high-opportunity years, incumbent defeats are twice as large as a portion of the contests won by newly elected Republicans (24.4 percent vs. 12.2 percent). Second, among the small number of newly elected Republicans who ousted Democratic incumbents, in normal-opportunity elections just one of the six (16.7 percent) Republicans was an amateur, whereas in high-opportunity years, seven of the eleven (63.6 percent) Republicans were amateurs.

11. For instance, at the time of their study, Canon and Sousa (1992) estimated that over 40 percent of southern Republicans currently serving in the U.S. House were at some point party-switchers (erstwhile Democrats).

12. Although this chapter has not dealt at length with the reasons why amateurs are more likely to emerge during high-opportunity years, the following three complementary explanations appear the most credible: (1) The pool of experienced Republican candidates is too small (thus you see evidence for the woodwork theory and party switching); (2) Experienced candidates are more risk averse than amateurs; the former do not want to take a gamble, but instead prefer to wait for a much more certain chance of victory; and (3) viable Republican amateurs have more credibility as agents of change during an electoral period that is anti-incumbent and anti-Democratic. On this last point, consider the following data from national exit polls: In 1990, among southern whites who voted for the House, for those who agreed with the statement that "It's time to give new people a chance" in Congress, 51.2 percent voted Democratic and 48.8 percent voted Republican (50.8 percent of voters agreed with the posi-

tion of giving new people a chance in Congress; contested districts only; 1990 VRS data). In 1994, among those southern white voters who wanted to give new people a chance to serve in Congress, 18.3 percent voted Democratic for the House and 81.7 percent voted Republican (61.2 percent of voters agreed with the position of giving new people a chance in Congress; contested districts only; 1994 VNS data). Commenting on the 1994 House elections, Gaddie and Bullock write: "In the region where for generations the politically ambitious paid their dues, in the state legislature or local office awaiting the retirement of the member of Congress, the old formula lost its magic. Rather than paving the way to Congress, political activities seemed to cost southern Democrats votes in 1994" (2000, 50).

5

National Implications of Southern Republican Ascendancy

[I]nsofar as the southern realignment solidifies and southerners dominate the Republican Party, the result could be such a strongly conservative party that more moderate electorates elsewhere in the nation could become alienated from the party's policy stances. (2005, 439)

—Lawrence C. Dodd

What a difference an election can make. Not long after the 2004 presidential contest, the media (see Hamburger and Wallsten 2006) and scholars alike (see Dodd and Oppenheimer 2005) talked openly of the advent of Karl Rove's construction of a permanent Republican majority. But following a disastrous attempt to reform Social Security (Jacobs 2006), a bungled response to the nation's most devastating natural disaster, a lopsided string of Republican congressional scandals (Hendry et al. 2009), and growing discontent with the Iraq War (Jacobson 2007a, 2007b), President George W. Bush acknowledged that his Grand Old Party took a "thumping" in the 2006 midterm. After Republicans ceded thirty House seats to the Democrats en route to losing their lower chamber majority for the first time in twelve years, the new Democratic majority followed up in 2008 with an additional twenty-one seats and the presidency.[1]

This chapter takes a detailed look at the short- and potentially longterm national implications of Republican success in southern U.S.

House contests. Like all elections, the dramatic results of the 2006 and 2008 races are the product of short-term and long-range changes in the political behavior and composition of the American electorate. Since the 1960s, the tremendous dynamism of American politics has most clearly been exhibited below the Mason-Dixon Line. The rise of southern Republicans has had—and continues to have—far-reaching electoral consequences that reverberate both in and outside the region as well as directly in the halls of Congress.

With an emphasis on the South's contribution to national partisan change at home and in Washington, this chapter chronicles the ascendancy of the GOP and its subsequent fall in the aftermath of the 2006 and 2008 elections. We begin with a review of southern Republican advancement in electoral politics that is juxtaposed against the pattern of GOP performance in the North. From the 1950s to the present, it is apparent that growing southern Republicanism fostered a long-term pattern of national convergence that plateaued in the 1990s (Black and Black 2002) and has since revealed increasing divergence.

The South was the linchpin of the unraveling of the New Deal coalition and, with it, the reconstitution of two markedly more homogenous and ideologically polarized political parties. Due to its distinctive but perhaps waning cultural milieu (see the next and final chapter), the South's Republican realignment made possible a national House majority, and yet the region is also a primary explanation for the party's later demise. Compared to the rest of the nation, the South used to be substantially more Democratic, and now it is much more Republican. The persistence of southern exceptionalism makes the region a precarious foundation for building the base of a national party majority. Since the 1960s, southern politics has gone from being a leading to a lagging indicator of national political change.

This Ain't Your Daddy's Dixie

Growing up in a culturally conservative "Deep South" small town[2] in east Texas, the foremost scholars of southern politics, Earl and Merle Black, never cease to be amazed by the contemporary prevalence of

Republicans in their native land. As they have explained to their fellow attendees on several occasions at the biennial meeting of the Citadel Symposium on Southern Politics, with the exception of an eccentric "village idiot," they just did not know anyone who professed allegiance to the Republican Party. Coming of age in the 1950s, the Black brothers belonged to the last generation to witness the final act of Jim Crow—a time when the Solid Democratic South showed few signs of crumbling. Of course monumental changes lurked right around the corner, and the Black brothers assiduously documented and analyzed them in their book *Politics and Society in the South* (1987). The children of Earl and Merle's generation have grown up in a South that looks very different from their parents', and one of the most evident signs of change is of course the rise of southern Republicans in congressional politics.

Figure 5.1 presents the two-party percentage of House seats held by Republicans in the North, South, and nation from 1946 through 2008. It is obvious in the trends for the North and South that, since the conclusion of World War II, northern Republicanism began a gradual decline that extended through the 1980s. By contrast, like the mythical Phoenix rising from the ashes, eight decades after the Civil War, southern Republicanism had just begun its ascent. By the 1990s, the percentage of GOP Representatives in both regions converges and makes possible the advent of a Republican House majority for the first time in forty years. Clearly, the emergence of a viable Republican Party in Dixie was instrumental in bringing about a national GOP congressional majority. And more recently, it is interesting that shortly after the historic 1994 midterm, the pattern of Republican representation diverges—southern strength persists whereas the share of northern Republicans declines, especially after 2004. Indeed, the sharp drop in northern Republicans accounts for the revival of a Democratic congressional majority in 2006.

In the 1990s, for northern Republicans, their party's takeover in 1994 constituted the apex of their representation in the northern House delegation (54 percent). But for southern Members, 1994 was the beginning of a ten-year reign of unbroken GOP growth[3] that peaked in 2004 at 63 percent of the southern House delegation. In

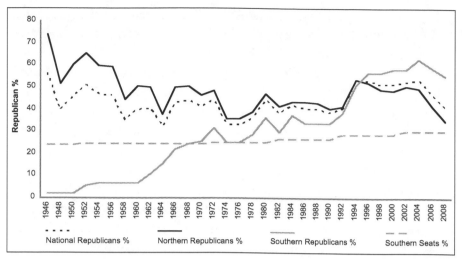

FIGURE 5.1 The Rise and Fall of the Republican Party in the U.S. House of Representatives

2006 and 2008, the share of Republicans dips in the South and plunges in the North. In the South, the percentage of Republicans drops 7.6 points from 2004 to 2008 (55 percent Republicans), while in the North, the share of Republicans falls off a cliff, going from 49.5 percent in 2004 to 34.9 percent in 2008—a difference of 14.6 points.[4]

A more visually insightful method of discerning North/South disparities in GOP representation in the U.S. House is displayed in Figure 5.2, which shows the regional percentage difference in Republicans (South minus North) from 1946 through 2008. Over the entire sixty-two-year span of House elections, it is evident that the height of regional convergence occurs in 1994, with just a 2.5 point difference in the regional percentages of Republicans (53.7 percent Republicans in the North and 51.2 percent Republicans in the South). After 1994, with one exception, the 2002 election—which took place during a short-term political environment nationally favoring the GOP because it "owned" the terrorism issue (see Jacobson 2003)—the regional gap in the percentage of Republicans has steadily widened. By 2008, the surplus in the share of southern GOP Representatives had expanded to 20 points. This regional difference in the percentage of Republicans was the widest since 1970, when the gap was 21 points and, of course,

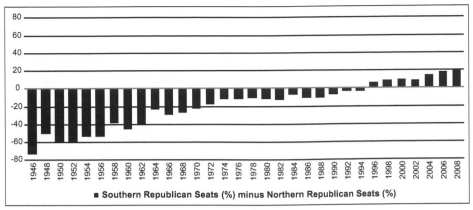

FIGURE 5.2 Regional Differences in the Republican Percentage of U.S. House Seats

northern Republicans were much more prevalent than their southern colleagues.

The contemporary regional divergence in Republican House representation speaks strongly to a long-term distinction in the viability of the major political parties. As the GOP steadily made inroads in the South, its strength outside the region was gradually declining. As the two regions converged, Republicanism in the South was rising and in the North it was waning. In 1994, regional convergence maximized at a moment when the political environment was running a national Republican tide (Petrocik and Desposato 1998; McKee 2008). The jump-shift pattern indicating a surge in Republican House seats between 1992 and 1994 was a national phenomenon, but the electoral structure supporting further GOP growth was confined to the South (Jenkins et al. 2007).[5] It was the only section of the country experiencing a long-term secular realignment in favor of the Republican Party. After the 1994 midterm, the shedding of northern GOP House seats and the persistence of southern Republican strength established a decade-long period of hyper-competitive national elections that maintained a razor-thin Republican House majority.

As Michael Barone described party competition in *The Almanac of American Politics* after the 2000 elections, America had become "The 49 percent Nation" (2001). In percentage terms, from 1994 through 2004 the GOP's largest national House majority was only 53.5 percent of the two-party distribution of congressional districts, and this was after the 2004 elections. Thus, the largest Republican House majority occurred right before they would lose it, and at this time the GOP's foundation of political support was at its weakest because it was disproportionately propped up by a region that, since 1994, was trending against the rest of the country. Commenting on the narrow Republican House majorities, Erikson and Wright note that:

> Even when the electoral landscape changed dramatically in the Republicans' favor with the 1994 Republican landslide, the swing was due to a small minority of voters. Between 1992 and 1994, the national major party vote shifted only six percentage points. During the 1994–2004 era of Republican control, the national vote for Congress hovered close to fifty-fifty. (2009, 73)

In hindsight, it is somewhat remarkable that political observers would contemplate a "permanent" Republican majority when the highest GOP seat margin would be eliminated with a partisan switch of only fifteen districts!

Hence it is crucial to understand the underpinnings of partisan strength in and outside the South because in the former region Republican growth was deeply rooted and enduring (Hayes and McKee 2008). By comparison, northern Republican success has been volatile because it is more sensitive to short-term conditions given the absence of a long-term Republican realignment.[6] In fact, what probably led so many scholars to overstate Republican congressional success was the fortuitous timing of short-term factors that boosted GOP performance not long after the party was losing support outside the South (e.g., the events of 9/11 redound to the electoral benefit of the GOP in 2002 after the share of northern Republicans had been declining since 1996).

As the anchor weight of the New Deal coalition, the steady exodus of white southerners from the Democratic Party eventually reached a point where this erstwhile dominant party reached parity with a partisan opponent that only a few generations ago was viewed by white southerners as anathema to the region's complex and tragic history. But as racial, economic, and social change progressed, Dixie would eventually become the regional redoubt of Republican electoral success.

Figures 5.3 and 5.4 illustrate the transition from the outsized presence of southern Democrats to the inordinate influence of southern Republicans, in terms of congressional representation and party affiliation, respectively. In Figure 5.3, the dotted line displays the southern percentage of all congressional districts. In Figure 5.4, the dotted line indicates the white southern percentage of all NES survey respondents who identify with either the Democratic or Republican Party (including independent leaners as partisans). What is notable about both figures is the inexorable upward trend in the southern Republican percentage of House seats and white southerners who identify as Republicans.

Figure 5.3 shows that in the 1950s southern Democrats accounted for 42 percent of the total Democratic share of House seats. By stark contrast, southern Republicans accounted for 3 percent of the total Republican House delegation in the 1950s. But by the 1990s, southern Republicans finally held the same share of districts (28.6 percent) as southern Democrats (28.3 percent). And by the next decade, the percentage of southern Republican seats was significantly greater than the southern share of all congressional districts (30 percent). From 2000 to 2008, 36 percent of all Republicans represented southern constituencies, whereas the southern portion of all Democratic Representatives had diminished to 24 percent.

Similarly, from the vantage of the electorate, Figure 5.4 shows the increase in Republican identification among southern whites and the decline in white Democrats. In the 1950s, as a share of all Democratic identifiers, southern whites were 21 percent. Southern white Republicans in the 1950s comprised a meager 8 percent of the total share of Republican identifiers. By the 1980s, however, southern whites comprised a greater portion of all GOP identifiers than Democrats (21 percent Republican versus 20 percent Democratic). This trend has continued to the point that, even though the southern white percentage of all partisans increased from 16 percent in the 1950s to 21 percent for 2000–2004, 28 percent of southern whites identified with the Republican Party from 2000 to 2004. In the 1950s, the white South

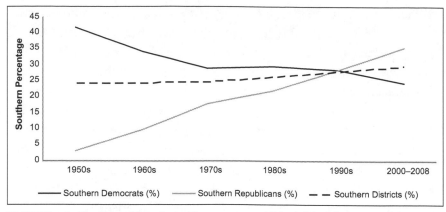

FIGURE 5.3 Decline of Southern Democrats and Rise of Southern Republicans

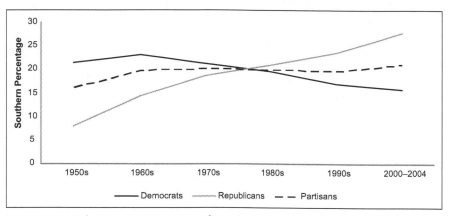

FIGURE 5.4 The Growing Presence of Southerners in the Republican Party

had a disproportionate influence on the Democratic Party, both in terms of representation and party identifiers. By the end of the twentieth century, compared to its size, the white South exhibits inequitable electoral might in the Republican Party—even more influence in terms of identifiers than was the case for white southern Democrats in the 1950s.

As Black and Black (2002) argued, in congressional elections, the advent of a competitive South led to a competitive America. But since the time of their definitive treatment on southern congressional politics, it seems that a Republican-advantaged South has contributed to a

Democratic America. In other words, in the 1990s the rightward shift in American politics was due primarily to the influence of southerners— both those holding leadership positions in the House and their more ideologically conservative constituencies back home. But the farther to the right the Southern-led Republican Party moved, the more electorally vulnerable were those northern GOP Representatives whose constituencies were decidedly less conservative and less supportive of the political dispositions of their southern neighbors, whose Members wielded a disproportionate amount of institutional influence. Under these conditions, Erikson and Wright contend that "[a] Congress that is off-center from the people ideologically would be a Congress out of equilibrium. To restore equilibrium, either Congress would realize its mistake and change its policy making, or the people would realize their mistake and vote in a more ideologically compatible Congress" (2009, 88).

Although predating the return of a national Democratic majority, Black and Black keenly understood the potential for southern Republicans to overreach:

> And just as segregationist southern Democrats once profoundly embarrassed northern Democrats and forced them to explain to their constituents that the southerners did, after all, ensure that the Democratic party controlled Congress, so moderate northern Republicans might have to explain to their constituents the reality that the southern congressional realignment was largely responsible for the Republicans' small national majorities. The southern Republicans' broad-ranging conservatism on economics, race, culture, and defense, particularly when communicated in crusading and absolute terms, may well have weakened the appeal of the party in the old strongholds of moderate to liberal Republicanism in the North. Just as the changing social bases of the Democratic party in the 1930s in time created tremendous strains and culminated in the exodus of conservative white southerners from the party, so, too, widespread perceptions of southern conservatives as proselytizing extremists, unless reversed by new and more inclusive Republican leadership styles, may well erode its appeal in parts of the North. (2002, 38)

The South and Partisan Polarization

One of the more talked about debates in contemporary American politics is the widening differences between the major political parties. The "red" state versus "blue" state banter is implicitly and often explicitly about the increasing polarization of the Democratic and Republican parties (Gelman et al. 2008). From an institutional perspective, there exists a broad scholarly consensus that Members of Congress are presently more polarized along partisan lines than they have been in over three decades and, depending on the measure, perhaps more polarized now than since the late 1800s (see Nivola and Brady 2006).

There are two characteristics that define what is meant by partisan polarization: (1) the ideological distance between Democratic and Republican Representatives has grown and (2) intraparty ideological cohesiveness has increased (Brady and Han 2006). On the basis of these two features, it is undeniable that the House of Representatives has become more polarized. Furthermore, it should come as no surprise that the southern realignment is a primary cause of the rising partisan polarization in the Congress. Joel D. Aberbach provides an excellent synopsis of the current state of partisan polarization:

> Whether one characterizes what has happened in the United States over the past few decades as sorting or polarization, the data seem rather conclusive that American politics is now more clearly structured than it was in the previous era. The Democratic Party was once an uncomfortable alliance of southern whites and more progressive northerners—an alliance often challenged from within by the crosscutting "conservative coalition" of southern Democrats and conservative Republicans. The Republican triumph in the South, a process that took many years but is now nearly complete, and the increasingly Democratic colorization of the North—to use the red state-blue state imagery so popular now—have produced a much more coherent set of parties. Today, both parties are much more internally consistent and, if only because of sorting, at greater ideological distance from one another. This consistency means that the cleavages in politics are more distinct, with less overlap on issues. (2008, 288)

For fear of rehashing all of the theoretical components of southern partisan change previously discussed (see Chapters 1 and 2), it should be noted that once the GOP established a foothold in the region, southern Democrats gradually moved toward the liberal pole of the ideological continuum. As northern Democratic Representatives fully embraced a pro-civil rights position and increased their share of the Democratic Caucus vis-à-vis their southern counterparts, growing pressure was placed on southern Democratic committee chairs to moderate their ideological positions (Black and Black 2002). The one-party Democratic legacy in the South came under attack by northern Democrats who sought to diminish the institutional influence of their more senior southern Democratic peers, who for decades chaired many of the most influential committees.[7]

The large influx of northern Democrats after the 1958 elections was a harbinger of the increasingly liberal direction that this larger regional faction would impose on the Democratic Caucus (see Carmines and Stimson 1989).[8] By the 1970s, the northern wing of the Democratic Party centralized House rules in order to move the balance of power away from committee chairs and in favor of the party leadership (Rohde 1991). The 1970s were the peak of dealignment in both the House and the electorate (Bartels 2000), and thus these institutional reforms had a direct bearing on setting in motion a more partisan political era (Jacobson 2007c). As Smith and Gamm (2009, 157) point out, in the early 1970s, "Democrats enhanced the formal powers of their central party leader at the lowest point in party polarization in the history of the two parties ... Sharp intraparty factionalism [i.e., northern versus southern Democrats], more than interparty differences, stimulated liberals to strengthen their central party leader and weaken the power of full committee chairs, many of whom were conservatives."

With respect to policy-making, the centralization of agenda-setting in the hands of House party leaders endowed them with more leverage to enforce ideological discipline on rank-and-file Members. From Democratic Speaker Thomas P. "Tip" O'Neill (1977–1987) to Speaker Nancy Pelosi (2007–present), the influence of party leadership in the post-reform House has grown and partisan polarization has become a fixture of congressional behavior (Pearson and Schickler 2009). The increasing clout of party leaders has been a bipartisan endeavor. For instance, after the 1994 Republican revolution, Speaker Newt Gingrich (1995–1999) amassed a level of power in the leadership not witnessed since the days of Speaker Joseph Cannon (1903–1911). In the distribution of committee chairs, senior Members were routinely passed over in favor of junior Members known to be ideologically closer to the positions promoted by the GOP leadership (Fenno 1997). Committee chairs were term-limited after six years, and legislation favored by the leadership was frequently taken out of the hands of committee chairs and addressed directly by the Rules Committee—an agent of the party leadership (see Dodd and Oppenheimer 2005).[9]

The strengthening of party leadership in Congress would not have been possible if not for the reality that the membership of both major party delegations was in fact becoming significantly more ideologically homogeneous. The increasingly liberal persuasion of Democrats and the even more conservative tilt of Republicans was a function of both Member adaptation and Member replacement (see Jacobson 2007c; Theriault 2006). Representatives in Congress who altered their voting behavior to better correspond with the ideological direction of their party were engaging in adaptation. Further, having an even greater impact on partisan polarization was the replacement (through retirement, defeat, death, etc.) of Republican (Democratic) Members with newly elected Republicans (Democratic) who proved even more conservative (liberal) than their predecessors. This kind of change was particularly evident in the South—especially in the case of the replacement of moderate Democrats with conservative Republicans. In a study of partisan polarization that spanned the 93rd (1973–1974) through 108th (2003–2004) Congresses, Theriault (2006, 498) finds that "58.5 percent of the replacement polarization and 48.1 percent of the total polarization results from the replacement of moderate southern Democrats by conservative Republicans."

One of the most common methods to estimate partisan polarization is with the use of Poole and Rosenthal's nominate scores for House Members.[10] Among several different indicators, the first dimension DW-NOMINATE scores are used the most often for assessing institutional polarization. The scores are a proxy for Representative

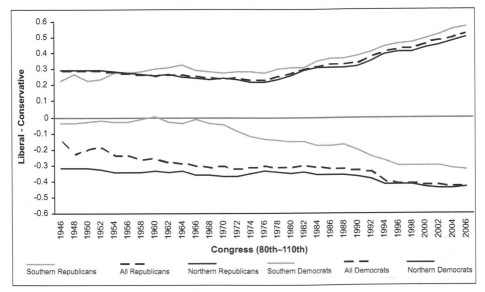

FIGURE 5.5 Diverging Parties in the U.S. House of Representatives

ideology, based on a liberal-to-conservative economic dimension of roll-call voting in Congress. The typical range for the DW-NOMINATE scores is from -1 (most liberal) to +1 (most conservative).

Figure 5.5 displays the median DW-NOMINATE scores for House Members from 1946 (80th Congress) through 2006 (110th Congress). These scores are presented for all Republicans and Democrats and according to the Representative's region (North or South). Three patterns are obvious to the naked eye. First, at the beginning of the time series, southern Democrats occupied the center of the ideological distribution of House Members. They were clearly a distinct group, much more conservative relative to northern Democrats. Over time, however, the movement of southern Democrats toward the liberal pole of the ideological continuum has made them much more similar to northern Democrats. Second, although southern Republicans were never as distant from northern Republicans as were southern Democrats compared to northern Democrats, since the 1960s southern Republicans have been consistently more conservative than northern Republicans. Finally, the increasing polarization of the Democratic and Republican parties takes flight in the 1970s and has continued ever since.

To determine the significance of regional and time-bound differences on partisan polarization, we can regress DW-NOMINATE scores onto whether or not a Member represents a southern district and the time period segmented by decade (covering 1946–2006). In addition, the region of the Representative can be interacted with time in order to see if there is a difference in the behavior of a given Member on the basis of region and a specific decade serving in the Congress. These analyses are evaluated separately for Democratic and Republican Members, respectively. A southern Representative is coded 1, and a northern Representative is coded 0. Time is partitioned into decades (1940s–2000s) with the baseline category comprised of the 1946–1948 elections (the 1940s). Finally, in the interactive models, "Southern Member" is multiplied by the corresponding decade. Since the DW-NOMINATE scores range from a negative value indicating a more liberal record to a positive value indicating a more conservative record, a positive (negative) coefficient means that the variable increases (decreases) conservative voting.

Table 5.1 presents the estimates of four models, two each for Democratic and Republican Members—an additive model followed by an interactive model (Southern Member x Decade). Starting with the additive model for House Democrats, as expected, southern Democrats are much more likely to exhibit conservative voting compared to northern Democrats. And with respect to time period, from the decade of the 1960s forward, Democratic Representatives display a more liberal voting record compared to the 1940s. The growing size of the negative values for the coefficients in each more recent decade indicates an increasingly stronger relationship between time and liberal voting.

The interactive model for Democratic Representatives is also quite revealing of what it shows regarding the relationship between region and time. As shown by the positive and significant interactions between southern Representatives and the 1950s as well as southern Representatives and the 1960s, in these decades southern Democrats were much more conservative on roll-call votes compared to northern Democrats. This finding is anticipated, but what is more noteworthy is that the pace of liberal polarization is swifter for southern Democrats

TABLE 5.1 **The Effects of Region and Time Period on the Ideology of U.S. House Members**

	Democrats	Democrats	Republicans	Republicans
Southern Member	.237 (.004)***	.281 (.015)***	.063 (.006)***	-.060 (.073)
1950s	-.010 (.009)	-.022 (.012)*	-.014 (.009)	-.014 (.010)
1960s	-.027 (.009)**	-.033 (.012)**	-.038 (.010)***	-.039 (.010)***
1970s	-.055 (.009)***	-.039 (.011)***	-.058 (.010)***	-.058 (.010)***
1980s	-.074 (.009)***	-.044 (.012)***	-.002 (.010)	-.005 (.010)
1990s	-.126 (.009)***	-.076 (.012)***	.090 (.010)***	.088 (.010)***
2000s	-.174 (.010)***	-.126 (.012)***	.187 (.010)***	.181 (.010)***
Southern *1950s	--	.034 (.018)*	--	.064 (.079)
Southern *1960s	--	.033 (.018)*	--	.114 (.075)
Southern *1970s	--	-.033 (.018)*	--	.117 (.075)
Southern *1980s	--	-.080 (.018)***	--	.130 (.074)*
Southern *1990s	--	-.152 (.019)***	--	.123 (.074)*
Southern *2000s	--	-.158 (.020)***	--	.136 (.074)*
Constant	-.301 (.008)***	-.321 (.010)***	.302 (.008)***	.304 (.008)***
Adjusted R^2	.38	.40	.23	.24
N	7,662	7,662	5,971	5,971

Note: Ordinary Least Squares Regressions (OLS) with standard errors in parentheses. Dependent variable is the first dimension coordinate on the DW-NOMINATE score; it ranges from -1.221 (most liberal) to 1.621 (most conservative).
***$p < .001$, **$p < .01$, *$p < .05$ (one-tailed tests).

from the 1970s onward. So, despite being more conservative than the typical northern Democrat, when southern Democrat and decade are interacted, we see that, beginning in the 1970s, southern Democrats exhibit more liberal voting records than northern Democrats. This result corroborates the pattern of greater polarization among southern Democrats vis-à-vis northern Democrats from the 1970s through 2006 (see Figure 5.5).

Similar to southern Democrats versus northern Democrats, in the Republican additive model we find that southern Republicans are significantly more conservative than northern Republicans. The effect of time, however, reveals a considerable delay in the growing conservatism of Republican Members. Compared to the 1940s, from the 1950s through the 1980s, Republican Representatives either exhibit more liberal voting behavior (in the 1960s and 1970s) or no difference in the ideological bent of their roll-call votes (in the 1950s and 1980s).

The results of the interactive model for Republicans supports the aforementioned claim that southern Republicans are primarily responsible for pulling the party farther to the right. Notice that, from the 1950s to the 1970s, there is no significant difference in the voting behavior of southern and northern Republicans. But starting in the 1980s and up through the 2000s, the interactive coefficients show that southern Republicans are significantly more conservative than northern Republicans—a development that may have indeed placed a GOP-controlled Congress out of equilibrium with the ideological preferences of the national electorate (Erikson and Wright 2009).

Since the 1970s, southern Democrats have moved at a swifter pace than northern Democrats toward the liberal end of the ideological spectrum, but, as a group, the former remain more moderate. With southern Republicans, on the other hand, not only has their more recent rate of conservative polarization exceeded northern Republicans, but up until the 2006 midterm, southern Republicans dominated the party leadership.[11] With this degree of southern influence over the direction of a Republican-held Congress, it appears that the GOP moved too far to the right and that this is at least one reason for the party's downfall in 2006. The vast majority of southern Republicans could take decidedly conservative positions without fear of electoral retribution because they were not very far from the ideological location of the median voter in their districts. By contrast, it is doubtful that the typical northern Republican could move very far to the right without paying a heftier electoral price.[12]

Up to this point, this section has emphasized polarization within Congress, but what about evidence of polarization in the mass public? This is one of the most intriguing and contentious questions currently capturing the attention of political scientists.[13] There is no debate that partisan polarization in Congress is much more pronounced than in the citizenry, but what scholars continue to disagree over is the extent to which the electorate has followed suit. The two camps most academically vested in the mass polarization debate are Fiorina et al. (e.g., 2005, 2008; see also Fiorina and Levendusky 2006) and Abramowitz and Saunders (e.g., 2008).

On one side of the debate stand Fiorina et al., who contend that it is a misnomer to characterize the tighter linkage between ideology and partisanship as evidence of mass polarization when in fact the ideological distribution of the American electorate has remained essentially constant since the 1970s. The median voter is still very much a political moderate even though partisans are now more likely to demonstrate a stronger relationship between ideology and political affiliation. Instead of polarization, what they see as going on within the mass public is an increase in political "sorting," with conservatives increasingly likely to identify with the GOP and liberals increasingly likely to align with the Democratic Party. By itself, sorting does not equate to polarization because, again, along the ideological spectrum the bulk of voters still remain centrists. What has changed is that liberals and conservatives, who still remain in the minority, are now better aligned with the political parties on the basis of ideology.

According to Fiorina et al., because of substantial elite polarization, mass voting behavior is often a faulty metric for assessing electoral polarization. In other words, since the ideological distance between the typical Democratic and Republican House candidate has widened, it makes it that much easier for a voter to make a choice, even though most voters have not moved away from the moderate middle of the ideological continuum.

In opposition to Fiorina et al. are Abramowitz and Saunders (1998, 2006, 2008), who, through a series of articles, have demonstrated that, for a nontrivial share of the electorate, political ideology drives party affiliation, and this has the effect of moving voters away from the center of the ideological distribution. Furthermore, political awareness is a critical factor increasing mass polarization because those citizens who are more politically knowledgeable demonstrate the highest levels of polarization. Contrary to Fiorina et al., Abramowitz and Saunders use data to show that greater ideological cohesiveness and movement away from the middle of the ideological spectrum is not a phenomenon confined to officeholders and political activists; polarization has also infected the mass electorate—especially among those more politically aware.

So who is right? Fiorina et al., or Abramowitz and Saunders? Ironically, since this debate is about mass polarization, the truth probably rests somewhere in the middle, between the positions staked out by these scholars. One the one hand, Fiorina et al. are essentially correct in claiming that the ideological distribution of the American electorate has moved very little over time, with most voters continuing to reside in the moderate middle. Also, it is indisputable that elites (i.e., candidates and party activists) have polarized, and this makes vote choice a simpler calculus, with partisans much less likely to split their tickets. Nonetheless, it is not true that what we have witnessed among the mass public is 100 percent sorting and 0 percent polarizing. In fact, Fiorina et al. admit that in addition to sorting has come some polarization, but just not very much. Unfortunately, this admission clouds the debate because of a lack of agreed upon criteria for what constitutes *a lot* of polarization—especially when the degree of polarization among elites dwarfs the level observed within the mass electorate.

What is abundantly clear is that it stretches credulity to suggest that elites can polarize to the extent that they have without capturing the attention of the mass public. To be sure, many voters (probably most) are not very politically informed, but a large enough segment of the electorate is. And among those who closely follow politics, the growing divergence among partisans in Congress has not gone unnoticed; the revival of mass partisanship since its nadir in the 1970s is largely a function of voters being aware of the growing and considerable ideological differences between Democrats and Republicans in Congress (Hetherington 2001). To modify a phrase from Aldrich et al. (1989), House Representatives are not "waltzing before a blind audience." Not only is a portion of the electorate cognizant of partisan differences, but these voters will take the next step and punish those Members whose behavior strays too far from the ideological preferences of their constituency (Erikson and Wright 2009).

Elite clarification of partisan differences across a broad range of issues has served to strengthen the relationship between party affiliation and ideology among the mass public, and this in turn has allowed Representatives to further polarize in their congressional voting behavior. Highlighting the importance of political geography, congressional districts are never configured at random. Instead, they are drawn to further some political objective—usually the election of one party over the other. Thus, even if most voters are politically moderate, most districts are drawn to favor either a Democrat or Republican. As Erikson and Wright (2009, 84) point out:

> Not only are Democratic and Republican House members ideologically distinct, but Democratic and Republican House members also represent different constituencies. Not surprisingly, Democrats represent Democratic (and liberal) districts, and Republicans represent Republican (and conservative) districts. The battleground is the set of somewhat moderate and competitive districts in the middle, which sometimes elect Republicans and sometimes Democrats.

Figures 5.6 and 5.7 show the increasing relationship between party identification and ideology among white NES survey respondents. Respondents are partitioned according to whether they live in the North or South. The first time the NES used the seven-point ideology scale was in 1972. The data are pooled according to decade: 1970s, 1980s, 1990s, and 2000–2004.

Figure 5.6 presents the percentage of white liberals who identify with the Democratic Party.[14] In 1970, 17 percent of all white Democrats were liberals, 11 percent of white southern Democrats were liberals, and 19 percent of northern whites were liberals. From the 1970s through 2004, there is a steady increase in the percentage of white Democrats who consider themselves liberals. By the end of the time series (2000–2004), three out of ten white Democrats were liberals. Over a quarter (26 percent) of white southern Democrats were liberals, and almost one out of three northern white Democrats were liberals (32 percent). As the percentage of liberal Democrats has increased, the gap between northern and southern Democratic liberals has narrowed (from 8 percentage points to 6). Finally, as the percentage of liberal Democrats has increased, the percentage of moderate Democrats has gone from 72 percent (1970s) to 63 percent (2000–2004).

Figure 5.7 presents the percentage of white conservatives who identify with the Republican Party. Like the pattern observed among Democrats, there has been a significant amount of ideological sorting for Republicans. The rate of sorting has been essentially the same for both parties, but the relationship between ideology and party affiliation is

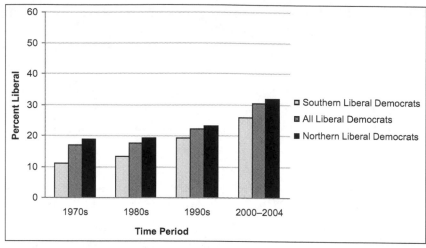

FIGURE 5.6 Liberal White Democrats

much stronger for Republicans. As expected, among white Republicans, southerners are more conservative. In 1970, 31 percent of all white Republicans were conservatives, 37 percent of white southern Republicans were conservatives, and 29 percent of northern white Republicans were conservatives. By the end of the time series (2000–2004), better than four out of ten white Republicans were conservatives (47 percent). Of white northern Republicans, 45 percent were conservatives, as were a majority of white southern Republicans (51 percent). As the percentage of conservative Republicans has increased, the gap between southern and northern Republican conservatives has narrowed (from 8 percentage points to 6). Finally, as the percentage of conservative Republicans has increased, the percentage of moderate Republicans has sharply declined, going from 66 percent (1970s) to 51 percent (2000–2004).

Whether the component of partisan polarization is at the elite (i.e., in Congress) or mass level, the South has played a fundamental role in this process. Before the 1970s, southern Democrats occupied the center of the ideological distribution in the House of Representatives. Their relatively faster movement toward greater liberalism, as measured by roll-call voting behavior, was the most important factor contributing to the increasing partisan polarization in Congress. Although

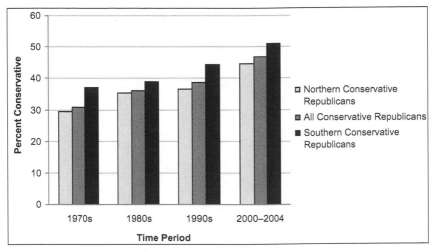

FIGURE 5.7 Conservative White Republicans

not as substantial as the polarization occurring among Representatives, it is evident that the mass public has also polarized. As partisans continue to sort themselves according to ideology, the portion of moderates affiliated with the Democratic and Republican parties has likewise declined.

The New Democratic Majority and the South

Special elections that take place before an upcoming general election are often viewed with great interest for what they might divulge about the political climate. The three special House elections held before the 2008 general contests signaled another Democratic tide (Nagourney and Hulse 2008). All three districts were being vacated by Republicans, and all three appeared to be GOP strongholds. The most marginal of the three was Illinois 14 (2004 Republican presidential vote = 56 percent), the district that since 1986 had been represented by erstwhile Republican Speaker of the House Dennis Hastert. The other two districts, both in the South (Louisiana 6 and Mississippi 1) were decidedly Republican (2004 Republican presidential vote = 59 percent and 63 percent, respectively). The defeats of all three GOP candidates in

TABLE 5.2 **Membership Changes in the U.S. House in the 2006 and 2008 Elections**

House of Representatives	*Republicans*	*Democrats*	*Independents*
At the time of the 2006 election	232	202	1
Elected in 2006	202	233	
Incumbents reelected	188	191	
Incumbents defeated	22	0	
Open seats retained	14	12	
Open seats lost	8	0	
At the time of the 2008 election	202	233	
Elected in 2008	178	257	
Incumbents reelected	162	221	
Incumbents defeated	14	4	
Open seats retained	12	8	
Open seats lost	14	0	

Note: These data do not alter the classification of incumbent and open seat contests based on elections that occurred in the interim prior to the 2008 contests (e.g., the special elections in IL 14, LA 6, and MS 1). The data for 2006 are a reproduction of the table shown in Jacobson (Table 1, 2007, 2).

these special open seat elections did indeed foretell another rough cycle for the Republican Party.[15]

In 2006, on their way to winning back the House for the first time in a dozen years, Democrats netted thirty-one seats. In 2008, the Democratic Party took back the White House and expanded on their House majority by taking another twenty-four seats from Republicans. After only two elections, Democrats had gone from a 46 percent minority party to a 59 percent majority party in the House of Representatives. Thus, in a little over two years, the American political landscape was transformed. Table 5.2 documents the number of seats held by the political parties before 2006 and up through the aftermath of the 2008 elections. It shows that in 2006, Democrats retained all of their districts while defeating twenty-two Republican incumbents and capturing eight seats that were previously held by Republicans. Then, in 2008 Republicans managed to take four seats from Democratic Representatives, but Democrats picked up fourteen Republican-held open seats and another fourteen against Republican incumbents.

TABLE 5.3 The Democratic Share of the U.S. House Vote in 2006 and 2008

Democratic Vote (%)	2006	2008	2006–2008
Nation	50.2	55.4	52.1
(N)	(380)	(379)	(759)
North	53.6	58.7	56.5
(N)	(271)	(275)	(546)
South	40.2	43.6	42.1
(N)	(109)	(104)	(213)

Note: The data presented are the median share of the Democratic House vote in contested elections (Democrat vs. Republican) in 2006 and 2008.

The seat gains made by Democrats in the House after the 2006 and 2008 elections have occurred nationwide, but the South has clearly been much stingier in relinquishing Republican representation. All counted, there were fifty-nine districts between 2006 and 2008 that switched from Republican to Democratic control: forty-six in the North (78 percent) and thirteen in the South (22 percent).[16] After the 2004 elections, southern Republicans constituted 35 percent of the Republican House majority (82 out of 232 seats). Then, after the 2008 elections southern Republicans were 40 percent (72 out of 178) of the GOP's significantly reduced minority House delegation.

Table 5.3 presents the Democratic share of the two-party House vote in contested elections for 2006 and 2008. Dividing the data according to region reveals the substantial drop-off in Democratic electoral strength in the South. In 2006, the national Democratic vote was just over 50 percent. By 2008, it was a much more comfortable 55 percent. By comparison, the northern share of the Democratic House vote increased from 54 percent in 2006 to 59 percent in 2008. Although the Democratic trend is also apparent in the South, the Democratic vote is markedly lower and increases at a lower rate between 2006 and 2008 (3.4 percentage points). From 2006 through 2008, the northern Democratic vote is 4.4 points above the national average, whereas the southern Democratic vote is 10 points below the national average.

A more stringent way to discern a regional difference in support for the new Democratic House majority is to assess the relationship between presidential voting and the House vote garnered by all fifty-nine Republicans who relinquished seats to Democrats in 2006 and 2008. This can be done by displaying a scatter plot of the Republican House vote on the vertical axis and the 2004 Republican presidential vote on the horizontal axis. In Figure 5.8, the data points are distinguished by region, with northern Republican House losers depicted by a hollow circle and southern Republican losers denoted by a black square. It is readily apparent that the biggest losers (the outliers with the lowest Republican House vote shares) represented northern districts.

What is more difficult to discern, however, is a relationship between the House vote and presidential vote. The dotted and solid lines graph the linear fit for the House vote and presidential vote for southern Republicans and northern Republicans, respectively. Although the slopes of the two lines are not displayed, it is worth noting what they are. In the case of southern Republican losers, the slope of the line is +.03, which means that a 10 percent increase in the Republican presidential vote increases the Republican House vote by 3 percentage points. By contrast, for northern Republican losers the slope of the line is -.05; a 10 percent increase in the Republican presidential vote decreases the Republican House vote by 5 points.

Hence, we find that in the South, district-level support for President Bush positively affected the House vote, whereas in the North, support for President Bush actually depressed the House vote for these Republicans who lost in either 2006 or 2008. This evidence suggests that, even among the population of hapless Republican House candidates, in 2006 and 2008 the roots of Republicanism remained resilient in the South but not in the North.

Finally, we can determine whether there remains a significant regional difference in the Democratic share of the House vote (1 = South, 0 = North) after controlling for several factors expected to impact congressional voting in 2006 and 2008. Some of the standard factors that usually affect the congressional vote are the previous vote in the district (Democratic House vote in the preceding election), the presidential vote in the district (2004 Democratic presidential vote), the district percentage black voting age population, median household income (in thousands), and district competitiveness as rated by Con-

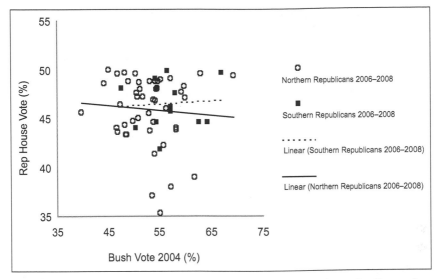

FIGURE 5.8 The Relationship Between the House Vote and District Share of the Presidential Vote for Republicans Who Lost in 2006 and 2008

gressional Quarterly (0 = safe Republican, 1 = favors Republican, 2 = leans Republican, 3 = no clear favorite, 4 = leans Democrat, 5 = favors Democrat, 6 = safe Democrat).

In addition to these factors, the 2006 and 2008 contests involved an unusually high number of candidates associated with scandals. The bulk of these candidates were Republican incumbents, but there were also a handful of Democrats (all of whom were incumbents). The coding scheme for deciding which candidates were associated with a scandal is adopted from Hendry et al. (2009, 90).[17] Many scandal-plagued candidates lost in 2006, but if they won and sought reelection in 2008, then they remain coded as part of a scandal. Thus there are two scandal dummies: "Democratic Scandal" and "Republican Scandal."

Finally, there are controls for the type of candidate and election year (1 = 2006, 0 = 2008). Specifically, there are dummy variables for a Democratic incumbent and the type of Open Seat (previously represented by a Democrat or Republican). The base category is therefore Republican incumbent. Three ordinary least squares (OLS) regressions estimate the Democratic House vote in 2006 and 2008 as a function of all the aforementioned independent variables. The first model

TABLE 5.4 Factors Influencing the Democratic House Vote in the 2006 and 2008 Elections

	All Districts	Incumbents Only	Open Seats Only
South	-.009 (.005)*	-.003 (.005)	-.052 (.018)**
Previous Democratic Vote	.055 (.013)***	.069 (.013)***	-.028 (.040)
Dem Pres Vote (2004)	.442 (.025)***	.449 (.025)***	.230 (.109)*
Black VAP	.045 (.020)*	.025 (.020)	.281 (.075)***
Median Income (thousands)	-.0005 (.0002)**	-.0004 (.0002)*	-.0009 (.0007)$\pm$
Competitiveness (CQ rating)	.036 (.002)***	.037 (.002)***	.034 (.006)***
Democratic Scandal	-.047 (.019)**	-.046 (.019)**	--
Republican Scandal	.009 (.009)	.010 (.009)	.019 (.022)
Democratic Incumbent	.023 (.011)*	.012 (.012)	--
Open Seat (Dem-previous)	-.013 (.015)	--	.005 (.026)
Open Seat (Rep-previous)	.021 (.008)**	--	--
2006 Election	.013 (.004)***	.012 (.004)***	.023 (.014)$\pm$
Constant	.194 (.012)***	.181 (.012)***	.346 (.046)***
Adjusted R^2	.92	.92	.81
N	759	689	70

Note: Ordinary Least Squares (OLS) regressions with standard errors in parentheses. The dependent variable is the Democratic share of the two-party U.S. House vote in the 2006 and 2008 elections. Only contested districts (Democrat vs. Republican) are included in the analyses. There were no Democratic candidates in the open seat contests associated with a scandal.
***$p < .001$, **$p < .01$, *$p < .05$, $\pm p < .10$ (one-tailed tests).

includes all two-party contested districts. The second model is limited to incumbent races. The third and last model is confined to open seat elections. The explanatory variable of interest in all three models is the South dummy. Is it the case after controlling for all of these other factors that districts in the South significantly and negatively influence the Democratic House vote in the 2006 and 2008 elections?

Table 5.4 shows the results of the three models. In almost every instance, the control variables take on the expected sign, though they are not always statistically significant. Also, the 2006 election dummy indicates that it was a better year for House Democrats than 2008—exactly what we would expect given their greater gains in the midterm. As for the variable of interest, "South," we find that, after controlling for other factors, southern districts had a statistically significant and negative effect on the Democratic House vote in all contested districts and open seat contests. There is no regional difference with respect to contested districts limited to incumbents seeking reelection.

For all contested districts, districts in the South depressed the Democratic House vote by about 1 percentage point. What is more impressive, however, is the effect of the South in open seat contests. Open seat contests are a better gauge of short-term electoral effects because incumbents tend to dampen the vote for the party that is advantaged by the prevailing political climate (see Petrocik and Desposato 2004). We see that in open seat races, the Democratic tide in the South was not nearly as pronounced as it was in the North. Compared to an open seat district in the North, an open seat in the South reduced the Democratic House vote by 5 percentage points.

These analyses of the 2006 and 2008 House elections make it apparent that the South remains much less supportive of the new Democratic majority. To be sure, the South is not necessarily bucking the Democratic trend, but it clearly is lagging in pace vis-à-vis the North when it comes to the growing electoral support for the Democratic Party in House contests.

Short- and Long-Term Perspectives on the 2006 and 2008 Elections

There are multiple lenses and interpretations for ascribing meaning to the outcome of an election (Dodd 2005). And what further complicates any election postmortem is the fact that short- and long-term considerations always factor into the vote decision. Finally, what at the time appears to be a short-term occurrence may become grounds for a long-term shift in American politics. All of these points warrant attention when evaluating the 2006 and 2008 elections. In this concluding section, both a short- and long-term approach to assessing the impact of the 2006 and 2008 contests is undertaken.

Leading into the 2006 midterm, the short-term political climate had soured to the point that it was the worst for the GOP since the 1974 post–Watergate elections. Casting a wide and foreboding shadow over the Republican Party were the increasingly negative evaluations of the incumbent president, Republican George W. Bush. Despite not being on the ballot, President Bush proved to be a massive drag on the Republican House vote. Negative voting—or voting against the lesser-preferred option, instead of wholeheartedly affirming one's support for the favored candidate—was rampant in 2006. As Jacobson (2007b) documents, going back to 1982, at 36 percent, the portion of respondents who agreed that their vote was "against the president" in the 2006 midterm was by far the highest.[18] In addition, the polarization of partisan views on the Iraq War was historically unrivaled (Jacobson 2007a). Finally, Republican House incumbents had also not done themselves any favors, as a healthy number of them were implicated in scandals (Hendry et al. 2009).

For Republicans, in the background of these extremely unpromising short-term conditions was the harsh reality that the GOP, propelled by the influence of its southern base, had strayed considerably away from the middle of the electorate. When this happens, public opinion exhibits a countervailing effect, pushing in the opposite direction of the path taken by the party in power (Stimson 2004). As shown by Stimson,[19] since 2002 the policy mood of the electorate was trending in a liberal direction. With this ongoing trend pushing against the GOP—and given the poor evaluations of President Bush[20] due to several factors, including most prominently the handling of the Iraq War and the response to Hurricane Katrina—it is no surprise that macropartisanship benefited the Democratic Party. Erikson and Wright (2009, 75) note that, "Both macropartisanship and mood help to explain the Democratic resurgence in the 2006 election. The 2006 electorate was both more Democratic and more liberal (in terms of Stimson's mood measure) than it had been in recent years."

Unfortunately for the Republican Party, President Bush was still serving at the time of the 2008 elections. Except for the success of the surge policy in Iraq, which drastically lowered combat-related casualties, there was very little that happened between 2006 and 2008 that offered the Republican Party in Congress and its presidential nominee John McCain much reason to anticipate electoral success. In September, the financial crisis came to a head, delivering the final blow to any notion of a McCain Presidency (Dodd and Oppenheimer 2009).

Consequently, in 2008 another formidable Democratic tide drowned Republican hopes of a political comeback in the House, and the American electorate voted Democrat Barack Obama into the White House, the nation's first African American president. En route to securing an Electoral College majority, Obama won three southern states: Florida, North Carolina, and Virginia. The last time North Carolina voted Democratic for the presidency was in 1976 when Jimmy Carter bested Republican Gerald Ford, and the Old Dominion last favored a Democrat in 1964 when President Johnson smothered Republican Barry Goldwater.

The preeminent political scientist of his time, V. O. Key insisted that "voters are not fools" (1966, 7). They evaluate political conditions and punish the ruling party if its performance is less than satisfactory.[21] This is a strong statement in support of retrospective voting (see also Fiorina 1981). In 2006, it appears that voters assessed the past performance of the majority party, did not like what they saw, and threw the Republicans out.[22] Perhaps the strategy of most Democratic House candidates was not to offer a strong alternative agenda, but rather to let the GOP hang itself based on the unpopularity of its congressional leadership and overwhelming support of a discredited president. Mann and Ornstein (2009, 54) have this to say about the 2006 midterm:

> [T]he public response was far more a desire to throw out the miscreants than a vote for any specific policy change. But a vote against a do-nothing Congress inevitably is a vote to create a do-something Congress that would solve problems that Americans saw as important. In that sense the 2006 election was a replay of the 1994 election, in which the target was the Democratic Congress and Democratic president.

Given the miserable state of affairs for the GOP heading into the 2006 elections, coupled with the almost certain loss of seats for the president's party in a midterm year (especially in the sixth year or second midterm for a two-term incumbent), the outcome in 2006 is not necessarily far afield from what we would expect (see Jacobson 2007b).

The election of 2008, however, is much more difficult to understand. First, because presidential candidates send clear messages to the electorate, the question becomes whether the message is a primary explanation for why Barack Obama won. Second, we can identify salient issues on which the candidates disagreed (Exhibit A being the Iraq War) and correlate it with voting behavior to show its effect on the electoral outcome.[23] But we also know that a sinking economy will invariably damage the candidate of the president's party, and hence the financial crisis constituted an exogenous shock to the presidential campaign, dooming McCain's chances. Finally, the electoral map was altered by the winning coalition that Obama assembled.

A fascinating way to consider the significance of the Obama Presidency is provided by the scholarship of Stephen Skowronek in his work *Presidential Leadership in Political Time* (2008).[24] If there really is a cyclical component to the relative effectiveness of presidents that is tied to their place in political time, then it is conceivable that Obama's presidency marks the beginning of a new political regime in American politics. Skowronek considers the Reagan Presidency as the start of a new political order—what he dubs the "Politics of Reconstruction."[25] Presidents who serve at this moment in political history have the freest hand to initiate large-scale policy changes and steer their party and the nation in a new direction.

But after Reagan, the Republican presidential regime eventually exhausted itself. First, George H. W. Bush took office and furthered, or at least tried to maintain, the core principles advocated by his predecessor (the "Politics of Articulation").[26] Then, along came Democrat Bill Clinton, who opposed the Republican order. Although Clinton was constrained in political time by a Republican congressional majority,[27] when he could not lead, he did his best to co-opt the GOP's policies (the "Politics of Preemption")[28] and was met with a harsh rebuke (impeachment).

Finally, the last Republican affiliated with the Republican regime was George W. Bush—a president with the misfortune of serving at a time when the Republican order was crumbling and his efforts to save it proved futile (the "Politics of Disjunction").[29] Based on this interpretation of recent political history, Barack Obama may be serving during the "Politics of Reconstruction"—building a new Democratic majority with a coalition of voters (African Americans, Hispanics, women, liberals, the young, the lower and middle classes, urbanites, the highly educated, the non-religious, and northerners) who will prove loyal enough to usher in a new Democratic era.

The aforementioned discussion is certainly speculative, but it begs an important question that has direct bearing on the viability of the Democratic House majority: Can we conclude that President Obama constructed a new majority with staying power, or will a sharp political setback revive the Republican Party? Satisfactory performance in governing is perhaps the most important factor affecting how long the Democratic Party retains its majority status. It is still too early to tell what will become of the relative strength of the Democratic and Republican parties, but the early signs do not auger well for the GOP—a party whose coalition of voters continues to shrink, and its most supportive regional constituency, white southerners, lag significantly behind the national Democratic trend.

Notes

1. As the opening quote suggests, before the Democratic Party won back the Congress in 2006, Dodd (2005) discussed several of the factors that might serve to end the Republican's House majority, including the party moving too far to the right because of its southern leadership, the expanding role of African Americans and Hispanics in national and southern politics, and an unsustainable fiscal policy. Overall, Dodd's essay presents a picture showing that GOP consolidation of congressional power was much weaker and problematic than was generally thought to be the case in 2004—a time when so many political observers believed House Republicans had rigged the districting of seats to the point that the party could maintain long-term dominance even in spite of governing lapses.

2. Sulphur Springs, Texas; U.S. Census Bureau 2007 population estimate was 15,387. As noted previously, the Deep South technically consists of Alabama, Georgia, Louisiana, Mississippi, and South Carolina.

3. In percentage terms, the Republican share of the two-party southern House delegation dropped a miniscule amount between 2000 (58.1 percent) and 2002 (58.0 percent), even though the party actually experienced a net gain in seats in the reapportionment election of 2002 (going from seventy-two Republican-held seats in 2000 to seventy-six Republican-controlled seats in 2002).

4. From 1994 through 2004 in the northern House delegation the GOP was the majority party three times: in 1994, 1996, and 2002.

5. According to Jenkins et al. (2007, 367): "Republican gains in non-Southern states—in congressional delegations, in governorships, and in state legislatures— were almost entirely confined to the 1994 election."

6. Within the North, the New England states (Connecticut, Maine, Massachusetts, New Hampshire, Rhode Island, and Vermont) have clearly undergone a contemporary realignment in favor of the Democratic Party that surpasses any other region with respect to the magnitude of its partisan shift. After the 2008 elections, all twenty-two House seats were won by Democrats, and out of twelve Senate seats, only three are held by Republicans.

7. Perhaps the most threatening reform for senior southern Democrats occurred in January 1973, with the adoption of a secret ballot for electing committee chairs (Pearson and Schickler 2009, 170).

8. Between 1956 and 1958, the northern share of the Democratic House delegation went from 58 percent to 65 percent.

9. One particular irritation for the minority party (whether they are Democrats post–1994 or Republicans post–2006) has been the increase in the percentage of bills given a closed rule that prohibits amending the legislation during House floor debate.

10. These data are made available through the following website: http:// voteview.com/default.htm.

11. After the 1994 elections, "[a]ll three of the most influential leaders of the Republican majority in the House of Representatives—Speaker of the House Newt Gingrich, of Atlanta, Georgia; Majority Leader Dick Armey of Dallas, Texas; and Whip Tom DeLay, of Houston, Texas—represented overwhelmingly white, suburban, middle-class districts in key southern metropolitan areas" (Black and Black 2002, 5).

12. This is an admittedly crude way of investigating this claim, but it roughly supports the point. First, between 2006 and 2008, there were fifty-nine House districts that switched from Republican to Democratic control. Of these districts, 78 percent were located in the North. Second, to the extent that the presidential vote is an acceptable proxy for district partisanship, among the forty-six northern Republican candidates who lost, in these districts the mean and median share of the 2004 Republican presidential vote was 53.1 percent and 53.5 percent, respectively. For the thirteen southern Republicans who lost in 2006 or 2008, the mean and median share of the 2004 Republican presidential vote was 56.9 percent and 56.5 percent, respectively. At least with respect to district partisanship, as indicated by the presidential vote, these northern Republicans represented more marginal districts, and

thus significant movement away from the ideological center should have been more costly.

13. For an excellent review of the polarization literature see Layman et al. (2006).

14. Independent leaners are classified as partisans and slightly ideological respondents are classified as liberals or conservatives (e.g., slightly liberal, liberal, and extremely liberal are all considered liberals; slightly conservative, conservative, and extremely conservative are all considered conservatives).

15. In the ensuing 2008 contest, a Republican won Louisiana 6.

16. This total does not account for Louisiana 6, a district that switched from Republican to Democratic in the interim before the 2008 general election, but was then won by a Republican in the 2008 general contest (technically a "primary" in Louisiana). Three districts in the South that were won by Democrats in 2006 were then won by Republicans in 2008 (Florida 16, Louisiana 2, and Texas 22). Furthermore, in the North, one district captured by a Democrat in 2006 was subsequently won back by a Republican in 2008 (Kansas 2).

17. Not all candidates had to be directly involved with a scandal to be coded as associated with a scandal. For example, in some open seat contests a Republican candidate is disadvantaged if the departed incumbent was of the same party and directly involved in a scandal—this was the case in Texas 22, the district vacated by Republican Tom DeLay. In addition to all of the candidates listed as associated with a scandal in Hendry et al. (2009, 90), I have added four more: Democrat Tim Mahoney in Florida 16 in 2008, Democrat William Jefferson in Louisiana 2 for 2006 and 2008, Democrat Charlie Rangel in New York 15 in 2008, and Republican Vito Fossella in New York 13 in 2008 (he retired, but this seat is coded as a Republican scandal because Fossella damaged the chances of the Republican candidate seeking the office in 2008).

18. Jacobson also notes that in 2006, "Democrats lost not a single seat in either body, the first election in U.S. history in which a party retained all of its congressional seats" (2007b, 1).

19. His data are available online at: http://www.unc.edu/~jstimson/time.html.

20. Bush had approximately a 35 percent approval rating on Election Day (Herrnson and Curry 2009, 103).

21. Of course the number of voters who behaved in this fashion did not have to be terribly large, and they were certainly not a majority. As in the past, most partisans voted in line with their affiliations.

22. As Riker (1982) once argued, it is much easier to understand the reasons for voting out politicians as opposed to voting them in. In an earlier work (as noted by Bartels 2008, 125–126), Key (1964, 567–568) made it very clear that it

was much more difficult to comprehend the rationale guiding the voting behavior of the electorate in midterm contests.

23. Based on data from the 2006 Cooperative Congressional Election Study (CCES), the four most important issues for the electorate in the 2006 midterm and the percentage of survey respondents who selected each issue were: 1. The War in Iraq (22 percent), 2. Terrorism (17 percent), 3. Corruption in Government (11 percent), and 4. Immigration (10 percent). According to the 2008 national exit poll, the four most important issues for the electorate in the 2008 general election and the percentage of survey respondents who selected each issue were: 1. The Economy (63 percent), 2. The War in Iraq (10 percent), 3. Terrorism (9 percent), and 4. Health Care (9 percent). The 2008 data are from CNN's website: http://www.cnn.com/ELECTION/2008/.

24. Lest it be misunderstood, Skowronek (2008) does not think that presidents are wholly captives of political time, but rather that they play a fundamental role in shaping the course of their fates (see Skowronek 1993).

25. President Reagan was of course hamstrung by a divided government—the absence of unified Republican control of Congress during his tenure. Other "Politics of Reconstruction" presidents include Andrew Jackson, Abraham Lincoln, and Franklin Delano Roosevelt.

26. Some other "Politics of Articulation" presidents include James K. Polk, John F. Kennedy, and Lyndon Baines Johnson.

27. A Republican Congress that Clinton had a major part in electing because of his failed policy agenda before the 1994 midterm.

28. Impeachment or threatened impeachment is a rare occurrence associated with two other "Politics of Preemption" presidents: Andrew Johnson and Richard M. Nixon.

29. Other unfortunate "Politics of Disjunction" presidents include Franklin Pierce, Herbert Hoover, and Jimmy Carter.

6

The Future of Southern Congressional Politics

A few studies have also found more pronounced regional differences when the "Deep South" (Louisiana, Mississippi, Alabama, Georgia, and South Carolina) is distinguished from the "Outer South" (Texas, Arkansas, Tennessee, Florida, North Carolina, and Virginia . . .). (2005, 676)

—Nicholas A. Valentino and David O. Sears

In what has come to be viewed by southern politics scholars as the political bible, V. O. Key's most impressive work, *Southern Politics in State and Nation* (1949, [1996][1]), explains the rationale for the South's one-party system and how it operated outside and within the region itself. Sixty years after the publication of Key's classic, we see that the South remains distinct from the rest of the nation. Yet instead of being hyper-Democratic, the South is now markedly more Republican than the North. So what makes Dixie so different from the rest of America? Of course there is no simple answer to this question—in fact it is the central question that motivates so many southern politics scholars, and once upon a time it was the reason why electoral studies often had a standard caveat: "except for the South. . . ."

Yet there are some, like Shafer and Johnston (2006), who have challenged the notion of southern exceptionalism, providing evidence that the region's politics is no longer significantly different. Since the end of World War II, the changes in the South—economic, social, and political—have been massive (Black and Black 1987). But have we come so far that the region has permanently parted ways with its peculiar historical legacy? Yes and no. Yes, because the apparatus of Jim Crow segregation is dead. No, because the culture is still tied to a distinctive racial history that continues to affect contemporary southern politics. The well known Faulkner (1975) quote, "The past is never dead, it's not even past," still resonates in academic studies on the South.[2] For instance, a recent and well-received book on the campaign styles of southern congressmen is titled: *The Hand of the Past in Contemporary Southern Politics* (Glaser 2005).

The purpose of this final chapter is to consider the leading factors that may serve to either perpetuate or alter the current state of southern congressional politics. First, for a party that has staked its electoral viability on the overwhelming support of white voters, increasing racial and ethnic diversity is a net loser for southern Republicanism. Second, a short-term factor that can have long-term consequences is reapportionment and redistricting. The party balance in southern state legislatures and governorships will have an important impact on House elections—especially if the political climate at the time when the new congressional boundaries are valid (in the 2012 elections) strongly favors one party. Third, performance in office is a crucial component affecting how many seats might change partisan hands. Finally, and most compelling as an explanation for why the southern GOP may find its majority status disintegrate, is that there really are two Souths, the Deep and Peripheral South,[3] and the diverging political behavior in these southern subregions advantages the Democratic Party. The political differences in these sections of the South take us full circle back to a discussion of why the past, at least in some parts of Dixie, is in many ways very much connected with the present.

Racial and Ethnic Change

It is well known that the Republican Party, especially the southern wing, relies almost completely on white support to elect an almost entirely white GOP House delegation.[4] And although demography clearly is not destiny, the American South is becoming more and more racially and ethnically diverse. With the exception of the Cuban American population in South Florida and a sizable share of Hispanics in Texas, in House contests the southern GOP lacks a history of attracting the votes of minorities. Thus, at least in the near term, the decline in the white percentage of the electorate invariably aids Democrats. Furthermore, the harsher stance that the GOP has recently taken on the immigration issue has caused a sharp decline in Hispanic support for Republican House candidates.[5]

Table 6.1 documents the racial (white and black) and ethnic (Hispanic)[6] compositions of all eleven southern states from 1950 through 2007. There are several things to note from this substantial amount of data. First is the issue of measurement; prior to 1980, the white share of the state population did not account for Hispanic ethnicity. Second, the U.S. Census Bureau slightly altered its racial categories in 2000 for the purpose of providing people with the option of claiming multiple racial classifications. The data reported for race in 2000 and 2007 are for those who claimed one race only. The denominator for every reported calculation in the table is the total state population. The last column, "Change," is the difference in the reported value for a racial/ethnic category from the latest to the earliest time the data are displayed (e.g., percent African American in 2007 minus percent African American in 1950, or percent Hispanic in 2007 minus percent Hispanic in 1980). Because of changes to the numerator for the above mentioned reasons, and because the denominator is always the total state population, estimates of the black and Hispanic populations are probably somewhat understated.

The most cautious way to assess the changes in Table 6.1 is by looking at changes in those years when the census calculations are consistent: 1950–1970 and 2000 versus 2007. Nonetheless, the last column ("Change") does violate this rule by calculating changes between the latest and earliest dates for a given racial classification. With this in mind, the difference in the white populations between 1950 and 2007 is particularly problematic for Florida and Texas, since their Hispanic populations have exploded and Hispanic ethnicity is not removed

TABLE 6.1 Race and Ethnicity Percentages in the South, 1950–2007

State	1950	1960	1970	1980[a]	1990	2000[b]	2007	Change[c]
AL								
White	68	70	74	73	73	70	69	+1
Black	32	30	26	26	25	26	26	-6
Hispanic	NA	NA	NA	1	1	2	3	+2
AR								
White	78	78	81	82	82	79	76	-2
Black	22	22	18	16	16	16	16	-6
Hispanic	NA	NA	NA	1	1	3	5	+4
FL								
White	78	82	84	77	73	65	61	-17
Black	22	18	15	14	14	15	16	-6
Hispanic	NA	NA	NA	9	12	17	21	+12
GA								
White	69	71	74	72	70	63	59	-10
Black	31	28	26	27	27	29	30	-1
Hispanic	NA	NA	NA	1	2	5	8	+7
LA								
White	67	68	70	68	66	63	62	-5
Black	33	32	30	29	31	32	32	-1
Hispanic	NA	NA	NA	2	2	2	3	+1
MS								
White	55	58	63	64	63	61	59	+4
Black	45	42	37	35	36	36	37	-8
Hispanic	NA	NA	NA	1	1	1	2	+1
NC								
White	73	75	77	75	75	70	68	-5
Black	26	24	22	22	22	22	22	-4
Hispanic	NA	NA	NA	1	1	5	7	+6
SC								
White	61	65	69	68	69	66	65	+4
Black	39	35	30	30	30	30	29	-10
Hispanic	NA	NA	NA	1	1	2	4	+3
TN								
White	84	83	84	83	83	79	77	-7
Black	16	16	16	16	16	16	17	+1
Hispanic	NA	NA	NA	1	1	2	3	+2
TX								
White	87	87	87	66	61	52	48	-39
Black	13	12	12	12	12	12	12	-1
Hispanic	NA	NA	NA	21	26	32	36	+15

(*continues*)

TABLE 6.1 (*continued*)

State	1950	1960	1970	1980[a]	1990	2000[b]	2007	Change[c]
VA								
White	78	79	81	78	76	70	67	-11
Black	22	21	19	19	19	20	20	-2
Hispanic	NA	NA	NA	1	3	5	7	+6
SOUTH								
White	75	77	79	73	70	64	61	-14
Black	25	23	20	20	19	19	20	-5
Hispanic	NA	NA	NA	7	9	13	16	+9

Note: Data were compiled by the author from the U.S. Census Bureau.
[a]1980 is the first time Hispanic origin data are shown and the White population is now classified as non-Hispanic.
[b]In the 2000 census the racial classifications for Whites (non-Hispanics) and Blacks is one race.
[c]Change is the difference between 2007 and 1950 or between 2007 and 1980 for Hispanics. All percentages were calculated with total state population as the denominator.

from the calculation for whites from 1950 through 1970. This is not much of an issue for the other states regardless of racial/ethnic category because (1) the Hispanic percentage is measured the same way for every year (1980–2007), and (2) the black percentage is slightly undercounted in every state because the 2000 and 2007 calculations use the one race category for the numerator.

Without getting bogged down in the changes for any one state, there are several important findings to be gleaned from the data in Table 6.1. First, from the 1950s to the 1970s, the white percentage in the South increased (+4 points), and hence the percentage of blacks declined (-5 points). This finding is noteworthy because the initial growth of the southern GOP occurred at a time when the relative share of whites was increasing. Second, for the last two time periods, 2000 and 2007, we now see the white percentage is declining (-3 points) and the black (+1 point) and Hispanic (+3 points) percentages are increasing. Third, although there are some measurement issues, it is most likely true that between 2007 and 1950, the decline among the percentage of whites (-14 points) is substantially greater than the reduction in the black percentage (-5 points) of the southern population. Finally, there is no question that the long-term reduction in the percentage of blacks and whites is a direct consequence of the growing Hispanic population

(+9 points). In fact, in every state between 1980 and 2007, the percentage of Hispanics has increased.

With the exception of Florida and Texas, the growth of Hispanics is a very recent development for most southern states. Hispanic growth has occurred from a very small base in percentage terms, but the magnitude of these increases has been astounding in several states that lack a history of Hispanic residents (Georgia, North Carolina, and Virginia). And in regard to Florida and Texas, the remarkable growth of Hispanics constitutes a real threat to the Republican Party. In these two states, their numbers are great enough that the GOP must make appeals and actively seek Hispanic support in House contests. Nonetheless, the biggest impediment to growing Hispanic influence in southern electoral politics centers on questions of citizenship. As is true in Florida and Texas, in the other states experiencing Hispanic population booms, a very large share of these residents are noncitizens—which of course severely discounts their political influence (see Bullock and Hood 2006).[7]

Finally, the racial/ethnic changes show different patterns depending on subregion: Deep South (Alabama, Louisiana, Mississippi, Georgia, and South Carolina) versus Peripheral South (Arkansas, Florida, North Carolina, Tennessee, Texas, and Virginia). In the Deep South, between 1950 and 2007 the black percentage has declined in every state. In three of the Deep South states, over the same time span the white percentage has increased (Alabama, Mississippi, and South Carolina). The Hispanic population, on the other hand, has essentially grown from scratch in the Deep South. Only in Georgia and South Carolina has the rate of Hispanic growth been notable. By comparison, between 1950 and 2007, the white percentage of the population has declined in every Peripheral South state. The decline in the black percentages in the Peripheral South are typically smaller than in the Deep South, and, even outside of Florida and Texas, Hispanic growth has been considerable in the Peripheral South (in Arkansas, North Carolina, and Virginia).

So, although the black percentages are higher in the Deep South, the rate of Hispanic growth is much lower, and the decline in the percentage of whites is much lower vis-à-vis the Peripheral South. The engine

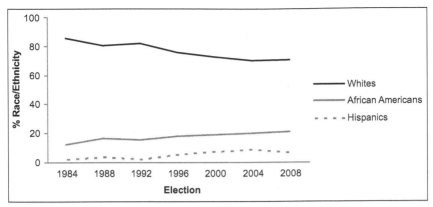

FIGURE 6.1 The Southern Voting Electorate in Presidential Years, 1984–2008
Note: Data are from national exit polls.

of racial and ethnic diversity is primarily found in the Peripheral South, where greater demographic changes have most likely contributed to the recent divergence in partisan electoral strength according to subregion. As will be shown, the road to a Democratic comeback runs through the Peripheral South.

It is necessary to provide demographic data to get a sense of the changing racial and ethnic composition of the southern population, but what really matters is how these data translate into electoral influence. To further this objective, Figure 6.1 presents data on the percentage of white (non-Hispanic), black, and Hispanic voters in the South for the 1984 to 2008 presidential elections.[8] It is apparent that, as a percentage of the voting electorate, whites are declining and African Americans and Hispanics are growing. In 1984, whites accounted for 85 percent of the southern electorate, African Americans 12 percent, and Hispanics 2 percent. By 2008, however, whites were down to 70 percent of the southern electorate, blacks comprised 21 percent, and Hispanics were 7 percent.

Thus, white influence at the southern ballot box is declining and, with it, Republican support in House elections. Nonetheless, the southern white electorate, at least for the time being, remains a formidable racial majority. Based on these data, in the short term it probably makes as much if not more sense for the Democratic Party to woo white voters as it does to narrowcast their appeals to a faster growing but much smaller minority voting electorate.

Reapportionment and Redistricting

According to a recent report,[9] congressional apportionment projections for 2010 based on 2008 population estimates show the South gaining between seven and eight seats, increasing the size of the southern House delegation from 131 to 138 or 139 total districts. Post-Katrina Louisiana is the only southern state expected to lose a seat. Texas would be the big winner with four new seats, followed by Florida with one or two pickups, and Georgia, North Carolina, and South Carolina each projected to gain one seat. Continuing a pattern since at least 1970, the 2010 reapportionment forecast has the Northeast and Midwest losing districts to the South and West. The Frostbelt loses representation to the Sunbelt—many erstwhile Frostbelt residents have permanently moved to the South (and West), greatly influencing the region's partisan politics.

In the 1990s, the South was ground zero for legal controversies surrounding the redrawing of congressional boundaries (see Cunningham 2001; Galderisi 2005; Grofman 1998; Lublin 1997). Although the Supreme Court has struck down the most blatant racial gerrymanders (e.g., see *Shaw v. Reno* [1993]), states must still perform a somewhat delicate balancing act—on the one hand making sure not to roll back the minority percentages in certain districts (retrogression), while at the same time not overly relying on race in the furtherance of partisan gerrymanders (Butler 2002). Nonetheless, there remains ample wiggle room for crafting district boundaries that obviously favor one party.

As shown in Chapter 3, reapportionment and redistricting in the 1990s proved a major catalyst to Republican ascendancy in southern House elections. Since the 2006 and 2008 elections, which have seen the cooling off of Republican growth, reapportionment and redistricting should play an integral role in affecting the partisan balance in the southern House delegation. In the case of those House candidates who will be elected in the newly drawn congressional districts, their active cultivation of the personal vote can fortify partisan gains made by Democrats or Republicans. Which party will be the net benefactor in southern House races as a consequence of reapportionment and redistricting is heavily conditioned by the partisan control of southern governorships and southern state legislatures—the political agents in charge of redrawing congressional boundaries.

Table 6.2 shows the party affiliation of the governor and when their term expires, along with the partisan control and margin of party control for the state senate and state house in all eleven southern states. As McDonald (2004) contends, the likelihood of a partisan gerrymander is high when one party has unified control of the state legislature and governorship (e.g., Georgia Democrats in 2002). Likewise, under split-partisan control, parties are more likely to broker a compromise that manifests itself in the crafting of a bipartisan gerrymander (e.g., Texas Democrats and Republicans in 2002) or an incumbent protection plan, particularly when a state neither gains nor loses a seat (e.g., Alabama in 2002).[10] Divided partisan control of the redistricting process also increases the likelihood of the courts stepping in as the final arbiter and architect of congressional boundaries.

Heading into the 2010 elections, in six southern states one party has unified control: Democrats in Arkansas and North Carolina, and Republicans in Florida, Georgia, South Carolina, and Texas. Coincidentally, omitting Arkansas, these are all the states projected to gain seats through the 2010 reapportionment. Based on these data, the GOP appears to have more opportunities to shape the redistricting process in their party's favor. Notice, however, that in Texas the Republican state house majority is very slim (just two seats), and with the exception of North Carolina (McDonald 2004), all southern governors can veto redistricting bills. Thus, the possible switch in party control of the governorship can significantly alter the decision calculus of these line drawers, who at the moment have unified partisan control over redistricting.

In the split partisan control states, some of the state senate and state house majorities are very narrow (e.g., Louisiana state house +2

TABLE 6.2 **Partisan Control of Southern Governorships and State Legislatures After the 2008 Elections**

State	Governor	State Senate	State House
Alabama	Republican – Bob Riley (2010—Term Limited)	Democratic, N = 35, +6	Democratic, N = 105, +19
Arkansas	Democratic – Mike Beebe (2010)	Democratic, N = 35, +19	Democratic, N = 100, +43
Florida	Republican – Charlie Crist (2010)	Republican, N = 40, +12	Republican, N = 120, +32
Georgia	Republican – Sonny Perdue (2010—Term Limited)	Republican, N = 56, +12	Republican, N = 180, +30
Louisiana	Republican – Bobby Jindal (2011)	Democratic, N = 39, +7	Democratic, N = 105, +2
Mississippi	Republican – Haley Barbour (2011—Term Limited)	Democratic, N = 52, +2	Democratic, N = 122, +26
North Carolina[a]	Democrat – Beverly Perdue (2012)	Democratic, N = 50, +10	Democratic, N = 120, +16
South Carolina	Republican – Mark Sanford (2010—Term Limited)	Republican, N = 46, +8	Republican, N = 124, +18
Tennessee	Democrat – Phil Bredesen (2010—Term Limited)	Republican, N = 33, +5	Republican, N = 99, +1
Texas[b]	Republican – Rick Perry (2010)	Republican, N = 31, +7	Republican, N = 150, +2
Virginia	Democrat – Tim Kaine (2009—Term Limited)	Democratic, N = 40, +2	Republican, N = 100, +8

Note: Data on governors are from The Green Papers: 2008 General Election (www.thegreenpapers.com/G08/). Data on the State Senate and State House are from the National Conference of State Legislatures (www.ncsl.org/statevote/partycomptable2009.htm).
[a]The North Carolina governor "does not have a veto over the redistricting plan" (McDonald 2004, 378).
[b]Texas does not have a gubernatorial term limit. For governors the next election date is in parentheses.

Democratic, Mississippi state senate +2 Democratic, Tennessee state house +1 Republican, and Virginia state senate +2 Democratic). Whether or not these slim majorities hold, the close party balance may serve to temper redistricting excesses. Also, with a change in party control of the governorship, three states would switch to unified Democratic control (Alabama, Louisiana, and Mississippi), but in Louisiana and Mississippi, the next gubernatorial election is in 2011. Likewise, assuming the partisan balance does not change in the state legislature, a 2010 Republican gubernatorial victory in Tennessee gives the GOP unified control.

In sum, if the party balance essentially remains the same for governorships and state legislatures after the 2010 elections, Republicans have an advantage because of their unified control in four states versus unified Democratic control in just two. Further, the greatest seat gains through reapportionment will occur in the states with the largest House delegations, and these states are also currently under unified GOP control (Texas, Florida, and Georgia stand to gain up to a total of seven seats, and these three states presently comprise 53 percent of the southern House delegation, or 70 out of 131 districts).

Of course much can happen between now and 2010 that affects the political climate, and short-term political conditions can strongly impact the actual electoral outcomes in reconfigured districts (see Desposato and Petrocik 2003; Grofman and Brunell 2005; McKee 2008; Petrocik and Desposato 1998). For instance, in 2004 the timing for a Republican "re-redistricting" in Texas could not have been much better. But in 2006—a decidedly Democratic year—a Republican-controlled redistricting in Georgia failed to change the partisan balance of the state's House delegation (see Hood and McKee 2008; Hood and McKee 2009).[11]

Finally, the courts have the last word on redistricting, making these political actors an ever present wild card with their authority to shape partisan outcomes. The most recent evidence of this was Texas in 2006. In *LULAC v. Perry* (2006), the U.S. District Court for the Eastern District of Texas redrew the congressional boundaries of five districts (Texas 15, 21, 23, 25, and 28). By substantially increasing the Hispanic population in Texas 23, the Republican incumbent Henry Bonilla lost a good deal of his core Anglo reelection constituency and was defeated in a runoff by former Texas Congressman Ciro Rodriguez.[12]

Performance in Office

Figure 6.2 shows the percentage of voters identifying with the Republican Party in each southern state for the 2004 and 2008 elections. The Republican percentage is out of all voters who claimed they were a

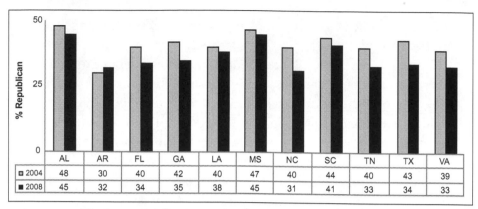

FIGURE 6.2 The Recent Decline in Southern Republican Identification

Democrat, Republican, or Independent. For both years, these data are from the individual state samples of the National Election Pool (NEP) exit polls. What is apparent in every state but Arkansas (a slight increase in GOP affiliates) is the decline in Republican voters between 2004 and 2008. These data clearly indicate evidence of "macropartisanship" (MacKuen et al. 1989). As the fortunes of a Republican president and his congressional majority soured, these aggregate data reflect a decline in GOP identifiers. This finding is not terribly surprising, but the consistency across states most friendly to the Republican Party is revealing. Performance is a fundamental component of maintaining a political party's electoral success.

There are two ways to consider performance in office: (1) the collective performance of a political party and (2) the individual performance of each Representative. As a new partisan era has come to fruition, Representatives have become less reliant on the incumbency advantage because of strong partisan majorities in any given district. Members have become much better aligned, both ideologically and in partisan affiliation, with the constituencies they represent (Erikson and Wright 2009). Ironically though, if the collective image of the party suffers, like it did for Republicans in 2006 and 2008, the incumbency advantage becomes more valuable as a means for surviving a short-term partisan tide running against an incumbent's party. Fenno's paradox that voters love their Representative but loathe Congress remains true, but as he made clear in *Home Style* (1978), when the brand name of a party takes a major hit (e.g., the GOP after Watergate), its individual adherents will suffer the electoral consequences.

Not long ago, Merle Black (2004) demonstrated with an impressive array of longitudinal data that the southern Democracy in the electorate had steadily declined since the 1950s. Likewise, Hayes and McKee (2008)[13] showed that southern Republican identification was expanding up through 2004. But since 2004, it appears at least in the short-term that Democratic identification is increasing. In 2006, data from the Cooperative Congressional Election Study (CCES) showed that the percentage of southern partisans was almost exactly even: 44.0 percent Republican and 43.5 percent Democratic (N = 10,481).[14] Given the massive size of the CCES sample, this is strong evidence that the southern Democracy has stanched the bleeding or, better yet, is experiencing a modest revival. A major source of consternation for the GOP is that a satisfactory record in office for the Democratic Congress and a Democratic president may serve to solidify Democratic identification among the youngest generation of southern voters.[15] This in turn could eventually reverse the current pattern of most southern parents transmitting a Republican affiliation to their children.

The incumbency advantage is a key component of how performance in office can produce electoral dividends. Recent studies have shown that there is considerable variability in the incumbency advantage. For example, short-term conditions can negatively influence incumbent vote shares (Desposato and Petrocik 2003). Also, the efforts of incumbents (or lack thereof) to cultivate a personal vote can elevate the incumbency advantage. As Erikson and Wright (2009) find, the incumbents who win the greatest share of the vote beyond what the partisanship of their district would predict are those who represent the most competitive districts—so the personal vote is a matter of political survival. For so many incumbents these days, as the partisan compositions of districts have become more one-sided (heavily Democratic or heavily Republican), the need to cultivate a personal vote has declined. According to a study by Oppenheimer:

> [N]ot all House members receive (or earn) incumbency advantage. It accrues the most to those who need it most to win reelection. Second,

it has not become constant. In fact, it declined markedly during the 1990s, to levels not seen in forty years, and should remain at lower levels for the foreseeable future. And third, these two findings are linked. It is precisely because fewer members need incumbency advantage that incumbency advantage in House elections has declined. The reason that fewer members need incumbency advantage is that the underlying partisan competitiveness of congressional districts today are overwhelmingly safe Democratic or safe Republican districts than at any point since 1960, at least. (2005, 135)

With the rise of southern Republicans has come the benefits that incumbency affords to those Representatives who actively cultivate a personal vote for reducing the likelihood of losing their next election. Hayes and McKee (2008) document that, over time, southern Republicans have been more electorally successful as the base of GOP incumbents has expanded. Placed within the context of a secular GOP realignment, as the Republican Party in the electorate has grown, so has the Republican incumbency advantage in southern House races (Stonecash 2008).[16] Now that Republicans are the majority party in the southern House delegation, the incumbency advantage can—and most certainly has—been used to limit the extent of House defeats in 2006 and 2008.[17] As Petrocik and Desposato (2004) find with NES data, compared to open seat contests, incumbency has the effect of reducing voter defections when short-term conditions clearly benefit one party (e.g., a partisan tide). Thus, incumbency truly is more important when a political party finds itself playing electoral defense.

As others have documented (e.g., Campbell 1997; Jacobson 2007b; Nivola and Galston 2008), since the 1970s there has been a marked decline in the number of split-results House districts—those in which the majority vote for the House and president differed according to party (i.e., the Democratic House candidate prevails, but a majority of voters supported the Republican presidential candidate). This development was of course most evident in the South where a disproportionate number of Democratic congressional districts voted Republican in presidential contests (Campbell 2006; Jacobson 2006). As a growing percentage of the electorate has better sorted itself along partisan lines, for most Representatives the incumbency advantage has indeed become less important for securing reelection. And to the degree that lopsided numbers of partisans in any given district indicates more loyalty in partisan voting, there remain fewer and fewer seats in the South that contain politically vulnerable Republicans. But this is also true for southern Democratic Representatives. Under these conditions, performance in office plays a critical role in affecting the short- and long-term partisan balance of the southern House delegation.

The End of Southern Exceptionalism?

There are many theoretical and empirical reasons to take issue with what Shafer and Johnston (2006) refer to as the seven myths of southern politics (pp. 177–185) in their book *The End of Southern Exceptionalism*. But for the sake of brevity and its relevance for the implications of this work, one of their myths deserves special attention, for it is by no means a myth. Shafer and Johnston devote a good deal of effort (see pp. 128–133, 178–180), both theoretical and empirical, to discrediting the notion of "Two Souths": the Deep South (DS) and the Peripheral South (PS). As stated by Shafer and Johnston, the fourth myth of southern politics in their list of seven is "that the resulting collapse of the old Democracy began in one distinctive subregion, the Peripheral South, and culminated in another, the Deep South" (2006, 178). By all accounts (even their own), the general pattern of Republican advancement in southern House elections clearly demonstrates that initial Republican growth was much more robust in the Peripheral South, and the Deep South lagged behind until the 1990s. Yet despite acknowledging this distinction in subregional Republican advancement (see p. 179), this does not refute the aforementioned myth because "[t]he *reason* the Deep South held the line on Republican gains was that it was more-black. Yet more-black districts in the Peripheral South or white-collar districts in the Deep South—and their denizens—did not behave appreciably differently from the same districts in the opposite sub-region" (2006, 179). In other words, culturally there is only one South, and it is merely the degree of racial concentration and variation in class disparities that influences the rate of Republican electoral success on the basis of subregion.

Shafer and Johnston apparently recognize that a rigorous empirical demonstration of their claim that the subregional classification of the South is a myth is in order. Therefore, they present the results of a multivariate test to bolster their argument. Using individual-level data (from the NES), they regress the Republican House vote (1 = Republican vote, 0 = Democratic vote) in the 1960s through 1980s on "Income Tercile" (a district-level measure), "Percentage Black" (a district-level measure), and "Deep South." If there are in fact two Souths, then the Deep South dummy (1 = Deep South, 0 = Peripheral South) should be significant in its effect on House vote choice. One might hypothesize, given the pattern of Republican advancement in the 1960s through the 1980s, that because this analysis spans a time period when Republican growth was stronger in the Peripheral South, the Deep South coefficient would be negative and significant: *Compared to Peripheral South voters, Deep South residents were significantly less likely to vote Republican in House races in the 1960s through 1980s.*

After presenting the results of the regression in Table 4.5 (p. 132), however, Shafer and Johnston aver that "a dummy variable for subregion has almost zero effect on the relationship between Republican voting and either income tercile or racial context. . . . At bottom, then, a geographic distinction—the purported 'Two Souths'—has nothing really to contribute: nothing to contribute to voting behavior for the House, and nothing to contribute to voting behavior for the Senate either" (2006, 132). Curiously, Table 4.5 does not designate with asterisks whether any of the coefficients are statistically significant. But since the coefficients and their corresponding standard errors are presented, it is easy enough to determine if any variables significantly influence House vote choice.

With this in mind, there is a serious problem with Shafer and Johnston's dismissal of "Two Souths." At least in the model for House vote choice,[18] with a coefficient of .40 and a standard error of .15, the Deep South variable is highly significant ($p < .05$, two-tailed). Additionally, because the Deep South coefficient takes on a positive sign, it means that after controlling for economic status (income tercile) and racial context (percentage black), in the 1960s through the 1980s, compared to Peripheral South denizens, Deep South residents were more likely to cast Republican ballots in House contests. So, given the correct interpretation of Shafer and Johnston's empirical analysis, there really is something to the notion that political behavior varies depending on southern subregion.

There is another fundamental problem with the work of Shafer and Johnston. As they contend and show with empirical evidence (see Chapter 4), in the 1960s through the 1980s, white southerners in blacker areas [i.e., the Deep South] voted more Republican in presidential contests and more Democratic in House races. After the 1980s, this pattern changes and they find that "white Southerners in blacker areas voted more *Republican* [original emphasis] both for Congress and for President in the 1990s" (Shafer and Johnston 2006, 110). The central revision that Shafer and Johnston attempt to impose on the southern politics literature is that, not only did class predate race in the Republican realignment, but, relative to race, it has been a more important factor. "For the white South, on the other hand, the story as told here clearly privileges the impact of economic development and an associated politics of class" (2006, 178).

This claim is dubious, especially when one considers that Shafer and Johnston find that, by the 1990s, whites in blacker areas were more disposed to vote Republican in House contests. Again, using a Deep/ Peripheral South distinction, not only is the Deep South "blacker," but it is also of a much lower SES—there are indeed fewer white collar/ upper-class residents (black or white) in the Deep South vis-à-vis the Peripheral South. Since this is indisputable, it naturally follows that if white southerners in blacker areas since the 1990s are more likely to vote Republican in House contests, then race must be a relatively more important factor than class in its impact on vote choice.

The evidence of a diverging pattern in Republican support according to southern subregion can be demonstrated with data on the 2006 and 2008 House elections. But before focusing on these more recent contests, it is worth documenting the long-term pattern of Republican growth in the South. Figure 6.3 presents David's Index of Republican Party strength in the South from 1952–2008 (for further details

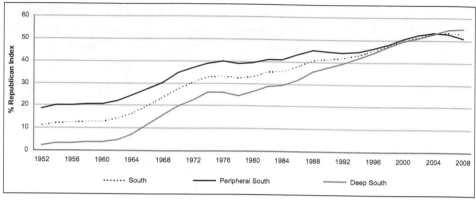

FIGURE 6.3 David's Index of Republican Party Strength in the South, 1952–2008

on the index, see David 1972, Hayes and McKee 2008, Hood et al. 2004, 2008, Lamis 1988, 1999).[19] The index is in Composite B form, a summary measure of the Republican share of the vote, which is calculated as follows:

(percent Republican Vote [Senate Election] + percent Republican Vote [Gubernatorial Election] + percent Republican Vote [Average Republican Congressional Vote]) / 3.

The Republican vote is out of the entire vote cast, not just the two-party vote in these contests. Figure 6.3 displays David's Index for the entire South and according to subregion, DS and PS. Finally, the patterns for each of the three geographic areas are highly reliable because they are based on a ten-year moving average. Hence, the trends are very conservative indicators of political change.

There are four important points to mention with respect to Figure 6.3. First, Republican growth takes off in the 1960s. Two, until the 1990s, Republican strength is substantially greater in the Peripheral South. Three, in the 1990s, increasing Republican strength indicates subregional convergence, as David's Indices for the PS and DS show little difference. Finally, in 2004, we see that the patterns for the DS and PS diverge, so Republican strength is sustained in the Deep South, whereas it declines in the Peripheral South.[20] Thus, the current state of southern congressional politics indicates that Republicanism is more electorally resilient in the Deep South. Consequently, more than any of the previously mentioned factors, the future of southern House elections is tied to recent changes in the electoral patterns of Republican success in the Deep South and Peripheral South.

So what is causing the recent divergence in Republican strength in southern subregions? The main culprit is population change through in-migration. For most of the post–World War II era, southern in-migration bolstered Republicanism. Most of the northerners who moved to all points below the Mason-Dixon Line were significantly more Republican than the native southern population (Black and Black 1987; Brown 1988). As the roots of Mountain Republicanism were finally joined to areas outside Appalachia, especially metropolitan areas in the Peripheral South (e.g., Republican Congressman Bill Cramer was first elected to a House district in St. Petersburg, Florida, in the 1954 midterm), the local bases of Republican support were heavily fortified by northern transplants (Polsby 2004). This was particularly true for GOP party activists (see Clark and Prysby 2004), who could easily fill a void since most native southerners were not affiliated with the Republican Party.

The long period of greater Republican in-migration has finally ended in many southern states. There are two reasons for this. First, because of the southern Republican realignment, the average southerner is now more Republican than the typical northern transplant. And second, many of the northern in-migrants are leaving some of the most Democratic sections of the North. Since at least the mid-1990s, in many parts of the South—particularly the Peripheral South—the newest northern migrants hail from parts of the North that clearly indicate they are more likely to be Democratic than the native southern population.

Table 6.3 presents 2000 census data on the place of birth for residents of each southern state.[21] In addition, the table shows the rate of population change in each state over three different time periods. Although there are numerous ways to evaluate these data, sticking with the subregion distinction is quite revealing. But before proceeding, it is necessary to point out that the definition of the South is the one employed by the U.S. Census Bureau. Under this classification, in addition to the eleven ex-Confederate states, the South includes Delaware, D.C., Kentucky, Maryland, Oklahoma, and West Virginia. Thus, the percentage of native-born southerners is a very liberal estimate that clearly understates the portion of northern in-migrants.

Unlike Al Gore and John Kerry, who were both shut out of every southern state in their Democratic presidential runs, in 2008 Barack Obama picked the lock on three states: Florida, North Carolina, and Virginia. Besides the fact that all three states are located in the Peripheral South, notice that among their non-southern-born populations, the highest percentage were born in the Northeast, the most Democratic region in the nation. Fully 20 percent of Florida residents were born in the Northeast, followed by Virginia at 11.4 percent, and then North Carolina at 8.4 percent. South Carolina is the only other southern state with its highest percentage of non-southern-born residents having been born in the Northeast.

Specific state-to-state migration patterns further emphasize the northern character of these states. In a 2000 census report detailing state-to-state migration flows from 1995–2000 (Perry 2003), the largest inflow of migrants to Florida and North Carolina was from New York. The greatest share of migrants to Virginia came from Maryland, a northern state that is categorized in the census-defined South. From 1995 to 2000, the single largest state-to-state migration flow in the nation was from New York to Florida (a net in-migration of 238,012 New Yorkers, Perry 2003, 2).

Furthermore, between 1995 and 2000, the only other southern state with its largest single state migrant inflow coming from outside the region was the PS state of Texas (California migrants). Thus, in Arkansas (Texas migrants), Tennessee (Florida migrants), and every Deep South state (Alabama: Georgia migrants, Georgia: Florida migrants, Louisiana: Texas migrants, Mississippi: Louisiana migrants, and South Carolina: North Carolina migrants), the largest single state migrant inflow came from another southern state (Perry 2003).

Returning to the data in Table 6.3, it is also the case that the percentage of native-born southerners is lower in most PS states. Under this classification, Florida stands out with only 45.7 percent of its population

TABLE 6.3 **Compositions and Changing Populations of Southern States**

State Population	AL	AR	FL	GA	LA	MS	NC	SC	TN	TX	VA
Native Southerners	88.4%	79.2%	45.7%	76.1%	90.5%	90.5%	77.8%	81.6%	82.1%	71.1%	69.6%
Born in the Northeast	2.4	1.6	20.0	6.3	1.6	1.4	8.4	7.7	3.3	2.8	11.4
Born in the Midwest	4.7	10.7	12.5	6.8	2.8	4.4	5.3	5.0	8.8	6.6	6.1
Born in the West	1.8	5.2	2.4	2.6	1.9	1.8	2.2	2.0	2.4	4.5	3.4
Born in U.S. Territories	0.7	0.5	2.6	1.1	0.6	0.5	0.9	0.8	0.7	1.1	1.5
Foreign Born	2.0	2.8	16.7	7.1	2.6	1.4	5.3	2.9	2.8	13.9	8.1
Non-Citizens	1.2	1.9	9.2	5.0	1.3	0.8	3.9	1.8	1.9	9.5	4.8
Population Change (1980–1990)	3.8	2.8	32.7	18.6	0.4	2.2	12.8	11.7	6.2	19.4	15.8
Population Change (1990–2000)	10.1	13.7	23.5	26.4	5.9	10.5	21.3	15.1	16.7	22.8	14.4
Population Change (2000–2007)	4.1	6.0	14.2	16.6	-3.9	2.6	12.6	9.9	8.2	14.6	8.9

Note: Place of birth and citizenship data are from the 2000 census (Census 2000 Summary File 3: P21. Place of Birth by Citizenship Status). Population change data are from the 2009 Statistical Abstract of the United States (Table 13: www.census.gov/prod/2008pubs/09statab/pop.pdf). Regions are based on census definitions: South = AL, AR, DE, D.C., FL, GA, KY, LA, MD, MS, NC, OK, SC, TN, TX, VA, WV; Northeast = CT, ME, MA, NH, NJ, NY, PA, RI, VT; Midwest = IL, IN, IA, KS, MI, MN, MO, NE, ND, OH, SD, WI; West = AK, AZ, CA, CO, HI, ID, MT, NV, NM, OR, UT, WA, WY.

born in the South. Additionally, although the correlation with noncitizens is high, due to the large influx of Hispanics in the PS states of
Florida and Texas, their foreign-born populations are in the double
digits (FL = 16.7 percent and TX = 13.9 percent).

Finally, the rate of population change is noticeably greater in the Peripheral South. There are exceptions to this rule, as the Deep South
states of Georgia and South Carolina have high rates of population
change.[22] In the DS states of Alabama, Louisiana, and Mississippi, on
the other hand, we find by far the lowest rates of population change.
And thanks to a big assist from Hurricane Katrina, between 2000 and
2007, the rate of population change in Louisiana was negative (-3.9
percent). For a PS state, Arkansas is the only one with a population
growth rate more in line with the Deep South than with its Peripheral
South neighbors.

With compositional change identified as a primary explanation for
the diverging pattern of Republican success in the Deep and Peripheral
South, we can now test for whether there really is a significant difference in Republican voting in these subregions after controlling for
other factors. Before presenting multivariate regressions, descriptive
data show that the Deep South has greater Republican strength in the
last two House elections. Between 2006 and 2008, Republicans made
up 61 percent of the DS House delegation, and the median Republican
vote (contested races only) in DS House elections was 61 percent. By
comparison, between 2006 and 2008 Republicans comprised 55 percent of the PS House delegation, and the median Republican vote
(contested races only) in PS House elections was 58 percent.[23]

The most straightforward method of evaluating the influence of
southern subregion on the House vote is to construct dummy variables
for districts residing in the Deep South and Peripheral South. With
district-level data, we can estimate a subregional effect on congressional
voting in all contested districts and those limited to the South. In addition, we can narrow the population of districts to only those contested
by incumbents—in the nation, and confined to the South.[24] In the
analyses that include all contested districts, the omitted dummy is for
the North (1 = northern district, 0 = southern district). In the analyses
limited to the South, the omitted dummy is for the Peripheral South.

Fortunately, it is not necessary to discuss in detail the control variables in the following regressions because they are exactly the same as those presented in Table 5.4 in the previous chapter. So, instead of a South dummy, we have simply added the subregional dummies (DS and PS) for the national-level regressions, and the single Deep South dummy for the regressions limited to the South.

Table 6.4 presents the ordinary least squares (OLS) estimates of the Democratic vote for the 2006 and 2008 House elections with the subregional dummies constituting the variables of interest. The consistent pattern is undeniable, regardless of which districts are included in the analyses, compared to the North and/or the Peripheral South: Deep South districts have a statistically significant and negative effect on the Democratic House vote in the 2006 and 2008 elections. For all contested districts, DS districts decrease the Democratic vote by 3 percentage points. In the remaining three models, DS districts reduce the Democratic vote by about 2 percentage points. Perhaps just as noteworthy is that the Peripheral South is not distinguishable from the North; there is no statistical difference in the effect that districts from these two regions have on the Democratic House vote in 2006 and 2008.

Finally, as Shafer and Johnston (2006) insist, if one really wants to demonstrate a difference in the political behavior of voters residing in the Deep South and Peripheral South, then it is more appropriate to use individual-level data. I could not agree more, and therefore data from the 2006 Cooperative Congressional Election Study (CCES) are employed to examine whether Deep South voters are less likely to vote Democratic after controlling for other factors expected to influence vote choice.

In the following models, most of the control variables are the same as those included in the district-level models: Competitiveness (CQ rating), Democratic Scandal, Republican Scandal, Democratic Incumbent, Open Seat (Dem-previous), and Open Seat (Rep-previous). The other variables included in Table 6.4 are omitted: Previous Democratic Vote, Dem Pres Vote (2004), Black VAP, and Median Income (thousands). In their place are measures for partisanship (1 = Strong Republican, 2 = Weak Republican, 3 = Independent Republican, 4 =

TABLE 6.4 Strong Evidence for the "Two Souths" Claim with District-Level Data on the 2006 and 2008 Elections

	Nation – All Districts	South – All Districts	Nation – Incumbents Only	South – Incumbents Only
Deep South	-.029 (.009)***	-.021 (.010)*	-.023 (.009)**	-.022 (.011)*
Peripheral South	-.005 (.005)	--	.000 (.005)	--
Previous Democratic Vote	.051 (.013)***	.024 (.021)	.065 (.013)***	.026 (.022)
Dem Pres Vote (2004)	.425 (.025)***	.356 (.057)***	.433 (.025)***	.353 (.060)***
Black VAP	.068 (.021)**	.052 (.043)	.047 (.022)*	.049 (.046)
Median Income (thousands)	-.0005 (.0002)**	-.0000 (.0004)	-.0004 (.0002)*	.0001 (.0004)
Competitiveness (CQ rating)	.036 (.002)***	.042 (.005)***	.037 (.002)***	.044 (.005)***
Democratic Scandal	-.043 (.019)*	-.109 (.032)***	-.042 (.019)*	-.104 (.033)**
Republican Scandal	.008 (.009)	.024 (.019)	.009 (.009)	.032 (.021)
Democratic Incumbent	.025 (.011)*	.012 (.023)	.014 (.012)	.001 (.026)
Open Seat (Dem-previous)	-.010 (.015)	.005 (.034)	--	--
Open Seat (Rep-previous)	.022 (.008)**	-.003 (.017)	--	--
2006 Election	.013 (.004)***	.005 (.008)	.012 (.004)**	.007 (.008)
Constant	.200 (.012)***	.214 (.026)***	.188 (.012)***	.207 (.027)***
Adjusted R²	.92	.90	.92	.90
N	759	213	689	197

Note: Ordinary Least Squares (OLS) regressions with standard errors in parentheses. The dependent variable is the Democratic share of the two-party U.S. House vote in the 2006 and 2008 elections. Only contested districts (Democrat vs. Republican) are included in the analyses.

***p < .001, **p < .01, *p < .05 (one-tailed tests).

Independent, 5 = Independent Democrat, 6 = Weak Democrat, 7 = Strong Democrat), race (1 = African American, 0 = otherwise), and family household income (fourteen total income categories, ranging from under $10,000 to $150,000 or more).

Similar to the four district-level regressions, the individual-level analyses include all contested districts in the nation and those limited to the South, as well as all incumbent-contested districts in the nation and those circumscribed to the South. Finally, the dependent variable is coded 1 for a Democratic House vote and 0 for a Republican House vote in the 2006 midterm. Since the dependent variable is binary, the models are estimated using logistic regression.

Table 6.5 shows the results for the four logistic regression models estimating the individual-level effect of southern subregion on the likelihood of voting Democratic in the 2006 House elections. Consistent with the district-level findings, in all four models Deep South voters were significantly less likely to vote Democratic in the 2006 House elections. Furthermore, Peripheral South voters were indistinguishable from northern voters with respect to their propensity to vote Democratic. In order to get a sense of the size of the effects, Table 6.6 shows the predicted probabilities of voting Democratic for each voter according to region (Deep South, Peripheral South, and North), when all of the control variables are set at their mean values. We see that while Peripheral South voters and northern voters have the same likelihood of voting Democratic, there is a significant and substantial—ranging from 10 to 13 points—difference in the probability of voting Democratic for Deep South voters versus those in the Peripheral South and North. In all four models, Deep South voters were more likely to vote for the Republican candidate in the 2006 House elections.

Concluding Remarks

This book began with a deceptively simple theory of partisan change in southern U.S. House elections. Republican ascendancy was the product of three interdependent and temporally related factors: (1)

TABLE 6.5 Strong Evidence for the "Two Souths" Claim with Individual-Level Data on the 2006 Elections

	Nation – All Districts	South – All Districts	Nation – Incumbents Only	South – Incumbents Only
Deep South Voter	-.420 (.092)***	-.408 (.098)***	-.533 (.102)***	-.493 (.108)***
Peripheral South Voter	.016 (.053)	--	-.007 (.056)	--
Partisanship	.940 (.013)***	.886 (.024)***	.932 (.013)***	.879 (.025)***
African American	.016 (.086)	-.202 (.135)	.031 (.090)	-.140 (.142)
Household Income	.001 (.006)	.012 (.012)	.002 (.007)	.012 (.013)
Competitiveness (CQ rating)	.167 (.023)***	.129 (.053)*	.166 (.027)***	.064 (.067)
Democratic Scandal	-.630 (.293)*	-1.682 (.943)	-.621 (.292)*	-1.612 (.943)
Republican Scandal	.216 (.087)*	.274 (.175)	.221 (.090)*	.362 (.182)*
Democratic Incumbent	.335 (.129)**	.547 (.314)	.335 (.150)*	.932 (.392)*
Open Seat (Dem-previous)	-.190 (.184)	.740 (.416)	--	--
Open Seat (Rep-previous)	.048 (.098)	.128 (.219)	--	--
Constant	-4.091 (.087)***	-3.947 (.163)***	-4.058 (.091)***	-3.920 (.171)***
Log Likelihood	-7305.80	-2054.00	-6631.45	-1846.85
Pseudo R^2	.45	.41	.44	.40
N	19,008	5,011	17,280	4,475

Note: Data are from the 2006 Cooperative Congressional Election Study (CCES). Dependent variable is vote choice: 1 = Democratic House Vote and 0 = Republican House Vote. Logistic regression coefficients with standard errors in parentheses. Only contested districts (Democrat vs. Republican) are included in the analyses. ***p < .001, **p < .01, *p < .05 (two-tailed tests).

TABLE 6.6 **Predicted Probabilities of Voting Democratic in the 2006 Elections**

	Nation – *All Districts*	*South –* *All Districts*	*Nation –* *Incumbents Only*	*South –* *Incumbents Only*
Deep South voters	.47	.39	.45	.36
Peripheral South voters	.58	.49	.58	.48
Northern voters	.57	--	.58	--

Note: Predicted probabilities were derived from the estimates presented in Table 6.5. All of the control variables were set at their mean values.

the increasing Republican identification of southern whites, (2) the 1990s redistricting, and (3) the emergence of viable Republican candidates. The most difficult component to fully explain is the mechanisms involved in setting in motion a secular partisan realignment. At the forefront was the strategic behavior of high-profile politicians—especially presidential candidates who successfully managed to alter the terms of party competition by stressing new issues of high salience to the mass public.

As a growing number of white southerners came to embrace the Republican Party—and specifically younger generations who came of age during and after the civil rights movement—a critical mass of GOP identifiers was finally assembled. But in order for Republicans to take back the House of Representatives in such a swift fashion in the mid-1990s, a highly disruptive event would have to transpire—one capable of weakening the Democratic incumbency advantage and thus prompting the emergence of opportunistic and viable Republican candidates. Redistricting accomplished this task and delivered a southern Republican House majority for the first time since 1874. A new electoral equilibrium, with the GOP firmly in control, took hold after the 1996 elections and persisted through 2004.

The unsatisfactory performance of a Republican president and Congress quickly reversed the national partisan balance in House elections. In the 2006 midterm, thanks to a marked shift in Democratic support outside the South, the Democratic Party reclaimed unified control of Congress for the first time since the 1994 Republican revolution. Then, the 2008 elections perpetuated the Democratic advantage as the party increased its presence in the House and Senate and captured the White House with the historic election of President Barack Obama. Although not enduring a reversal of partisan control, which is what occurred in the North, the 2006 and 2008 elections struck a heavy blow to Republican hegemony in the South. Indeed, the electoral equilibrium was shaken, particularly in the Peripheral South—a subregion showing considerably less Republican resiliency vis-à-vis the Deep South.

In addition to racial and ethnic change, performance in office, and reapportionment and redistricting, the strongest indication of a southern Democratic revival hinges on the diverging political behavior of voters in the Deep and Peripheral South. Not only are there significant differences in the voting behavior of DS and PS residents—with the former much more supportive of the Republican Party in the most recent House elections—the roots of this increasingly divergent pattern are firmly planted in the very old legacy of the South's exceptional racial history. Going back to Antebellum, the culture of the Deep South, with its much greater reliance on a slave economy, produced a more militant racial politics—a politics whose central objective was the concentration of power in the hands of planters and thus the denial of it to the vast majority of poor whites and blacks, the latter of whom were of course relegated to the status of property. Hence the pillars propping up the one-party Democratic Solid South rested squarely in the soil of the black belt[25] counties running across the heart of the Deep South states.

Key (1949) puts the racial issue at the forefront of southern politics, arguing that black belt whites were the main power brokers who managed to incite a Civil War and put down the populist revolt of the 1890s. At its heart, the notion of racial threat as explained by Key is a form of social dominance theory. The most threatened whites, those who lived in areas where they were the minority population, resorted to the legal sanctioning of segregation and the disenfranchisement of blacks—and even outright violence if nothing else worked—in order to maintain their political, economic, and social superiority. Thus, to understand southern politics, one must understand the integral role of race. Accordingly, the importance of race is dependent on the black percentage of southern states (see Hood et al. 2008).[26] The higher the African

American percentage, the more adversarial is a state's racial politics—hence the distinction between Deep South and Peripheral South states.

In short, the Democratic Party became the bulwark defending the southern system of Jim Crow segregation. The absence of two-party competition had dire consequences for the well-being of black and lower-class whites because the racial issue subverted the class issue and was thus effectively used to prevent the emergence of a biracial coalition capable of dismantling the white supremacist status quo. In the words of Key:

> This sketch of the broad outlines of the foundations of southern politics points to an extraordinary achievement of a relatively small minority—the whites of the areas of heavy Negro population—which persuaded the entire South that it should fight to protect slave property. Later, with allies from conservatives generally, substantially the same group put down a radical movement welling up from the sections dominated by the poorer whites. And by the propagation of a doctrine about the status of the Negro, it impressed on an entire region a philosophy agreeable to its necessities and succeeded for many decades in maintaining a regional unity in national politics to defend those necessities. (1996, 9)

So why rehash the political history of the Old South? Is there a need to dig up what would appear to be ancient history? Yes, because the remnants of this past, although very much diluted, are more likely to be encountered in the Deep South. It is here where the Republican Party for years made minuscule gains in House elections because "un-Reconstructed" Democratic Representatives refused to soften their resistance to civil rights. And it is here where the contemporary Republican Party, a party much more racially conservative, now has more political support in the most recent southern House contests. Relative to the Peripheral South, given the greater presence of African Americans in the Deep South, race always was and still remains a greater issue to Deep South whites. It is a primary reason why racial polarization in voting behavior is consistently more pronounced in the Deep South.

It is a fool's errand to once and for all attempt to decipher just how many parts a Republican vote is tied to economics and how many parts a Republican vote is tied to race (or say religiously motivated "values" issues).[27] As the parties have polarized on both issues, race and class have become much more tightly linked (Carmines and Stimson 1982). In addition, because of its sensitive nature and the social desirability to obfuscate one's true racial beliefs, it is exceedingly difficult to quantify the amount of southern racial conservatism. Yet when this has been attempted in a rigorous manner, there is little doubt that race persists as a much more important concern among southern whites (see Glaser 1994; Kuklinski et al. 1997; Valentino and Sears 2005).

What is now becoming clearer, however, is that the hand of the past in contemporary southern politics (with apologies to Glaser 2005) is becoming much less instructive for residents of the Peripheral South. It is here where we find the engine propelling political, economic, and social change. From within, and especially from without, because of a much larger mixture of non-southern migrants, in many parts of the Peripheral South population change has been of a magnitude great enough to reach the tipping point—permanently altering what used to be a southern culture.

The more recent residents of these states are typically more Democratic, less race-conscious, and thus less concerned with race-related issues. It is in the Peripheral South where southern exceptionalism faces its greatest threat. In short, it is here where the Democratic Party is positioned to make further electoral inroads in southern House contests. The Peripheral South is much larger[28] and much more diverse (racially, economically, socially, politically, etc.) than the Deep South. The future of southern congressional politics is becoming increasingly dependent on what happens in this southern subregion. For the GOP to retain its electoral advantage in southern House elections it has no choice but to broaden its appeal among this growing population that, with each passing day, looks less and less "southern."

Notes

1. Quotes attributed to *Southern Politics in State and Nation* are from the new edition published by the University of Tennessee Press in 1996.

2. During the Democratic nomination season, in his pivotal speech on race (March 18, 2008), in which Barack Obama definitively parted ways with the Rev-

erend Jeremiah Wright and addressed in candid language many of the intractable components of race relations in America, he paraphrased the above-mentioned Faulkner quote: "The past isn't dead and buried. In fact, it isn't even past" (http://www.themillionsblog.com/2008/03/obama-and-faulkner-quote.html).

3. The Peripheral South is also commonly referred to as the Rim South or Outer South (as mentioned in the quote at the start of this chapter).

4. Because of the scandal hanging over African American Democratic Representative William Jefferson in Louisiana 2, in 2008 he was vanquished by a Republican challenger who happened to be a Vietnamese immigrant, Joseph Cao.

5. According to national exit poll data, Hispanic support for Republican House candidates dropped 14 percentage points between 2004 and 2006. The Hispanic vote for Republican House candidates was 44.1 percent in 2004 versus 30.1 percent in 2006 (author's calculations). Because of issues of representativeness, given the disproportionately large samples for Florida and Texas, these statistics are for the nation as opposed to just the South.

6. Because Hispanic is an ethnicity, those who claim to be Hispanic can be of any race.

7. Also, Hispanic participation rates generally lag behind whites and African Americans.

8. Prior to 1984, the national exit polls did not provide a variable identifying a voter's state, just a region code that defined the South as the eleven ex-Confederate states plus Kentucky and Oklahoma. Because the raw data for the 2008 national exit poll were not released at the time of this writing, the South-wide percentages for race and ethnicity were calculated based on the percentage of whites, blacks, and Hispanics surveyed in each state, along with the total number of respondents surveyed in each state (this information is available at CNN's website: http://www.cnn.com/ELECTION/2008/results/polls/#USP00p1).

9. Election Data Services produced this report ["New Population Estimates Show Slight Changes for 2008 Congressional Apportionment, but Point to Major Changes for 2010"] that can be accessed online at: http://www.election dataservices.com/images/File/NR_Appor08wTables.pdf.

10. Bipartisan gerrymanders and incumbent protection plans are often synonymous.

11. Because of the limited and concentrated effects of the 2006 redistrictings in Texas and Georgia, these changes to voter compositions have not been modeled in any of the analyses of the 2006 and 2008 House elections in this chapter or the preceding chapter.

12. For the 2004 elections, in Texas 23 the Anglo voting age population was 45.1 percent and the Hispanic voting age population was 50.9 percent. In 2006,

in the reconfigured Texas 23, the Anglo voting age population was 33.7 percent and the Hispanic voting age population was 61.2 percent (data are from reports made available by the Texas Legislative Council).

13. Hayes and McKee (2008) include Kentucky and Oklahoma as southern states in all of their analyses.

14. These data are based on the seven-point scale for party identification, and independent leaners are classified as partisans. Strong Republicans = 20.7 percent, Weak Republicans = 12.1 percent, Independent Republicans = 11.2 percent, Independents = 12.5 percent, Independent Democrats = 11.9 percent, Weak Democrats = 12.0 percent, Strong Democrats = 19.6 percent.

15. Of course Republicans are hoping the usual pattern of midterm loss will materialize in the 2010 elections.

16. According to Stonecash (2008, 113), by evaluating the incumbency advantage according to political party, "Democrats have experienced little gain in recent decades, while Republicans have."

17. If the electoral outlook is truly abysmal, then incumbency is no savior, so there will be an increase in "strategic" retirements—exactly what we saw in the case of Republicans in 2006 and 2008.

18. The Deep South dummy is not significant in the Senate model.

19. I thank Trey Hood for making these data available to me. The calculation of David's Index is from Hood et al. (2008).

20. For the DS, David's Index of Republican strength was 2.5 percent in 1952 and 55.2 percent in 2008. For the PS, David's Index of Republican strength was 18.5 percent in 1952 and 51.0 percent in 2008.

21. See Black and Black (1987, 17) for an analysis that shows the percentage of native whites (born in the United States) born outside the South from 1950 through 1980.

22. Another way to analyze the results in the table is based on contiguity. For instance, the states connected along the Atlantic seaboard (Virginia, North Carolina, South Carolina, Georgia, and Florida) show the highest rates of residents born in the Northeast and highest rates of population growth. This alternative approach is outside the scope of the analysis, but it reveals another relationship underlying subregional political change.

23. Furthermore, after the 2008 elections, in the six PS states, only the mega-states of Florida and Texas have majority Republican House delegations. By contrast, in the five DS states, only Mississippi has a majority Democratic House delegation.

24. Open seat races are not examined, but it should be noted that in this much smaller set of districts (N = 70), it is the only instance where, compared to the North, both the Deep South (N = 5 districts) and Peripheral South (N =

11 districts) dummies indicate a significantly lower Democratic vote in the 2006–2008 House elections (results will be made available by the author upon request). A South-only analysis cannot be performed for open seats, since there are just sixteen total cases.

25. The black belt refers specifically to the rich dark soil that primarily covers the middle of the Deep South states (also the middle of Virginia, North Carolina, and parts of east Texas). The black belt was the locus of the South's slave economy.

26. Hood et al. (2008) find a distinctive pattern of partisan change in the Deep and Peripheral South states. Regardless of subregion, from 1960 to 2004, increasing black mobilization (i.e., number of registered blacks divided by the total number of registered voters) caused greater Republican strength (as measured with David's Index). Only in the Deep South, however, is the relationship recursive: Increasing Republican strength in the Deep South caused greater black mobilization. This is strong evidence of the Deep South's more racially polarized politics.

27. The importance of economic and racial issues is also variable, depending on the electoral context. For instance, economic issues matter more in an economic downturn like the one that manifested itself at the time of the 2008 elections.

28. The Peripheral South contains 72 percent (94 out of 131) of the South's congressional districts.

Appendix A

Documentation of Data Sources

A massive amount of data are presented in this book, and to every extent possible they have been documented either in the text, endnotes, or notes accompanying tables, figures, and maps. This appendix provides a list of the primary data sources for the individual-, district-, and state-level analyses.

Survey Data

1. American National Election Studies (NES) cumulative file (1948–2004).
2. Youth-Parent Socialization Panel Study, 1965–1997: Four Waves Combined.
3. National Exit Polls: State and National samples from 1982–2008. Polls were conducted by ABC/Washington Post, CBS, CBS/*New York Times*, Voter Research and Surveys, Voter News Service, and National Election Pool.
4. State Surveys for various years: Alabama (Capstone Poll), Arkansas (Arkansas Poll), Florida (Florida Annual Policy Survey), Georgia (Georgia Poll), Mississippi (Mississippi Poll), North Carolina (Carolina Poll), South Carolina (South Carolina State Policy Survey; South Carolina Omnibus Survey), Tennessee (Tennessee Survey), Texas (Texas Poll), and Virginia (Commonwealth Poll). These data were all accessed electronically through the Odum Institute for Research in Social Science at the University of North Carolina at Chapel Hill.
5. Survey data on Texas 19 in the 2004 U.S. House election were from Susan A. Banducci and Nathan K. Mitchell (The 2004 Race for the 19th Congressional District: A Rolling Cross Section Survey, Computer File and Documentation. Lubbock: Earl Survey Research Lab, Texas Tech University).
6. 2006 Cooperative Congressional Election Study (CCES): common data set.

District-Level Data

1. U.S. House vote returns are from various volumes of *The Almanac of American Politics, Congressional Elections 1946–1996* (Congressional Quarterly Inc. 1998), *Guide to U.S. Elections.* 5th ed. Volume II (CQ Press 2005); official U.S. House returns for 2006 and 2008 were from all fifty states' secretary of state websites and/or elections divisions.
2. Percent redrawn constituency data were from the Missouri Census Data Center and the Texas Legislative Council.
3. U.S. House Representatives' DW-Nominate scores were from Poole and Rosenthal (http://voteview.com/DWNL.htm).
4. Congressional district shapefiles were from the U.S. Census Bureau and the Texas Legislative Council.
5. David's Index of Republican Party strength, 1952–2008 (ten-year moving average), provided by Trey Hood (University of Georgia).
6. Congressional Quarterly's district competitiveness ratings were from *CQ Weekly Reports* and also provided by Brian Brox (Tulane University).
7. Data on primary candidates were from various volumes of *CQ Weekly Reports.*
8. Data on candidate quality, previous Democratic House vote in the district, seat typology (e.g., Democratic incumbent, open seat previously held by Republican), and which party won the district, were provided by Gary C. Jacobson (University of California, San Diego).
9. Data on candidate spending, district presidential vote, and median household income were from various volumes of *The Almanac of American Politics.*
10. Data on black, white, and Hispanic voting age populations were from the U.S. Census Bureau and the Texas Legislative Council (if just for the state of Texas).
11. Data on 2006 and 2008 House candidates associated with a scandal were from Hendry et al. (2009).

State-Level Data

1. State-level data on race and ethnicity, population change, place of birth, and state-to-state migration flows were from the U.S. Census Bureau.
2. Data on currently serving southern governors were from *The Green Papers: 2008 General Election* (http://www.thegreenpapers.com/G08/).
3. Data on the partisan composition of southern state legislatures were from the National Conference of State Legislatures (http://www.ncsl.org/).

Appendix B

Chapter 3 Supplementary Analysis

The Partisan Impact of Redistricting: District-Level Models for the 1992, 1994, 2002, and 2004 (Texas only) Southern U.S. House Elections

DEP VAR: Republican House vote (%)	Additive Model	Interactive Model
Variables of Interest		
Incumbent (1 = Dem, 0 = Rep)	-.233 (.012)***	-.279 (.016)***
Redrawn constituents (%)	.077 (.022)***	-.009 (.028)
Redrawn * Incumbent	--	.181 (.041)***
Control Variables		
Republican presidential vote (%)	.414 (.060)***	.424 (.057)***
Black voting age population (%)	-.045 (.048)	-.058 (.046)
Median income (in thousands)	.000 (.001)	.001 (.001)
Deep South	-.017 (.013)	-.016 (.012)
1994 election	.060 (.012)***	.062 (.011)***
2002 election	-.002 (.013)	-.006 (.012)
2004 election	-.022 (.019)	-.030 (.018)*
Constant	.388 (.042)***	.404 (.041)***
Adjusted R^2	.83	.84
N	230	230

Note: Estimates are ordinary least squares (OLS) coefficients with standard errors in parentheses. Dependent variable is the Republican district share of the two-party U.S. House vote. The models only include contested districts (Democrat vs. Republican) with incumbents seeking reelection. The variable of interest, "Redrawn constituents," is the district percentage of constituents an incumbent inherited after redistricting. The variable was calculated based on data from the following links: data for 1992 = http://oseda.missouri.edu/plue/geocorr/ and data for 2002 = http://mcdc2.missouri.edu/websas/geocorr2k.html.
***$p \leq .001$, **$p \leq .01$, *$p \leq .05$ (one-tailed tests)

Appendix C

Chapter 4 Supplementary Tables

Newly Elected Republican General Election Winners Who Ran in Unopposed Primaries, 1988–2004

Year	Name	State/ District	Election Type	Seat was held by Dem/Rep	Elective	Prior Occupation
1988	--	--	--	--	--	--
1990	--	--	--	--	--	--
1992	Jay Dickey	AR 4	Open	Democrat	No	Lawyer
	Tillie K. Fowler	FL 4	Open	NA	Yes	Jacksonville City Council ('85–'92)
	Charles T. Canady	FL 12	Open	Republican	Yes	Former State Representative ('84–'90)
	Bob Goodlatte	VA 6	Open	Democrat	No	Lawyer; Congressional Aide
1994	Saxby Chambliss	GA 8	Open	Democrat	No	Lawyer
	Walter B. Jones, Jr.	NC 3	Defeated Incumbent	Democrat	Yes	Former State Representative ('83–'92)
	Richard M. Burr	NC 5	Open	Democrat	No	Sales Manager
	Tom Davis	VA 11	Defeated Incumbent	Democrat	Yes	Fairfax County Board of Supervisors ('80–'94)
1996	Asa Hutchinson	AR 3	Open	Republican	No	Chairman Arkansas Republican Party
1998	**Robin Hayes**	NC 8	Open	Democrat	Yes	Former State Rep. ('92–'96); Concord Bd. of Alderman ('78–'81)

Year	Name	District	Seat	Party	Prev. Exp.	Office
2000	Adam Putnam	FL 12	Open	Republican	Yes	State Representative ('96–'00)
	±Johnny Isakson	GA 6	Open	Republican	Yes	Former State Senator ('93–'96) and State Representative ('76–'90)
	Edward Schrock	VA 2	Open	Democrat	Yes	State Senator ('95–'00)
2002	±**John Boozman**	AR 3	Open	Republican	No	Optometrist
	Tom Feeney	FL 24	Open	NA	Yes	State Representative ('90–'02)
	Mario Diaz-Balart	FL 25	Open	NA	Yes	State Representative ('88–'92, '00–'02); Former State Senator ('92–'00)
	±**Joe Wilson**	SC 2	Open	Republican	Yes	State Senator ('85–'01)
	±J. Randy Forbes	VA 4	Open	Democrat	Yes	State Senator ('97–'01); Former State Representative ('89–'97)
2004	±**Randy Neugebauer**	TX 19	Defeated Incumbent	NA	Yes	Lubbock City Council ('92–'98); Mayor Pro Tempore ('94–'96)

Data were compiled by the author from the Biographical Directory of the United States Congress and *The Almanac of American Politics*, various issues.

±Johnny Isakson was first elected in a special election in 1999 (Newt Gingrich resigned this seat), which was opposed by another Republican and a Democrat. John Boozman was first elected in a 2001 special election. He was opposed by a Republican in the first primary runoff, and a Democrat in the second general runoff. Joe Wilson was first elected in a special election in 2001, which was opposed by a Democrat. J. Randy Forbes was first elected in a 2001 special election, which was opposed by a Democrat. As discussed in detail in Chapter 3, Randy Neugebauer was first elected in a crowded special election in 2003, but his initial primary in 2004 was uncontested. As an incumbent at the time of the 2004 general election, Neugebauer faced off against another incumbent, Democrat Charles Stenholm in the reconfigured Texas 19. Representatives in bold have previous elective experience, but were not officeholders at the time they won their House seats. In all cases with "NA" entered for the party of the Representative who previously held the seat, this means that the district was drastically altered through redistricting—hence no one used to hold the seat.

Newly Elected Republican General Election Winners Who Ran in Contested Primaries, 1988–2004

Year	Name	State/ District	Election Type	Seat was held by Dem/Rep	Elective	Prior Occupation
1988	Craig T. James	FL 4	Defeated Incumbent	Democrat	No	Lawyer
	Clifford B. Stearns	FL 6	Open	Democrat	No	Motel Company Executive
	Porter J. Goss	FL 13	Open	Republican	Yes	Lee County Commissioner ('83–'88); Sanibel City Council ('74–'82)
	Larkin Smith	MS 5	Open	Republican	Yes	Harrison County Sheriff ('84–'89)
	John J. Duncan, Jr.	TN 2	Open	Republican	No	Knox County Judge
1990	Charles H. Taylor	NC 11	Defeated Incumbent	Democrat	Yes	Former State Senator ('73–'75) and State Representative ('67–'73)
1992	Terry Everett	AL 2	Open	Republican	No	Businessman; Newspaper Executive
	Spencer Bachus	AL 6	Defeated Incumbent	Democrat	Yes	Former State Representative ('84–'87) and State Senator ('83–'84)
	Tim Hutchinson	AR 3	Open	Republican	Yes	State Representative ('85–'92)
	John L. Mica	FL 7	Open	Republican	Yes	Former State Representative ('77–'81)
	Dan Miller	FL 13	Open	Republican	No	College Professor; Businessman
	Lincoln Diaz–Balart	FL 21	Open	NA	Yes	State Senator ('89–'92) and Former State Representative ('87–'89)
	Jack Kingston	GA 1	Open	Democrat	Yes	State Representative ('85–'93)
	Mac Collins	GA 3	Defeated Incumbent	Democrat	Yes	State Senator ('89–'93); Chair, Butts County Commission ('77–'81)
	John Linder	GA 4	Open	Democrat	Yes	Former State Representative ('76–'80, '82–'90)
	Bob Inglis	SC 4	Defeated Incumbent	Democrat	No	Lawyer
	Henry Bonilla	TX 23	Defeated Incumbent	Democrat	No	Television Executive
1994	Joe Scarborough	FL 1	Open	Democrat	No	Lawyer
	Dave Weldon	FL 15	Open	Democrat	No	Physician

	Name	District	Status	Party		Background
	Mark Foley	FL 16	Open	Republican	Yes	State Senator ('93–'95) and Former State Representative ('90–'92)
	Bob Barr	GA 7	Defeated Incumbent	Democrat	No	Former U.S. Attorney; U.S. Senate Candidate (1992)
	Charlie Norwood	GA 10	Defeated Incumbent	Democrat	No	Dentist
	Roger F. Wicker	MS 1	Open	Democrat	Yes	State Senator ('88–'94)
	David Funderburk	NC 2	Open	Democrat	No	Professional Lecturer and Writer ('88–'94)
	Fred Heineman	NC 4	Defeated Incumbent	Democrat	No	Raleigh, NC Police Chief
	Sue Myrick	NC 9	Open	Republican	Yes	Former Mayor of Charlotte ('87–'91); Senate Candidate (1992)
	Mark Sanford, Jr.	SC 1	Open	Republican	No	Owner of Real Estate Firm; Farmer
	Lindsey Graham	SC 3	Open	Democrat	Yes	State Representative ('92–'94)
	Zach Wamp	TN 3	Open	Democrat	No	Real Estate Broker
	Van Hilleary	TN 4	Open	Democrat	No	Textile Business Executive
	Ed Bryant	TN 7	Open	Republican	No	Former U.S. Attorney
	Steve Stockman	TX 9	Defeated Incumbent	Democrat	No	Accountant
	Mac Thornberry	TX 13	Defeated Incumbent	Democrat	No	Lawyer; Former Congressional Aide
1996	**Bob Riley**	AL 3	Open	Democrat	Yes	Former Ashland City Council Member ('72–'76); Businessman
	Robert B. Aderholt	AL 4	Open	Democrat	No	Haleyville Municipal Judge
	*John Cooksey	LA 5	Open	NA	No	Physician
	Chip Pickering	MS 3	Open	Democrat	No	Former Congressional Aide
	Bill Jenkins	TN 1	Open	Republican	Yes	Former State Representative ('62–'71, Speaker '69–'71); State Judge
	*Pete Sessions	TX 5	Open (Special)	Democrat	No	Retired Phone Company Executive
	*Kevin Brady	TX 8	Open (Special)	Republican	Yes	State Representative ('90–'96)
	Kay Granger	TX 12	Open	Democrat	Yes	Mayor of Fort Worth ('91–'95); Fort Worth City Council ('89–'91)
	#Ron Paul	TX 14	Open	Republican	Yes	Former U.S. Representative ('79–'85); Political Activist; Physician

Year	Name	State/District	Election Type	Seat was held by Dem/Rep	Elective	Prior Occupation
1998	Jim DeMint	SC 4	Open	Republican	No	Market Research Company Owner
2000	±David Vitter	LA 1	Open	Republican	Yes	State Representative ('92–'99)
	Ander Crenshaw	FL 4	Open	Republican	Yes	Former State Senator ('86–'93) and State Representative ('72–'78)
	Henry Brown, Jr.	SC 1	Open	Republican	Yes	State Representative ('85–'00); Hanahan City Council ('81–'85)
	John Culberson	TX 7	Open	Republican	Yes	State Representative ('86–'00)
	Jo Ann Davis	VA 1	Open	Republican	Yes	State Representative ('97–'00)
	Eric Cantor	VA 7	Open	Republican	Yes	State Representative ('91–'00)
2002	Jo Bonner	AL 1	Open	Republican	No	Senior Aide to U.S. Representative Sonny Callahan ('84–'02)
	Mike Rogers	AL 3	Open	Republican	Yes	State Representative ('94–'02)
	±Jeff Miller	FL 1	Open	Republican	Yes	State Representative ('98–'01); Real Estate Broker; Deputy Sheriff
	Ginny Brown–Waite	FL 5	Defeated Incumbent	Democrat	Yes	State Senator ('92–'02); Hernando County Commissioner ('90–'92)
	Katherine Harris	FL 13	Open	Republican	Yes	FL Secretary of State ('98–'02); Former State Senator ('94–'98)
	Phil Gingrey	GA 11	Open	NA	Yes	State Senator ('98–'02); Marietta School Board ('93–'97)
	Max Burns	GA 12	Open	NA	Yes	Former Screven County Commissioner ('93–'98); College Professor
	Gresham Barrett	SC 3	Open	Republican	Yes	State Representative ('96–'02)
	Marsha Blackburn	TN 7	Open	Republican	Yes	State Senator ('98–'02)
	Jeb Hensarling	TX 5	Open	Republican	No	Lawyer; Businessman; Staffer for Senator Phil Gramm ('85–'89)
	Michael Burgess	TX 26	Open	Republican	No	Obstetrician
	John Carter	TX 31	Open	NA	Yes	Williamson County District Court Judge ('81–'01); Lawyer

2004	Connie Mack	FL 14	Open	Republican	Yes	State Representative ('00–'03)
	Tom Price	GA 6	Open	Republican	Yes	State Senator ('96–'04)
	Lynn Westmoreland	GA 8	Open	Republican	Yes	State Representative ('92–'04, Minority Leader '00–'03)
	Virginia Foxx	NC 5	Open	Republican	Yes	State Senator ('94–'04); Watauga Bd. of Education ('76–'88)
	Patrick McHenry	NC 10	Open	Republican	Yes	State Representative ('02–'04)
	*Bobby Jindal	LA 1	Open	Republican	No	Government Administrator; Gubernatorial Candidate (2003)
	*Charles Boustany	LA 7	Open	Democrat	No	Surgeon
	Bob Inglis	SC 4	Open	Republican	Yes	Former U.S. Representative ('93–'99); Lawyer
	Louie Gohmert	TX 1	Defeated Incumbent	Democrat	Yes	Smith Cnty. Dist. Ct. Judge ('92–'02); Chief J, 12th Circuit ('02–'03)
	Ted Poe	TX 2	Defeated Incumbent	Democrat	Yes	Harris County Judge ('81–'03)
	Michael McCaul	TX 10	Open	NA	No	Government Lawyer
	Mike Conaway	TX 11	Open	NA	Yes	Midland School Board ('85–'88); U.S. House Candidate (2003)
	Kenny Marchant	TX 24	Open	NA	Yes	State Representative ('86–'04); Mayor of Carrollton ('84–'86)
	Thelma Drake	VA 2	Open	Republican	Yes	State Representative ('95–'04)

Data were compiled by the author from the Biographical Directory of the United States Congress and *The Almanac of American Politics*, various issues.

*Denotes open party primaries. For example, in 1996 Texas held open party primaries in thirteen districts that were redrawn; and like Louisiana, a runoff was required if the primary winner failed to secure a majority of the vote.

#Ron Paul defeated Republican incumbent Greg Laughlin in the primary. Laughlin switched from Democrat to Republican in June 1995 (Barone and Ujifusa 1997).

±David Vitter was first elected in a special election in 1999, which was opposed by several Republicans and a Democrat. He defeated another Republican in the runoff.

Jeff Miller was first elected in a special election in 2001, which was opposed by a Democrat and a third party candidate.

Representatives in bold have previous elective experience, but were not officeholders at the time they won their House seats.

Representatives whose names are italicized were defeated by Democrats in their first bids for reelection. In all cases with "NA" entered for the party of the Representative who previously held the seat, this means that the district was drastically altered through redistricting—hence no one used to hold the seat.

References

Aberbach, Joel D. 2008. "Comments on 'Toward Depolarization.'" In *Red and Blue Nation? Consequences and Correction of America's Polarized Politics*, eds. Pietro S. Nivola and David W. Brady. Washington, D.C.: Brookings Institution Press.

Abramowitz, Alan I. 1991. "Incumbency, Campaign Spending, and the Decline of Competition in U.S. House Elections." *Journal of Politics* 53(1): 34–56.

———. 1994. "Issue Evolution Reconsidered: Racial Attitudes and Partisanship in the U.S. Electorate." *American Journal of Political Science* 38(1): 1–24.

———. 1995. "The End of the Democratic Era? 1994 and the Future of Congressional Election Research." *Political Research Quarterly* 48(4): 873–889.

Abramowitz, Alan I., and Kyle L. Saunders. 1998. "Ideological Realignment in the U.S. Electorate." *Journal of Politics* 60(3): 634–652.

———. 2006. "Exploring the Bases of Partisanship in the American Electorate: Social Identity vs. Ideology." *Political Research Quarterly* 59(2): 175–187.

———. 2008. "Is Polarization a Myth?" *Journal of Politics* 70(2): 542–555.

Abramson, Paul R., John H. Aldrich, and David W. Rohde. 1994. *Change and Continuity in the 1992 Elections*. Washington, D.C.: Congressional Quarterly.

Adams, Greg D. 1997. "Abortion: Evidence of Issue Evolution." *American Journal of Political Science* 41(3): 718–737.

Aistrup, Joseph A. 1996. *The Southern Strategy Revisited: Republican Top-Down Advancement in the South*. Lexington: University Press of Kentucky.

Aldrich, John H. 1995. *Why Parties: The Origin and Transformation of Political Parties in America*. Chicago: University of Chicago Press.

———. 2000. "Southern Parties in State and Nation." *Journal of Politics* 62(3): 643–670.

Aldrich, John H., and David W. Rohde. 1997–1998. "The Transition to Republican Rule in the House: Implications for Theories of Congressional Politics." *Political Science Quarterly* 112(4): 541–567.

Aldrich, John H., John L. Sullivan, and Eugene Borgida. 1989. "Foreign Affairs and Issue Voting: Do Presidential Candidates 'Waltz Before a Blind Audience'?" *American Political Science Review* 83(1): 123–141.

Ansolabehere, Stephen, James M. Snyder, Jr., and Charles Stewart, III. 2000. "Old Voters, New Voters, and the Personal Vote: Using Redistricting to Measure the Incumbency Advantage." *American Journal of Political Science* 44(1): 17–34.

Arbour, Brian K., and Seth C. McKee. 2006. "Cracking Back: The Effectiveness of Partisan Redistricting in the Texas House of Representatives." *American Review of Politics* 26 (Winter): 385–403.

Banducci, Susan A., and Nathan K. Mitchell. 2004. *The 2004 Race for the 19th Congressional District: A Rolling Cross Section Survey*, Computer File and Documentation. Lubbock: Earl Survey Research Lab, Texas Tech University.

Barone, Michael, and Richard E. Cohen. 2001. *The Almanac of American Politics: 2002*. Washington, D.C.: National Journal.

———. 2003. *The Almanac of American Politics: 2004*. Washington, D.C.: National Journal.

———. 2005. *The Almanac of American Politics: 2006*. Washington, D.C.: National Journal.

Barone, Michael, and Grant Ujifusa. 1993. *The Almanac of American Politics: 1994*. Washington, D.C.: National Journal.

———. 1997. *The Almanac of American Politics: 1998*. Washington, D.C.: National Journal.

Bartels, Larry M. 2000. "Partisanship and Voting Behavior, 1952–1996." *American Journal of Political Science* 44(1): 35–50.

———. 2002. "Beyond the Running Tally: Partisan Bias in Political Perceptions." *Political Behavior* 24(2): 117–150.

———. 2008. *Unequal Democracy: The Political Economy of the New Gilded Age*. Princeton, NJ: Princeton University Press.

Bartley, Numan V., and Hugh D. Graham. 1975. *Southern Politics and the Second Reconstruction*. Baltimore, MD: Johns Hopkins University Press.

Bass, Jack, and Walter De Vries. 1976. *The Transformation of Southern Politics: Social Change and Political Consequence since 1945*. New York: Basic Books.

Baumgartner, Frank R., and Bryan D. Jones. 1993. *Agendas and Instability in American Politics*. Chicago: University of Chicago Press.

Beck, Paul Allen. 1977. "Partisan Dealignment in the Postwar South." *American Political Science Review* 71(2): 477–496.

———. 1979. "The Electoral Cycle and Patterns of American Politics." *British Journal of Political Science* 9(2): 129–156.

Black, Earl. 1998. "Presidential Address: The Newest Southern Politics." *Journal of Politics* 60(3): 591–612.

Black, Merle. 2004. "The Transformation of the Southern Democratic Party." *Journal of Politics* 66(4): 1001–1017.

Black, Earl, and Merle Black. 1987. *Politics and Society in the South*. Cambridge, MA: Harvard University Press.

———. 2002. *The Rise of Southern Republicans*. Cambridge, MA: Harvard University Press.

Brady, David W., and Hahrie C. Han. 2006. "Polarization Then and Now: A Historical Perspective." In *Red and Blue Nation? Characteristics and Causes of America's Polarized Politics*, eds. Pietro S. Nivola and David W. Brady. Washington, D.C.: Brookings Institution Press.

Brown, Thad A. 1988. *Migration and Politics: The Impact of Population Mobility on American Voting Behavior*. Chapel Hill: University of North Carolina Press.

Bullock, Charles S., III. 1995a. "Affirmative Action Districts: In Whose Faces Will they Blow Up?" *Campaigns & Elections* April: 22–23.

———. 1995b. "Comment: The Gift that Keeps on Giving? Consequences of Affirmative Action Gerrymandering." *American Review of Politics* 16 (Spring): 33–39.

———. 1996. "The South and the 1996 Elections." *PS: Political Science and Politics* 29(3): 450–455.

———. 1998. "Georgia: Election Rules and Partisan Conflict." In *The New Politics of the Old South: An Introduction to Southern Politics*, eds. Charles S. Bullock III and Mark J. Rozell. Lanham, MD: Rowman & Littlefield.

———. 2000. "Partisan Changes in the Southern Congressional Delegation and the Consequences." In *Continuity and Change in House Elections*, eds. David W. Brady, John F. Cogan, and Morris P. Fiorina. Stanford, CA: Stanford University Press.

Bullock, Charles S., III., Donna R. Hoffman, and Ronald Keith Gaddie. 2005. "The Consolidation of the White Southern Congressional Vote." *Political Research Quarterly* 58(2): 231–243.

Bullock, Charles S., III., and M. V. Hood, III. 2006. "A Mile-Wide Gap: The Evolution of Hispanic Political Emergence in the Deep South." *Social Science Quarterly* 87(5): 1117–1135.

Burnham, Walter Dean. 1991. "Critical Realignment: Dead or Alive?" In *The End of Realignment? Interpreting American Electoral Eras*, ed. Byron E. Shafer. Madison: The University of Wisconsin Press.

———. 1996. "Realignment Lives: The 1994 Earthquake and its Implications." In *The Clinton Presidency: First Appraisals*, eds. Colin Campbell and Bert A. Rockman. Chatham, NJ: Chatham House Publishers.

Butler, Katharine Inglis. 2002. "Redistricting in a Post-*Shaw* Era: A Small Treatise Accompanied by Districting Guidelines for Legislators, Litigants, and Courts." *University of Richmond Law Review* 36 (1): 137–270.

Cain, Bruce E. 1984. *The Reapportionment Puzzle*. Berkeley: University of California Press.

———. 1985. "Assessing the Partisan Effects of Redistricting." *American Political Science Review* 79(2): 320–333.

Cain, Bruce E., John A. Ferejohn, and Morris P. Fiorina. 1987. *The Personal Vote: Constituency Service and Electoral Independence*. Cambridge, MA: Harvard University Press.

Cameron, Charles, David Epstein, and Sharon O'Halloran. 1996. "Do Majority-Minority Districts Maximize Substantive Black Representation in Congress?" *American Political Science Review* 90(4): 794–812.

Campbell, Angus, Philip E. Converse, Warren E. Miller, and Donald E. Stokes. 1960. *The American Voter*. New York: John Wiley and Sons.

Campbell, Colin, and Bert A. Rockman, eds. 1996. *The Clinton Presidency: First Appraisals*. Chatham, NJ: Chatham House Publishers.

Campbell, James E. 1997. "The Presidential Pulse and the 1994 Midterm Congressional Election." *Journal of Politics* 59(3): 830–857.

———. 2006. "Party Systems and Realignments in the United States, 1868–2004." *Social Science History* 30(3): 359–386.

Canon, David T. 1990. *Actors, Athletes, and Astronauts: Political Amateurs in the United States Congress*. Chicago: University of Chicago Press.

Canon, David T., and David J. Sousa. 1992. "Party System Change and Political Career Structures in the U.S. Congress." *Legislative Studies Quarterly* 17(3): 347–363.

Carmines, Edward G. 1991. "The Logic of Party Alignments." *Journal of Theoretical Politics* 3(1): 65–80.

Carmines, Edward G., and James A. Stimson. 1980. "The Two Faces of Issue Voting." *American Political Science Review* 74(1): 78–91.

———. 1982. "Racial Issues and the Structure of Mass Belief Systems." *Journal of Politics* 44(1): 2–20.

———. 1989. *Issue Evolution: Race and the Transformation of American Politics*. Princeton, NJ: Princeton University Press.

Carmines, Edward G., and James Woods. 2002. "The Role of Party Activists in the Evolution of the Abortion Issue." *Political Behavior* 24(4): 361–377.

Carsey, Thomas M., and Geoffrey C. Layman. 1999. "A Dynamic Model of Political Change among Party Activists." *Political Behavior* 21(1): 17–41.

———. 2006. "Changing Sides or Changing Minds? Party Identification and Policy Preferences in the American Electorate." *American Journal of Political Science* 50(2): 464–477.

Carson, Jamie L. 2005. "Strategy, Selection, and Candidate Competition in U.S. House and Senate Elections." *Journal of Politics* 67(1): 1–28.

Carson, Jamie L., Erik J. Engstrom, and Jason M. Roberts. 2006. "Redistricting, Candidate Entry, and the Politics of Nineteenth Century U.S. House Elections." *American Journal of Political Science* 50(2): 283–293.

Carson, Jamie L. and Jason M. Roberts. 2005. "Strategic Politicians and U.S. House Elections, 1874–1914." *Journal of Politics* 67(2): 474–496.

Carter, Dan T. 1996. *From George Wallace to Newt Gingrich: Race in the Conservative Counterrevolution, 1963–1994.* Baton Rouge: Louisiana State University Press.

Clark, John A., and Charles L. Prysby, eds. 2004. *Southern Political Party Activists: Patterns of Conflict and Change, 1991–2001.* Lexington: University Press of Kentucky.

Clayton, Dewey M. 2000. *African Americans and the Politics of Congressional Redistricting.* New York: Garland Publishing.

Connelly, William F., Jr., and John J. Pitney, Jr. 1994. *Congress' Permanent Minority? Republicans in the U.S. House.* Lanham, MD: Rowman & Littlefield Publishers.

Converse, Philip E. 1964. "The Nature of Belief Systems in Mass Publics." In *Ideology and Discontent,* ed. David E. Apter. London: Free Press of Glencoe.

Cowden, Jonathan A. 2001. "Southernization of the Nation and Nationalization of the South: Racial Conservatism, Social Welfare and White Partisans in the United States, 1956–92." *British Journal of Political Science* 31(2): 277–301.

Cox, Gary W., and Jonathan N. Katz. 2002. *Elbridge Gerry's Salamander: The Electoral Consequences of the Reapportionment Revolution.* Cambridge: Cambridge University Press.

Cunningham, Maurice T. 2001. *Maximization, Whatever the Cost: Race, Redistricting and the Department of Justice.* Westport, CT: Praeger.

David, Paul T. 1972. *Party Strength in the United States: 1872–1970.* Charlottesville: University Press of Virginia.

Davidson, Chandler. 1990. *Race and Class in Texas Politics.* Princeton, NJ: Princeton University Press.

Davidson, Roger H., and Walter J. Oleszek. 2000. *Congress and Its Members.* 7th ed. Washington, D.C.: CQ Press.

Desposato, Scott W., and John R. Petrocik. 2003. "The Variable Incumbency Advantage: New Voters, Redistricting, and the Personal Vote." *American Journal of Political Science* 47(1): 18–32.

Dimock, Michael A., and Gary C. Jacobson. 1995. "Checks and Choices: The House Bank Scandal's Impact on Voters in 1992." *Journal of Politics* 57(4): 1143–1159.

Dodd, Lawrence C. 2005. "Re-Envisioning Congress: Theoretical Perspectives on Congressional Change—2004." In *Congress Reconsidered,* eds. Lawrence C. Dodd and Bruce I. Oppenheimer. Washington, D.C.: CQ Press.

Dodd, Lawrence C., and Bruce I. Oppenheimer, eds. 2005. *Congress Reconsidered*. 8th ed. Washington, D.C.: CQ Press.

Dodd, Lawrence C., and Bruce I. Oppenheimer. 2009. "Congressional Politics in a Time of Crisis: The 2008 Elections and Their Implications." In *Congress Reconsidered*, eds. Lawrence C. Dodd and Bruce I. Oppenheimer. Washington, D.C.: CQ Press.

Downs, Anthony. 1957. *An Economic Theory of Democracy*. New York: Harper.

Ehrenhalt, Alan. 1991. *The United States of Ambition: Politicians, Power, and the Pursuit of Office*. New York: Random House.

Epstein, David, and Sharyn O'Halloran. 1999a. "Measuring the Electoral and Policy Impact of Majority-Minority Voting Districts." *American Journal of Political Science* 43(2): 367–395.

———. 1999b. "A Social Science Approach to Race, Redistricting, and Representation." *American Political Science Review* 93(1): 187–191.

———. 2000. "Majority-Minority Districts and the New Politics of Congressional Elections." In *Continuity and Change in House Elections*, eds. David W. Brady, John F. Cogan, and Morris P. Fiorina. Stanford, CA: Stanford University Press.

Erikson, Robert S., and Gerald C. Wright. 2005. "Voters, Candidates, and Issues in Congressional Elections." In *Congress Reconsidered*. 8th ed., eds. Lawrence C. Dodd and Bruce I. Oppenheimer. Washington, D.C.: CQ Press.

———. 2009. "Voters, Candidates, and Issues in Congressional Elections." In *Congress Reconsidered*, eds. Lawrence C. Dodd and Bruce I. Oppenheimer. Washington, D.C.: CQ Press.

Faulkner, William. 1975. *Requiem for a Nun*. New York: Vintage Books.

Fenno, Richard F., Jr. 1978. *Home Style: House Members in Their Districts*. Boston: Little, Brown.

———. 1997. *Learning to Govern: An Institutional View of the 104th Congress*. Washington, D.C.: Brookings Institution Press.

Fiorina, Morris P. 1977. *Congress: Keystone of the Washington Establishment*. New Haven, CT: Yale University Press.

———. 1981. *Retrospective Voting in American National Elections*. New Haven, CT: Yale University Press.

———. 2002. "Parties and Partisanship: A 40-Year Perspective." *Political Behavior* 24(2): 93–115.

———. 2005. "*Keystone* Reconsidered." In *Congress Reconsidered*. 8th ed., eds. Lawrence C. Dodd and Bruce I. Oppenheimer. Washington, D.C.: CQ Press.

Fiorina, Morris P., Samuel J. Abrams, and Jeremy C. Pope. 2005. *Culture War? The Myth of a Polarized America*. New York: Pearson Longman.

———. 2008. "Polarization in the American Public: Misconceptions and Misreadings." *Journal of Politics* 70(2): 556–560.

Fiorina, Morris P., and Matthew S. Levendusky. 2006. "Disconnected: The Political Class versus the People." In *Red and Blue Nation? Characteristics and Causes of America's Polarized Politics*, eds. Pietro S. Nivola and David W. Brady. Washington, D.C.: Brookings Institution Press.

Flanigan, William H., and Nancy H. Zingale. 2007. *Political Behavior of the American Electorate*. Washington, D.C.: CQ Press.

Fowler, Linda L. 1993. *Candidates, Congress, and the American Democracy*. Ann Arbor: The University of Michigan Press.

Franklin, Charles H. 1992. "Measurement and the Dynamics of Party Identification." *Political Behavior* 14(3): 297–309.

Frymer, Paul, Thomas P. Kim, and Terri L. Bimes. 1997. "Party Elites, Ideological Voters, and Divided Party Government." *Legislative Studies Quarterly* 22(2): 195–216.

Gaddie, Ronald Keith, and Charles S. Bullock, III. 2000. *Elections to Open Seats in the U.S. House: Where the Action Is*. Lanham, MD: Rowman & Littlefield.

Galderisi, Peter F., ed. 2005. *Redistricting in the New Millennium*. Lanham, MD: Lexington Books.

Gelman, Andrew, and Gary King. 1994. "A Unified Method of Evaluating Electoral Systems and Redistricting Plans." *American Journal of Political Science* 38(2): 514–554.

Gelman, Andrew, David Park, Boris Shor, Joseph Bafumi, and Jeronimo Cortina. 2008. *Red State, Blue State, Rich State, Poor State: Why Americans Vote the Way They Do*. Princeton, NJ: Princeton University Press.

Gimpel. James G. 1996. *Legislating the Revolution: The Contract with America in its First 100 Days*. Boston: Allyn and Bacon.

Glaser, James M. 1994. "Back to the Black Belt: Racial Environment and White Racial Attitudes in the South." *Journal of Politics* 56(1): 21–41.

———. 1996. *Race, Campaign Politics, and the Realignment in the South*. New Haven, CT: Yale University Press.

———. 2005. *The Hand of the Past in Contemporary Southern Politics*. New Haven, CT: Yale University Press.

Green, Donald, Bradley Palmquist, and Eric Schickler. 2002. *Partisan Hearts and Minds: Political Parties and the Social Identities of Voters*. New Haven, CT: Yale University Press.

Grofman, Bernard, ed. 1998. *Race and Redistricting in the 1990s*. New York: Agathon Press.

Grofman, Bernard, and Thomas L. Brunell. 2005. "The Art of the Dummymander: The Impact of Recent Redistrictings on the Partisan Makeup of Southern House Seats." In *Redistricting in the New Millennium*, ed. Peter F. Galderisi. Lanham, MD: Lexington Books.

Grose, Christian R., and Antoine Yoshinaka. 2003. "The Electoral Consequences of Party Switching by Incumbent Members of Congress, 1947–2000." *Legislative Studies Quarterly* 28(1): 55–75.

Hadley, Charles D. 1985. "Dual Partisan Identification in the South." *Journal of Politics* 47(1): 254–268.

Hamburger, Tom, and Peter Wallsten. 2006. *One Party Country: The Republican Plan for Dominance in the 21st Century.* Hoboken, NJ: John Wiley & Sons.

Handley, Lisa, Bernard Grofman, and Wayne Arden. 1998. "Electing Minority-Preferred Candidates to Legislative Office: The Relationship between Minority Percentages in Districts and the Election of Minority-Preferred Candidates." In *Race and Redistricting in the 1990s*, ed. Bernard Grofman. New York: Agathon Press.

Hayes, Danny, and Seth C. McKee. 2008. "Toward A One-Party South?" *American Politics Research* 36(1): 3–32.

Hendry, David J., Robert A. Jackson, and Jeffrey J. Mondak. 2009. "Abramoff, Email, and the Mistreated Mistress: Scandal and Character in the 2006 Elections." In *Fault Lines: Why the Republicans Lost Congress*, eds. Jeffrey J. Mondak and Dona-Gene Mitchell. New York: Routledge.

Herrnson, Paul S., and James M. Curry. 2009. "Issue Voting in the 2006 Elections for the U.S. House of Representatives." In *Congress Reconsidered*, eds. Lawrence C. Dodd and Bruce I. Oppenheimer. Washington, D.C.: CQ Press.

Hetherington, Marc J. 2001. "Resurgent Mass Partisanship: The Role of Elite Polarization." *American Political Science Review* 95(3): 619–631.

Hetherington, Marc J., Bruce A. Larson, and Suzanne Globetti. 2003. "The Redistricting Cycle and Strategic Candidate Decisions in U.S. House Races." *Journal of Politics* 65(4): 1221–1235.

Hill, Kevin A. 1995. "Does the Creation of Majority Black Districts Aid Republicans? An Analysis of the 1992 Congressional Elections in Eight Southern States." *Journal of Politics* 57(2): 384–401.

Hill, Kevin A., and Nicol C. Rae. 2000. "What Happened to the Democrats in the South? US House Elections, 1992–1996." *Party Politics* 6(1): 5–22.

Hogan, Robert E. 2003. "Institutional and District-Level Sources of Competition in State Legislative Elections." *Social Science Quarterly* 84(3): 543–560.

———. 2004. "Challenger Emergence, Incumbent Success and Electoral Accountability in State Legislative Elections." *Journal of Politics* 66(4): 1309–1329.

Hood, M. V., III., Quentin Kidd, and Irwin L. Morris. 2004. "The Reintroduction of the *Elephas Maximus* to the Southern United States: The Rise of Republican State Parties, 1960–2000." *American Politics Research* 32(1): 68–101.

————. 2008. "Two Sides of the Same Coin? Employing Granger Causality Tests in a Time Series Cross-Section Framework." *Political Analysis* 16(3): 324–344.

Hood, M. V., III., and Seth C. McKee. 2008. "Gerrymandering on Georgia's Mind: The Effects of Redistricting on Vote Choice in the 2006 Midterm Election." *Social Science Quarterly* 89(1): 60–77.

————. 2009. "Trying to Thread the Needle: The Effects of Redistricting in a Georgia Congressional District." *PS: Political Science & Politics* Forthcoming.

Jacobs, Lawrence R. 2006. "The Presidency and the Press." In *The Presidency and the Political System*, ed. Michael Nelson. Washington, D.C.: CQ Press.

Jacobson, Gary C. 1990. *The Electoral Origins of Divided Government: Competition in U.S. House Elections, 1946–1988*. Boulder, CO: Westview Press.

————. 1991. "Explaining Divided Government: Why Can't the Republicans Win the House?" *PS: Political Science and Politics* 24(4): 640–643.

————. 1996. "The 1994 House Elections in Perspective." *Political Science Quarterly* 111(2): 203–223.

————. 2000. "Reversal of Fortune: The Transformation of U.S. House Elections in the 1990s." In *Continuity and Change in House Elections*, eds. David W. Brady, John F. Cogan, and Morris P. Fiorina. Stanford, CA: Stanford University Press.

————. 2001. *The Politics of Congressional Elections*. 5th ed. New York: Addison-Wesley.

————. 2003. "Terror, Terrain, and Turnout: Explaining the 2002 Midterm Elections." *Political Science Quarterly* 118(1): 1–22.

————. 2004. *The Politics of Congressional Elections*. 6th ed. New York: Longman.

————. 2005. "All Quiet on the Western Front: Redistricting and Party Competition in California House Elections." In *Redistricting in the New Millennium*, ed. Peter F. Galderisi. Lanham, MD: Lexington Books.

————. "Comments: Disconnected, or Joined at the Hip?" In *Red and Blue Nation? Characteristics and Causes of America's Polarized Politics*, eds. Pietro S. Nivola and David W. Brady. Washington, D.C.: Brookings Institution Press.

————. 2007a. *A Divider, Not a Uniter: George W. Bush and the American People*. New York: Pearson Longman.

————. 2007b. "Referendum: The 2006 Midterm Congressional Elections." *Political Science Quarterly* 122(1): 1–24.

————. 2007c. "Explaining the Ideological Polarization of the Congressional Parties since the 1970s." In *Party, Process, and Political Change in Congress: Further New Perspectives on the History of Congress*, eds. David W. Brady and Matthew D. McCubbins. Palo Alto, CA: Stanford University Press.

Jacobson, Gary C., and Samuel Kernell. 1983. *Strategy and Choice in Congressional Elections*. 2nd ed. New Haven, CT: Yale University Press.

Jenkins, Shannon, Douglas D. Roscoe, John P. Frendreis, and Alan R. Gitelson. 2007. "Ten Years after the Revolution: 1994 and Partisan Control of Government." In *The State of the Parties: The Changing Role of Contemporary American Parties*, eds. John C. Green and Daniel J. Coffey. Lanham, MD: Rowman & Littlefield.

Karp, Jeffrey A., and Marshall W. Garland. 2007. "Ideological Ambiguity and Split Ticket Voting." *Political Research Quarterly* 60(4): 722–732.

Keith, Bruce E., David B. Magleby, Candice J. Nelson, Elizabeth Orr, Mark C. Westlye, and Raymond E. Wolfinger. 1992. *The Myth of the Independent Voter*. Berkeley: University of California Press.

Key, V. O., Jr. 1949. *Southern Politics in State and Nation*. New York: A. A. Knopf.

———. 1955. "A Theory of Critical Elections." *Journal of Politics* 17(1): 3–18.

———. 1959. "Secular Realignment and the Party System." *Journal of Politics* 21(2): 198–210.

———. 1964. *Politics, Parties, and Pressure Groups*. New York: Crowell.

———. 1966. *The Responsible Electorate: Rationality in Presidential Voting, 1936–1960*. Cambridge, MA: Belknap Press of Harvard University Press.

———. 1996. *Southern Politics in State and Nation*. Knoxville: University of Tennessee Press.

Knuckey, Jonathan. 2006. "Explaining Recent Changes in the Partisan Identifications of Southern Whites." *Political Research Quarterly* 59(1): 57–70.

Kousser, J. Morgan. 1996. "Estimating the Partisan Consequences of Redistricting Plans—Simply." *Legislative Studies Quarterly* 21(4): 521–541.

Kuklinski, James H., Michael D. Cobb, and Martin Gilens. 1997. "Racial Attitudes and the 'New South.'" *Journal of Politics* 59(2): 323–349.

Ladd, Everett Carll. 1995. "The 1994 Congressional Elections: The Postindustrial Realignment Continues." *Political Science Quarterly* 110(1): 1–23.

Lamis, Alexander P. 1988. *The Two-Party South*. Oxford: Oxford University Press.

Lamis, Alexander P., ed. 1999. *Southern Politics in the 1990s*. Baton Rouge: Louisiana State University Press.

Layman, Geoffrey C., and Thomas M. Carsey. 1998. "Why Do Party Activists Convert? An Analysis of Individual-Level Change on the Abortion Issue." *Political Research Quarterly* 51(3): 723–749.

———. 2002a. "Party Polarization and Party Structuring of Policy Attitudes: A Comparison of Three NES Panel Studies." *Political Behavior* 24(3): 199–236.

———. 2002b. "Party Polarization and 'Conflict Extension' in the American Electorate." *American Journal of Political Science* 46(4): 786–802.

Layman, Geoffrey C., Thomas M. Carsey, and Juliana Menasce Horowitz. 2006. "Party Polarization in American Politics: Characteristics, Causes, and Consequences." *Annual Review of Political Science* 9: 83–110.

Lublin, David. 1997. *The Paradox of Representation: Racial Gerrymandering and Minority Interests in Congress.* Princeton, NJ: Princeton University Press.

———. 2004. *The Republican South: Democratization and Partisan Change.* Princeton, NJ: Princeton University Press.

Lublin, David, and D. Stephen Voss. 2000. "Boll-Weevil Blues: Polarized Congressional Delegations into the 21st Century." *American Review of Politics* 21(Winter): 427–450.

MacKuen, Michael B., Robert S. Erikson, and James A. Stimson. 1989. "Macropartisanship." *American Political Science Review* 83(4): 1125–1142.

———. 1992. "Peasants or Bankers? The American Electorate and the U.S. Economy." *American Political Science Review* 86(3): 597–611.

Mann, Thomas E., and Norman J. Ornstein. 2009. "Is Congress Still the Broken Branch?" In *Congress Reconsidered*, eds. Lawrence C. Dodd and Bruce I. Oppenheimer. Washington, D.C.: CQ Press.

Mayhew, David R. 2002. *Electoral Realignments: A Critique of an American Genre.* New Haven, CT: Yale University Press.

McDonald, Michael P. 2004. "A Comparative Analysis of Redistricting Institutions in the United States, 2001–02." *State Politics and Policy Quarterly* 4(4): 371–395.

McKee, Seth C. 2002. "Majority Black Districts, Republican Ascendancy, and Party Competition in the South, 1988–2000." *American Review of Politics* 23 (Summer): 123–139.

———. 2004. "Review Essay: The Impact of Congressional Redistricting in the 1990s on Minority Representation, Party Competition, and Legislative Responsiveness." *Journal of Political Science* 32: 1–46.

———. 2008. "The Effects of Redistricting on Voting Behavior in Incumbent U.S. House Elections, 1992–1994." *Political Research Quarterly* 61(1): 122–133.

McKee, Seth C., and Daron R. Shaw. 2005. "Redistricting in Texas: Institutionalizing Republican Ascendancy." In *Redistricting in the New Millennium*, ed. Peter F. Galderisi. Lanham, MD: Lexington Books.

McKee, Seth C., Jeremy M. Teigen, and Mathieu Turgeon. 2006. "The Partisan Impact of Congressional Redistricting: The Case of Texas, 2001–2003." *Social Science Quarterly* 87(2): 308–317.

Miller, Warren E. 1991. "Party Identification, Realignment, and Party Voting: Back to the Basics." *American Political Science Review* 85(2): 557–568.

———. 1998. "Party Identification and the Electorate of the 1990s." In *The Parties Respond: Changes in American Parties and Campaigns*, ed. L. Sandy Maisel. Boulder, CO: Westview Press.

———. 2001. "Generational Changes and Party Identification." In *Controversies in Voting Behavior*, eds. Richard G. Niemi and Herbert F. Weisberg. Washington, D.C.: CQ Press.

Nadeau, Richard, Richard G. Niemi, Harold W. Stanley, and Jean-Francois God-bout. 2004. "Class, Party, and South/Non-South Differences: An Update." *American Politics Research* 32(1): 52–67.

Nagourney, Adam, and Carl Hulse. 2008. "Republican Election Losses Stir Fall Fears." *New York Times*. May 15. Online at http://www.nytimes.com/2008/05/15/us/politics/15repubs.html.

Nie, Norman H., Sidney Verba, and John R. Petrocik. 1976. *The Changing American Voter*. Cambridge, MA: Harvard University Press.

Nivola, Pietro S., and David W. Brady, eds. 2006. *Red and Blue Nation? Characteristics and Causes of America's Polarized Politics*. Washington, D.C.: Brookings Institution Press.

Nivola, Pietro S., and William A. Galston. 2008. "Toward Depolarization." In *Red and Blue Nation? Consequences and Correction of America's Polarized Politics*, eds. Pietro S. Nivola and David W. Brady. Washington, D.C.: Brookings Institution Press.

Oppenheimer, Bruce I. 2005. "Deep Red and Blue Congressional Districts: The Causes and Consequences of Declining Party Competitiveness." In *Congress Reconsidered*, eds. Lawrence C. Dodd and Bruce I. Oppenheimer. Washington, D.C.: CQ Press.

Pearson, Kathryn, and Eric Schickler. 2009. "The Transition to Democratic Leadership in a Polarized House." In *Congress Reconsidered*, eds. Lawrence C. Dodd and Bruce I. Oppenheimer. Washington, D.C.: CQ Press.

Perry, Marc J. 2003. "State-to-State Migration Flows: 1995 to 2000." U.S. Census Bureau.

Petrocik, John R. 1981. *Party Coalitions: Realignment and the Decline of the New Deal Party System*. Chicago: University of Chicago Press.

Petrocik, John R. 1987. "Realignment: New Party Coalitions and the Nationalization of the South." *Journal of Politics* 49(2): 347–375.

Petrocik, John R., and Scott W. Desposato. 1998. "The Partisan Consequences of Majority-Minority Redistricting in the South, 1992 and 1994." *Journal of Politics* 60(3): 613–633.

———. 2004. "Incumbency and Short-Term Influences on Voters." *Political Research Quarterly* 57(3): 363–373.

Phillips, Kevin P. 1969. *The Emerging Republican Majority*. New Rochelle, NY: Arlington House.

Polsby, Nelson W. 2004. *How Congress Evolves: Social Bases of Institutional Change*. New York: Oxford University Press.

Rae, Nicol C. 1994. *Southern Democrats*. New York: Oxford University Press.

———. 1998. *Conservative Reformers: The Republican Freshmen and the Lessons of the 104th Congress*. Armonk, NY: M. E. Sharpe.

Rice, Tom W. 1994. "Partisan Change Among Native White Southerners: 1965–1982." *American Politics Quarterly* 22(2): 244–251.

Riker, William H. 1980. "Implications from the Disequilibrium of Majority Rule for the Study of Institutions." *American Political Science Review* 74(2): 432–446.

———. 1982. *Liberalism Against Populism*. Prospect Heights, IL: Waveland Press.

———. 1986. *The Art of Political Manipulation*. New Haven, CT: Yale University Press.

Rohde, David W. 1991. *Parties and Leaders in the Postreform House*. Chicago: University of Chicago Press.

Schattschneider, E. E. 1960. *The Semisovereign People: A Realist's View of Democracy in America*. New York: Holt, Rinehart, and Winston.

Schweers, Maureen. 2003. "U.S. House Races: Republican Resurgence after Eight Lean Years." In *Midterm Madness: The Elections of 2002*, ed. Larry J. Sabato. Lanham, MD: Rowman & Littlefield.

Shafer, Byron E. 1991. "The Notion of an Electoral Order: The Structure of Electoral Politics at the Accession of George Bush." In *The End of Realignment? Interpreting American Electoral Eras*, ed. Byron E. Shafer. Madison: The University of Wisconsin Press.

Shafer, Byron E., and Richard Johnston. 2006. *The End of Southern Exceptionalism: Class, Race, and Partisan Change in the Postwar South*. Cambridge, MA: Harvard University Press.

Shotts, Ken. 2001. "The Effect of Majority-Minority Mandates on Partisan Gerrymandering." *American Journal of Political Science* 45(1): 120–135.

Skowronek, Stephen. 1993. *The Politics Presidents Make: Leadership from John Adams to George Bush*. Cambridge, MA: Belknap Press.

———. 2008. *Presidential Leadership in Political Time: Reprise and Reappraisal*. Lawrence: University Press of Kansas.

Smith, Steven S., and Gerald Gamm. 2009. "The Dynamics of Party Government in Congress." In *Congress Reconsidered*, eds. Lawrence C. Dodd and Bruce I. Oppenheimer. Washington, D.C.: CQ Press.

Stanley, Harold W. 1988. "Southern Partisan Changes: Dealignment, Realignment or Both?" *Journal of Politics* 50(1): 64–88.

Stimson, James A. 2004. *Tides of Consent: How Public Opinion Shapes American Politics*. Cambridge: Cambridge University Press.

Stonecash, Jeffrey M. 2008. *Reassessing the Incumbency Effect*. New York: Cambridge University Press.

Stonecash, Jeffrey M., Mark D. Brewer, and Mack D. Mariani. 2003. *Diverging Parties: Social Change, Realignment, and Party Polarization*. Boulder, CO: Westview Press.

Sundquist, James L. 1983. *The Dynamics of the Party System.* Washington, D.C.: The Brookings Institution.

Theriault, Sean M. 2006. "Party Polarization in the US Congress: Member Replacement and Member Adaptation." *Party Politics* 12(4): 483–503.

Thielemann, Gregory S. 1992. "Party Development in the South: The Case for Southern Exceptionalism." *Social Science Quarterly* 73(1): 141–143.

Valentino, Nicholas A., and David O. Sears. 2005. "Old Times There Are Not Forgotten: Race and Partisan Realignment in the Contemporary South." *American Journal of Political Science* 49(3): 672–688.

Wattenberg, Martin P. 1991. "The Building of a Republican Regional Base in the South: The Elephant Crosses the Mason-Dixon Line." *Public Opinion Quarterly* 55(3): 424–431.

Woodward, C. Vann. 2002. *The Strange Career of Jim Crow.* Oxford: Oxford University Press.

Index